One hundred practical texts of perception and spiritual discernment from Diadochos of Photike

BELFAST BYZANTINE TEXTS AND TRANSLATIONS

General editor: Professor M.E. Mullett

Editorial board: Dr R.H. Jordan
                  Professor M.J. McGann
                  Dr E.A.M. Haan

Advisory board: Professor M.J. Angold
                  Professor A.A.M. Bryer
                  Professor R. Cormack
                  Professor J. Herrin

TITLES

BBTT1:   The Life of Michael the Synkellos
         Mary B. Cunningham
BBTT4:   Alexios I Komnenos, I
         Margaret Mullett and Dion Smythe
BBTT6.1: The Theotokos Evergetis and eleventh-century monasticism
         Margaret Mullett and Anthony Kirby
BBTT6.2: Work and worship at the Theotokos Evergetis 1050-1200
         Margaret Mullett and Anthony Kirby

One hundred practical texts of perception and spiritual discernment from Diadochos of Photike

Text, translation and commentary by Janet Elaine Rutherford

BELFAST BYZANTINE TEXTS AND TRANSLATIONS, 8

First published in 2000
by Belfast Byzantine Enterprises
Institute of Byzantine Studies
The Queen's University of
Belfast, BT7 1NN

© 2000 Belfast Byzantine Enterprises

All rights reserved. No part of this publication may be reproduced, stored in a retrieval system, or transmitted, in any form or by any means, electronic, mechanical, photocopying, recording or otherwise, without the prior permission of the publisher.

ISBN: 0 85389 782 4
ISSN: 0960-9997

British Library Cataloguing-in-Publication Data

A catalogue record for this book is
available from the British Library

Printed and bound in Northern Ireland by
The Universities Press

Contents

Editor's preface	vii
About this translation	ix
Foreword	xi
Abbreviations	xiii
Introduction	1
One hundred practical texts of perception and spiritual discernment Text and translation	12
Commentary	159
Bibliography	181

About this translation

This translation has been made on the basis of two principles: respect for the text's linguistic and grammatical integrity, and respect for the reader's right to be presented with as accurate a reflection of the text's language and grammar as possible–warts and all. Diadochos is not easy to read in Greek, and the English translation reflects that. The desire of translators to make good English (or Latin, or whatever) prose out of difficult Greek has, I believe, been responsible for the theological stature of Diadochos remaining unrecognised for so long. The practice of translating words which may have a technical significance on the assumption that they have none leads to using different English words for the same Greek word when it appears in different sentences, in order to make individual sentences sound right in English. But the result is that the Greek word, and all the sentences in which it appears, become theologically meaningless. This volume is the end product of a long process which began with the assumption that if Diadochos referred repeatedly to γνῶσις or αἴσθησις, for example, there was a high degree of likelihood that these words had a precise meaning for him. I therefore collected every instance in which Diadochos used a Greek root which might have a technical significance, and compared them to see if there might indeed be a common sense behind all the instances of their use. Of the hundred or so roots I examined, some dozen emerged as having distinct technical meanings–and also distinct relationships to each other. At this point I began to realise that Diadochos was not only a precise thinker but also a systematic one. Further examination of the relationships between his technical terms revealed a degree of complexity and coherence in his thinking which scholars had hitherto not recognised. This complexity makes it very difficult to present his technical vocabulary as a list of terms. Instead, each term is discussed in the commentary as it arises, in the context of the other terms to which it relates; and thus the translation and commentary must be used together. If this seems laborious, it is because the Greek of Diadochos is laborious. Fluent Greek readers of his day would have had to work at understanding him, and so will readers of this translation. But the balance, harmony, and coherence of his theological vision well repay the effort. Once his technical vocabulary has been mastered and his theological preoccupations understood (they are discussed in the Introduction), the text acquires a growing clarity and beauty which can only be the reward of those who start reading it under the full impact of its seeming opacity.

In memory of my father

The Reverend Richard Marshall Harding
(United Methodist Church)

late of the U.S. Army Chaplains' Department

ὁ θεὸς ἀγάπη ἐστίν, καὶ ὁ μένων ἐν τῇ ἀγάπῃ
ἐν τῷ θεῷ μένει, καὶ ὁ θεὸς ἐν αὐτῷ μένει.

Foreword

I am very grateful for the help which I have received at every stage of this volume, as it grew out of my doctoral dissertation. At a very early point I received encouragement from The Very Reverend Dr Kallistos Ware, who also kindly sent me his article on the Jesus Prayer in Diadochos. It was in a footnote to this article that I first learned of the existence of an unedited uncial manuscript of the *One hundred practical texts*; thus the project of a new edition was indicated from the outset of my study of Diadochos. I would like to thank Mr Nigel Wilson, Dr David Parker and Dr Jeffrey Featherstone for looking at samples of the manuscript in an attempt to date it. Their thoughts are discussed in the introduction to the text. My particular thanks go to Dr Robert Jordan, whose advice on the more obscure grammatical puzzles of the text has been generously given over the whole course of my study of Diadochos, from dissertation to critical apparatus. I am also very grateful to Professor John Dillon for his painstaking appraisal of the text, and for casting a philosophical eye over the translation, introduction and commentary. This was done within severe time constraints, which calls for special thanks. I am only too aware of the many philosophical and patristic resonances which Professor Dillon quite rightly feels should be explored. As I explain in the Introduction, I hope this slim volume will encourage other scholars to pursue the many Diadochan links there must be with other authors. I have limited myself strictly to a consideration of his relation to his two overt sources, Evagrios and pseudo-Makarios, and even here I have been far from complete. This is for a reason; before looking for influence and relationship between Diadochos and other authors, it is necessary to elucidate the thinking of Diadochos in its own right. The task of translating Diadochos could be continued forever, and I am glad to be able to call a halt here. Professor Dillon was able to suggest some additional refinements to the translation, and in at least one case to resolve an outstanding mystification. I am also indebted to the attention which The Reverend Professor Brian Daley gave to the volume, again under severe time constraints. His comments have led to the inclusion of the note on the translation, and the summary of Diadochan anthropology which can be found in the Introduction. I am alive to the fact that my principles of translation, both in general terms and with specific reference to Diadochos's technical vocabulary, might be controversial, and I hope that the inclusion of these two features will clarify the reasoning behind my methodology. I must also thank Professor Michael McGann for last minute proof reading and further correction of the translation, which caught many residual errors. Finally I must mention the debt which all students of Diadochos owe to Édouard des Places for his exhaustive editing of all the works of Diadochos. This edition of the *One hundred practical texts* is based on his, and at every stage of my editing I have been conscious of the enormous debt I owe him. It goes without saying that any shortcomings in the text, translation, and comments contained in this volume are my own, and in no way reflect on the scholars who have so kindly advised me, or those upon whose work I have endeavoured to build.

Janet Elaine Rutherford   Belfast, 2000

Abbreviations

Bibliotheke	Photios, μυριοβιβλίον ἢ βιβλιοθήκη ed. R. Henry, *Bibliothèque*, (Paris, 1959)
Gnostic chapters	Evagrios, κεφάλαια γνωστικά, ed. A. Guillaumont, *Patrologia Orientalis* 28.i
Homilies	pseudo-Makarios, εὐχαί ed. H. Dörries, E. Klostermann, M. Kroeger, *Die 50 geistlichen Homilien des Makarios* (Berlin, 1964)
Œuvres spirituelles	E. des Places, *Œuvres spirituelles–Diadoque de Photicé* (Paris, 1966)
On Prayer	Evagrios, περὶ προσευχῆς, ed. J. Migne, *Patrologia Graeca* (Paris, 1857-1866), 79, 1165-1200
Praktikos	Evagrios, λόγος πρακτικός, ed. A. and C. Guillaumont, *Évagre le Pontique, Traité pratique ou Le moine* (Paris, 1971)
Sermon on the Ascension	Diadochos, εἰς τὴν ἀνάληψιν, ed. E. des Places, *Œuvres spirituelles–Diadoque de Photicé* (Paris, 1966)
REB	*Revue des études byzantines*
SPBS	Society for the Promotion of Byzantine Studies

Introduction

Diadochos of Photike's *One hundred practical texts of perception and spiritual discernment* has been an important work of devotional theology in the Orthodox church since its composition in the fifth century. Unfortunately it has been difficult to assess the full scope and significance of Diadochos's place within the history of the church, since he has a highly technical vocabulary, which he uses in a very precise and idiosyncratic way. This volume is the result not only of the discovery of a new and important manuscript of the text, but also of painstaking analysis of the exact significance of Diadochos's use of deceptively common ascetic language. The translation and commentary are designed to be used together to gain a clear understanding both of the author's highly developed theology, and of his place in the history of Christian prayer and theology–both in his own day and as a continuing influence within Orthodoxy to the present day.

Diadochos, like any important and original thinker, should be read on his own terms, and understood through his own words. In his case this is also a practical necessity, since almost nothing is known of his life. He seems to have become bishop of Photike in Epiros in northern Greece some time between the Council of Chalcedon in 451 and the death of the patriarch Proterios of Alexandria in 457.[1] Victor Vitensis describes him as having written 'many works of catholic doctrine,'[2] but of these only three remain[3]–the substantial work contained in this volume, a short reflection on the differences between divine, angelic, and human nature,[4] and part of a sermon on the Ascension,[5] which seems to have been preserved because of a single reference to Christ not being of 'one

---

[1] see Photios, μυριοβιβλίον ἢ βιβλιοθήκη ed. R. Henry, *Bibliothèque*, (Paris, 1959), III, 100; F. Dörr, *Diadochus von Photike und die Messalianer* (Freiburg, 1937).

[2] Victoris Vitensis, *Historia persecutionis Africanae provinciae*, ed. E. Schwartz (Vienna, 1866).

[3] A fourth work, ἐρωτήσεις καὶ ἀποκρίσεις, though attributed to Diadochos in some manuscripts, is more frequently attributed to Symeon the New Theologian, which is certainly correct. See J. Darrouzès, 'La Catéchèse de Diadoque', *REB*, 15 (1957), 172-175.

[4] ὅρασις, ed. E. des Places, *Œuvres spirituelles - Didaoque de Photicé* (Paris, 1966), 169-179.

[5] εἰς τὴν ἀνάληψιν, ed. E. des Places, *Œuvres spirituelles*, 164-168.

confused nature', and which was almost certainly written after the Council of Chalcedon, and probably after Diadochos had become a bishop.

Of these three works it is the *One hundred practical texts* which represents the apex of Diadochos's theological achievement, and which exerted the most profound influence upon the church. This work however was probably written before the Council of Chalcedon and Diadochos's accession as bishop. Diadochos gives no indication here that he is aware of contemporary Christological debates, and draws upon a Trinitarian theology and Christology which would have been familiar to Christians of the third century. As we shall see from reading the text and commentary, Diadochos has a very clear conception of the relationship of the persons of the Trinity–the Father from whom all existence flows, his Son the Logos inherent in the world as the Father's manifest presence, guiding creation, illumining it and giving it life, and the Spirit conveying the Son's risen presence into the individual soul, as baptismal grace first of all, and subsequently as the grace of illumination. This Trinitarian theology is perfectly suited to tackle the problem Diadochos confronts in his *practical texts*. His task in this work is to counter the more radical doctrinal suppositions of Messalianism, a heresy which was condemned at the Council of Ephesus in 431.

Arising in Mesopotamia in the mid-fourth century, Messalianism was a movement of intensely penitential piety which quickly influenced ascetics throughout Syria, Asia Minor, and Thrace. As with Diadochos himself, little is known of the details of Messalianism, beyond summaries of belief recorded by Timothy of Constantinople and John of Damascus. The status of various extant patristic works as being 'Messalian' or not has been hotly debated, given the sparse information we have of the movement.[6] We cannot even be certain that it constituted a formal 'sect' at all; it seems rather to have been an ascetic culture which inclined towards an exaggerated emphasis on human culpability. The errors Diadochos addresses can almost all be found in the version of the Makarian *Homilies* which has long been familiar to scholars in the West,[7] and references to this text will be given in the commentary as appropriate. Diadochos does not seem to have had personal experience of Messalians; he speaks of them vaguely, and often in the past tense. But if the more

---

[6] For a summary of this debate see E. des Places, *Œuvres spirituelles*, Introduction.

[7] Εὐχαί, ed. H. Dörries, E. Klostermann and M. Kroeger, *Die 50 geistlichen Homilien des Makarios* (Berlin, 1964).

dubious theological premises of Messalianism were not a concrete reality for him, the ascetic culture associated with it certainly was. Both its terminology and its emphasis on prayer as an emotional experience were very important to him, and to those to whom he wrote.

Like Diadochos himself, we know very little about the audience for whom his instruction was intended. He speaks of them in general terms, as those who practise asceticism in groups, or as hermits. It is not clear that they were all in one region, nor, on the assumption that Diadochos was writing between the councils of Ephesus and Chalcedon, can we even be sure that at this time he was in Old Epiros at all. But the tone of his writing makes it clear that he considered himself to have pastoral responsibility for instructing a diverse group of ascetics in the fundamentals of both the practice and theology of prayer. Perhaps we can find a clue in his name, which is a very curious one for a Christian ascetic, and later a bishop, to have. Meaning 'successor', 'diadochos' is most usually associated with the heads of philosophical schools, who succeeded to the responsibility both to safeguard and to interpret and develop the traditions which they inherited. While we cannot be sure that there was an association of ascetics who were formally grouped into some sort of Evagrian 'school' of asceticism, there is no doubt that Diadochos writes with authority to a dispersed group of monks whom he expected would regard his words as authoritative, instructing them in the right theory and practice of a form of prayer whose basis is Evagrian, but which has been developed to incorporate Makarian terminology and practice.

Because he attempted to preserve what was valuable in writings such as the Makarian *Homilies*, confusion arose earlier this century over whether Diadochos was himself Messalian. Ironically, this resulted from the method Diadochos used to attack Messalianism. Diadochos did not wish to give up devotional practices which so many ascetics, himself included, found very valuable. But something, possibly the Council of Ephesus, had roused him into an understanding of the doctrinal errors which could so easily arise from this form of asceticism. Over-emphasis on human unworthiness had led Messalians to doubt the capacity of human beings to be saved at all; baptism was seen as only imperfectly cleansing the soul from sin, with Satan still indwelling us and only ever retreating to the edges of our souls through human efforts of unceasing prayer and penitence. On the evidence of the Makarian *Homilies* there seems to have been a corresponding emphasis on the merit of Christ's sacrifice on the cross as the necessary payment for the unpayable debt of sin which each human being owes to God. Penitence, unceasing prayer, attention to one's experience of prayer to give evidence of the presence of grace–all these must be valuable tools for an ascetic. Diadochos attempts to wrench the language and culture of Messalian prayer away from its heretical associations by demonstrating that Messalians have misinterpreted the Scriptural references on which they have based their theology, and from which they have drawn their terminology–in short, he uses both their language and their proof-texts against them, to claim both for orthodox asceticism.

But this is not the sum of Diadochos's achievement. In trying to counter Messalian claims that their doctrines were validated by their spiritual experiences and Scripture, Diadochos realised that in order for ascetics to dare to pray at all it would be necessary to address a question which has haunted thinkers throughout the ages, and which is no less pressing today: How can we know that anything we experience or reason for ourselves is true? On what basis can we validly interpret our experiences and intuitions of God, or of Scripture? Diadochos saw that to answer this question it is necessary to relate it to every other important question of theology: What is the state of the human soul as a result of original sin? Is it capable of recognising evidence validly, and validly interpreting it, at all? What exactly is our human predicament, and how can God help us out of it? How much does God do for us, and what must we do to make his gifts of grace effective? It is probable that the condemnation of Messalianism was the crisis of Diadochos's life, since through it he came to realise that neither appealing to Scripture nor making unceasing petitions to God can guarantee freedom from serious doctrinal error. And since the goal of those who pray is to find God in truth–a true experience of true reality–he saw that it was necessary to find a way forward that would safeguard both our experience of prayer and our interpretation of that experience. This necessitated a precise theory of both the state of the fallen human intellect and the nature of God's saving intervention.

Starting from his own experience of the ascetic life, Diadochos found validation of both the practice and theory of prayer in a thorough and reflective reading of Scripture, combined with analysis of one's experiences during prayer. Of course, these were precisely the criteria claimed by Messalians. But Diadochos believed that Messalian error derived from flaws in both criteria–they had no means of discriminating between spiritual experiences which might be of either divine or demonic origin, and consequently they did not have a sound basis for interpreting

INTRODUCTION

Scripture. Diadochos finds the reason for these and all similar theological errors in the innate vulnerability of the human intellect due to original sin. He sees three components to the human intellect: Will, Sense, and Reason–all of which must be integrated in completely harmonious Recollection of God in order for the intellect accurately to assess the true significance of both spiritual experience and Scripture. The intellect's Sense perceives spiritual experiences, which must be closely examined by Reason against the criterion of Scripture. It is for the human Will to hold Sense and Reason in an integrated disposition towards God. Unfortunately, as a result of Adam's fall, all three intellectual faculties–Will, Sense, and Reason–which were originally whole and integrated, have wavered from concentration on God and fragmented towards the created world. Thus all three must be assisted by grace to maintain the integrated disposition towards God which is necessary for valid assessment of spiritual evidence–and it is valid assessment of spiritual evidence which enables us to know the state of our spiritual health and what to do about it. The damaged Will must be steadied through psalmody, but especially through recitation of the prayer 'Lord Jesus,' gathering Sense and Reason into integrated Recollection of God long enough for grace to complete the transformation of this imperfect, willed integration into a restoration of true wholeness. But this is a work which can never be completed in this life. The proper co-operation between the human will and grace not only enables God to restore the damaged human being to its pre-fallen state, but also makes it possible for the risen Christ to illumine each individual into a greater likeness to God than Adam and Eve had had to start with. Yet throughout life the tendency for our attention to wander back to the world remains. And so, ranging from the most intricate theology to a consideration of the most prosaic aspects of ascetic life, Diadochos presents an integrated picture of human nature, body and soul in relation to God and neighbour, so that the whole human being is reintegrated into proper relationship within creation. Every criterion Diadochos sets out is based on Scripture, sometimes explicit and sometimes implicit, as will be discussed in the commentary.

Diadochos's theological stature in addressing these fundamental problems is unique in patristic literature. Ironically, his technique of using Messalian terminology in a new way to demonstrate Messalian errors not only led to his language being very hard to understand; it has also led scholars to view his work primarily as a source for learning more about the legacy of pseudo-Makarios, and Diadochos's other main influence, Evagrios, rather than reading the *Texts* as an original theological work in its own right. In fact, Diadochos's problem of finding a criterion for judging spiritual evidence necessitated such a highly integrated theory of humanity, God, and the nature of sin, that it is not possible to learn much about Diadochos's use of his sources until one can understand them as integrated parts of his whole theology, aware of the precise meaning he gives their language. It is for this reason that explanations of the details of Diadochos's theology are best understood in the context of his arguments, and are presented here as a commentary. Any thematic treatment of Diadochos severs the multiplicity of relationships between one aspect of his thinking and all the others. Diadochos's treatment of his sources is correspondingly multifaceted, so that references to them in the commentary are not intended to be complete. An effort has been made to show the main aspects of Messalianism which Diadochos was countering, and the main aspects of Evagrian asceticism which he draws upon. But an author of such complexity, and such wide education, will doubtless raise a host of associations in the minds of his readers. This volume is not therefore intended to be the last word on Diadochos; rather it is meant to be a resource for further research, and a catalyst to restoring Diadochos to his rightful place both in Christian theology and in devotional tradition– since those who study and those who pray ought to be united in their need for precise and accurate texts and translations. Of all that Diadochos has to offer, this insight is not the least: that theological understanding and the practice of prayer are not distinct, separable aspects of human endeavour. As Immanuel Kant wrote in his *Critique of pure reason*, 'Thoughts without content are empty; intuitions without concepts are blind . . . they can supply objectively valid judgements of things only in conjunction with each other.' Dealing with spiritual sensation in a way which we are accustomed to do when dealing with physical sensation, Diadochos had an early understanding of just this relationship between reason and experience.

The human being according to Diadochos

Ἄνθρωπος refers both to the individual person and to corporate humanity. Each person is composed of body and SOUL (ψυχή), which are joined at the interface of the HEART (καρδία). The soul comprises three parts, of which the INTELLECT (νοῦς) is the guiding faculty. Because of the disobedience of Adam and Eve all human beings are subject to fragmentation of the intellect. The WILL (θέλησις) is the intellect's capacity to co-operate with God's grace to regain the HABIT (ἕξις) of RECOLLECTION (μνήμη) of God. The intellect apprehends and assesses

INTRODUCTION

experiential EVIDENCE (πεῖρα) of both divine and demonic activity in the heart through synergy between its two balancing faculties, SENSE (αἴσθησις) and REASON (διάνοια). Sense feels divine and demonic activity by a process of PERCEPTION (γνῶσις), which is the intellectual equivalent of bodily sense perception. Reason weighs this evidence in the light of Scripture. Grace communicates to Reason, and Reason articulates what grace communicates, by a process of DIVINE CONVERSE (θεολογία). Reason also assesses the Sense's feelings of conscience, by a process of SELF-EXAMINATION (ἔλεγχος) to determine whether the Will is in full harmony with the holy Spirit's activity of grace.

THE INTELLECT

```
                    Will
                  (habit)
              (recollection)

   Sense   ←——————————————→   Reason
(perception)               (divine converse)
(evidence)                 (self-examination)
```

The interrelatedness of these terms is an integral part of their significance for Diadochos. Trying to define any one of them in isolation is misleading, and for this reason there is no index of terms in this volume. Each term will be discussed in the commentary, in the context in which it arises, in order to emphasise the coherence of Diadochos's thinking.

INTRODUCTION

The text

This edition grew out of a footnote. In his article, 'The Jesus Prayer in St Diadochus of Photike', [8] Kallistos Ware signalled his discovery in the Lavra monastery of Mt. Athos of an uncial manuscript containing the works of Mark the Monk and this work of Diadochos of Photike. This manuscript, Γ 42, had been mistakenly dated in the catalogue as fourteenth century, and had not been examined by Édouard des Places in preparing his excellent edition of the works of Diadochos. [9] Having devoted my doctoral thesis to an examination of Diadochos's technical vocabulary and an English translation of des Places's text, the next stage was obviously to prepare a new edition, taking account of a manuscript which must pre-date all the others extant by at least a century, if not significantly more. It is, unfortunately, not possible to date uncials with precision unless there is some external evidence upon which to do so. But I am grateful to Mr Nigel Wilson, Dr Jeffrey Featherstone, and Dr David Parker for looking at prints of the manuscript, and confirming that its most likely date is late eighth to early ninth century–though this estimate is made primarily on historical grounds, and the manuscript might indeed be older. The need for a new edition and translation was also indicated by the fact that des Places's edition is no longer in print, nor is there an English translation of Diadochos in print. In addition, having untangled the precise significance of Diadochos's technical vocabulary, and the intricate theology he constructs with it, lucid translation of Diadochos is now much easier to achieve with confidence, without relying on paraphrase, as has so often been necessary in the past.

Finding an early manuscript is of course not enough reason to embark on a new edition of a text; the quality of text represented by the manuscript is the important thing. So I was excited to discover that, apart from many standard orthographic errors (exacerbated by the lack of diacriticals in uncial manuscripts), the text of Diadochos in Lavra Γ 42 is not only complete, it is also an excellent witness, supplying in many cases the missing link between variant readings of the two main manuscript families identified by des Places. In some cases the uncial gives what is obviously the origin of the variants; in others, it gives weight to one or other reading; and in at least one case it is the only witness to a very necessary noun, where all other manuscripts have a dangling adjective. This text is in fact not dissimilar to des Places's own; where they do

---

[8] *Aksum-Thyateira* (Athens, 1985), 558 note 3.
[9] *Œuvres spirituelles.*

INTRODUCTION

diverge, it is usually due to the inclusion of primitive features either not present in other manuscripts, or present in so few of them as not to have been convincing to des Places. These features present a very convincing witness to what is now known of the Diadochan lexis. In some cases they pertain to *nomina sacra*; Diadochos is precise in the use of all his language, and this is true of his references to the persons of the Trinity. *Lord*, apart from quotations from the Old Testament, invariably refers to Jesus; so in some places the reading *God* is preferred to *Lord*, since the reference is to the Father; in others *Spirit* is preferred to *God* with reference to the conveyance of grace. There are many more references to the name *Jesus* in most of the later manuscripts than there are in this one, but that does not indicate a serious flaw in any of them. Diadochos very clearly articulates the use of the prayer 'Lord Jesus', but he often refers to Jesus simply as *the Lord*, or *our Lord*, to which subsequent scribes have quite legitimately added *Jesus* or *Jesus Christ*. Because it is now known how precisely Diadochos used language, it has in most cases been a straightforward task to identify primitive readings in establishing this text.

This edition is, then, intended to complement the painstaking work of Édouard des Places. His manuscript designations have been retained, and the new uncial has been designated accordingly; since it most often agrees with S (manuscript family 2), and T (manuscript family 1), it is referred to as R. As well as taking account of the new uncial, I have also been able to obtain a copy of M (Mosqu. gr. 184), which des Places was unable to consult himself, having to rely on notes from a previous edition by Weis-Liebersdorf.[10] Unfortunately this important manuscript has not fared well since Weis-Liebersdorf examined it, and is now incomplete and in very bad condition. Des Places examined or re-examined the manuscripts AaBbcFGHNSTtV. Apart from the edition of Weis-Liebersdorf, which was based on AabcM, there had been an edition by Popov (Kiev, 1903) which had as its foundation AM and the *Philokalia* of St Nikodemos of the Holy Mountain. It will be obvious then that in Diadochan textual scholarship the lion's share of the work has been done by des Places; this edition is based on his work, and it is hoped that the unravelling of Diadochan vocabulary together with the exciting witness of Lavra Γ 42 provide the foundations of a not unworthy successor.

---

[10] Leipzig, 1912.

INTRODUCTION

Manuscripts appearing in the critical apparatus are as follows:

A	Vindob. theol. gr. 93 (olim 158), 10th century
a	Paris. gr. 913, 10th century
B	Monac. gr. 498, 10th century
b	Paris. gr. 1053, 10th century
c	Paris. Coislin. 123, 11th century
F	Paris. gr. 1056, 11th century
G	Vatic. Chis. gr. R IV 7, 10th century
H	Hierosol. Sabait. 157, 10th century
K	Casensis LL 231, 11th century
M	Mosqu. gr. 184 (olim 145), 10th century
N	Cryptensis B α. 19, 10th century
P	Patmos 189, 11th century
R	Athos Lavra Γ 42, 8th-9th centuries(?)
S	Mutin. Estens. gr. α. U. 2. 12, 11th century
T	Athen. Bibl. nat. 549, 11th century
t	Vatic. gr. 392, 12th-13th centuries
V	Vatic. gr. 2028, 10th century

Details of the characteristics of the manuscripts and of their relationships can be found in des Places's introduction. They are not replicated here since both the reliability of variant readings and the relationship between witnesses should be clear from the critical apparatus. The prevalence of itacism in R sometimes leads to ambiguity as to which manuscript family it agrees with; in these cases it will appear where agreement is most likely, but as (R). Because there are so many good witnesses to the text, neither Photios's *Bibliotheke* nor the *Philokalia* of Nikodemos of the Holy Mountain has been referred to in the critical apparatus; neither of them provides evidence which is not more strongly witnessed in the above manuscripts.

One hundred practical texts of perception and spiritual discernment from Diadochos of Photike

Text and translation

Διαδόχου ἐπισκόπου Φωτικῆς τῆς Παλαιᾶς Ἠπείρου
τοῦ Ἰλλυρικοῦ κεφάλαια πρακτικὰ γνώσεως καὶ
διακρίσεως πνευματικῆς ρ΄

5   Πρῶτος ὅρος τῆς πίστεως· ἔννοια περὶ θεοῦ ἀπαθής.
     Δεύτερος ὅρος τῆς ἐλπίδος· ἐκδημία τοῦ νοῦ ἐν ἀγάπῃ πρὸς τὰ
     ἐλπιζόμενα.
     Τρίτος ὅρος τῆς ὑπομονῆς· τὸν ἀόρατον ὡς ὁρατὸν ὁρῶντα τοῖς τῆς
     διανοίας ὀφθαλμοῖς ἀδιαλείπτως καρτερεῖν.
10   Τέταρτος ὅρος τῆς ἀφιλαργυρίας· οὕτω θέλειν τὸ μὴ ἔχειν ὡς θέλει τις
     τὸ ἔχειν.
     Πέμπτος ὅρος τῆς ἐπιγνώσεως· ἀγνοεῖν ἑαυτὸν ἐν τῷ ἐκστῆναι θεῷ.
     Ἕκτος ὅρος τῆς ταπεινοφροσύνης· λήθη τῶν κατορθουμένων προσεχής.
     Ἕβδομος ὅρος τῆς ἀοργησίας· ἐπιθυμία πολλὴ τοῦ μὴ ὀργίζεσθαι.
15   Ὄγδοος ὅρος τῆς ἁγνείας· αἴσθησις ἀεὶ κεκολλημένη θεῷ.
     Ἔνατος ὅρος τῆς ἀγάπης· αὔξησις φιλίας πρὸς τοὺς ὑβρίζοντας.
     Δέκατος ὅρος τῆς τελείας ἀλλοιώσεως· ἐν τρυφῇ θεοῦ χαρὰν ἡγεῖσθαι τὸ
     στυγνὸν τοῦ θανάτου.

20   Λόγοι κρίσεως καὶ διακρίσεως πνευματικῆς Διαδόχου ἐπισκόπου
     Φωτικῆς τῆς Ἠπείρου. Διὰ ποίας δεῖ γνώσεως εἰς τὴν προδεδηλωμένην
     τοῦ κυρίου ἡμᾶς ὁδηγοῦντος καταφθάσαι τελειότητα, ἵνα ἕκαστος ἡμῶν
     τῶν κατὰ τὸ σχῆμα τῆς ἐλευθερικῆς παραβολῆς τὸ τοῦ λόγου σπέρμα
     καρποφορήσωμεν.

1-3 Titulus sec. R: Διαδόχου ἐπισκόπου Φωτικῆς τῆς Ἠπείρου κεφάλαια γνωστικὰ
ρ΄ Nb (ρ om. b) τοῦ μακαρίου Διαδόχου ἐπισκόπου Φωτικῆς τῆς Ἠπείρου τοῦ
Ἰλλυρικοῦ λόγος ἀσκητικός· κεφάλαια ρ΄ ὅροι ι΄ προλεγόμενοι T titulum totum om.
MS ‖ 4 Definitiones om. RS ‖ 6 ἐν ἀγάπῃ om. T ‖ 8 ὁρῶντα] ὁρᾶν καὶ a ‖ 9 καρτερεῖν]
ἐγκαρτερεῖν T ‖ 12 ἐπιγνώσεως AMNa: γνώσεως BT ‖ 20-21 λόγοι - Ἠπείρου Nb:
τοῦ αὐτοῦ ἁγίου Διαδόχου . . . κεφάλαια ρ΄ B τοῦ αὐτοῦ κεφάλαια πρακτικὰ
γνώσεως καὶ διακρίσεως πνευματικῆς ἑκατόν T nihil AMRac ‖ 21-24 διὰ -
καρποφορήσωμεν om. MR ‖ 22 ἵνα] ἢν b ‖ ἕκαστος ἡμῶν Ac: ἕκαστος BNTab ‖ 23
ἐλευθερικῆς] εὐαγγελικῆς T ‖ τὸ τοῦ TV: τοῦ ceteri ‖ post καρποφορήσωμεν add. καὶ
εἰσὶν κεφάλαια ρ΄ A: κεφάλαια ρ΄ b τοῦ μακαρίου Διαδόχου ἐπισκόπου Φωτικῆς τῆς
Ἠπείρου λόγος ἀσκητικὸς κεφαλαίων ρ΄ c nihil BMNRTa.

One hundred practical texts of perception and spiritual discernment from Diadochos bishop of Photike in Old Epiros in Illyrikon

First definition:	*Faith: dispassionate intellectual conception concerning God.*
Second definition:	*Hope: journeying of the intellect in love towards things hoped for.*
Third definition:	*Steadfastness: to persevere ceaselessly, seeing what is unseen just as what is seen, with the eyes of reason.*
Fourth definition:	*Freedom from affection for money: to want not to have, in the same way as one wants to have.*
Fifth definition:	*Full perception: to be unaware of oneself in being taken away to God.*
Sixth definition:	*Humble-mindedness: being particularly oblivious to one's achievements.*
Seventh definition:	*Freedom from anger: a great desire not to be angry.*
Eighth definition:	*Purity: a Sense which always cleaves to God.*
Ninth definition:	*Love: the increase of affection towards those who are insulting.*
Tenth definition:	*Perfect transformation: in the sumptuousness of God to hold the hatefulness of death to be joy.*

Words of judgement and spiritual discernment of Diadochos bishop of Photike in Epiros. Through what sort of perception it is necessary to be guided by the Lord to arrive at that perfection which has been shown to us; so that each of us who accord with the pattern of the liberating parable[1] may bring to fruition the seed of the Logos.

---

[1] See Matthew 13:8f/ Mark 4:8f/ Luke 8:8f.

ΔΙΑΔΟΧΟΥ

α΄.

Πάσης πνευματικῆς, ἀδελφοί, ἡγείσθω θεωρίας πίστις ἐλπὶς ἀγάπη, πλέον δὲ ἡ ἀγάπη. Αἱ μὲν γὰρ καταφρονεῖν τῶν ὁρωμένων ἐκδιδάσκουσι καλῶν· ἡ δὲ ἀγάπη αὐταῖς συνάπτει τὴν ψυχὴν ταῖς ἀρεταῖς τοῦ θεοῦ, αἰσθήσει νοερᾷ τὸν ἀόρατον ἐξιχνεύουσα.

β΄.

Φύσει ἀγαθὸς μόνος ὁ θεός ἐστιν. Γίνεται δὲ καὶ ἄνθρωπος ἐξ ἐπιμελείας τῶν τρόπων ἀγαθὸς διὰ τοῦ ὄντως ἀγαθοῦ, εἰς ὅπερ οὐκ ἔστιν ἀλλασσόμενος, ὅταν ἡ ψυχὴ διὰ τῆς ἐπιμελείας τοῦ καλοῦ τοσοῦτον γένηται ἐν θεῷ ὅσον ἡ ταύτης δύναμις ἐνεργουμένη θέλει· γίνεσθε γάρ, φησίν, ἀγαθοὶ καὶ οἰκτίρμονες ὡς ὁ πατὴρ ὑμῶν ὁ ἐν τοῖς οὐρανοῖς.

γ΄.

Τὸ κακὸν οὔτε ἐν φύσει ἐστὶν οὔτε μὴν φύσει τίς ἐστι κακός· κακὸν γάρ τι ὁ θεὸς οὐκ ἐποίησεν. Ὅτε δὲ ἐν τῇ ἐπιθυμίᾳ τῆς καρδίας εἰς εἶδός τις φέρει τὸ οὐκ ὂν ἐν οὐσίᾳ, τότε ἄρχεται εἶναι ὅπερ ἂν ὁ τοῦτο ποιῶν θέλοι. Δεῖ οὖν ἀεὶ τῇ ἐπιμελείᾳ τῆς μνήμης τοῦ θεοῦ ἀμελεῖν τῆς ἕξεως τοῦ κακοῦ· δυνατωτέρα γάρ ἐστιν ἡ φύσις τοῦ καλοῦ τῆς ἕξεως τοῦ κακοῦ, ἐπειδὴ τὸ μὲν ἔστιν, τὸ δὲ οὐκ ἔστιν, εἰ μὴ μόνον ἐν τῷ πράττεσθαι.

δ΄.

Πάντες ἄνθρωποι κατ᾽ εἰκόνα ἐσμὲν τοῦ θεοῦ· τὸ δὲ καθ᾽ ὁμοίωσιν ἐκείνων μόνον ἐστὶ τῶν διὰ πολλῆς ἀγάπης τὴν ἑαυτῶν ἐλευθερίαν δουλωσάντων τῷ θεῷ. Ὅτε γὰρ οὐκ ἐσμὲν ἑαυτῶν, τότε ὅμοιοί ἐσμεν τῷ

---

3 ἐκδιδάσκουσι] διδάσκουσι B ∥ αὐταῖς] αὐτὴν MT ∥ 9 ὄντως] ὄντος AT ∥ 10 καλοῦ] ἀγαθοῦ M ∥ 11 γένηται BTa: γίνεται AMNS ∥ ταύτης AMNRS: αὐτῆς BTa ∥ 12 ὡς] ὥσπερ R ∥ ὑμῶν] ἡμων M ∥ 16 ἐν] ἐν τῇ a ∥ τίς ἐστι κακός] ἐστίν τι κακόν M ∥ 18 τι om. a ∥ ὅτε ABNST: ὅταν Ma ∥ τῇ om. a ∥ εἰς om. AM ∥ 18 τις ABNSTa: τι MR ∥ φέρει] ἄγοι a ∥ ὅπερ] καθ᾽ ὁ BNRS ∥ 19 ἀεὶ om. R ∥ θέου] θεοῦ καὶ παντὸς ἔργου ἀγαθοῦ a ∥ 20 τῆς ἕξεως τοῦ κακοῦ om. b ∥ 20-21 δυνατωτέρα - κακοῦ om. R ∥ εἰ μὴ BMRSTa: ἢ AN om. b ∥ 25 τοῦ θεοῦ ANRST et (+ τῷ νοερῷ τῆς ψυχῆς κινήματι) a: θεοῦ BM ∥ 26 μόνον BNa.c. c: μόνων AMNp.c.STab ∥ πολλῆς ἀγάπης] πολλὴν ἀγάπην R ∥ 27 τότε BNRSTa: om. AM.

DIADOCHOS

1.   Let faith, hope, and love guide all spiritual contemplation, brethren; but above all love.[2] For the former thoroughly teach us to despise those good things which are visible; but love binds the soul to the very virtues of God, tracking down, by an intellectual Sense, that which is unseen.

2.   God alone is good by nature. But a human being becomes good also through that which is really good, from attention to habits, being transformed into that which it is not whenever the soul (through attention to good) comes to be in God as much as its activated power decides. For it says, 'Become good and compassionate as your Father who is in heaven.'[3]

3.   What is bad does not exist by nature nor indeed is anyone bad by nature. For God did not make anything bad. But when, in the desire of the heart, one casts into a form that which is not in existence, then it begins to be whatever its maker may decide. And so, in paying attention to the recollection of God, one must always ignore the habit of that which is bad. For the nature of what is good is more powerful than the habit of what is bad, since the former exists but the latter does not exist, except in being performed.

4.   We are all of us in the image of God; but to be in the likeness is a characteristic only of those who, through great love, submit their own freedom to God. For when we are not our own then we are like him who

---

[2] See 1 Corinthians 13:13.
[3] See Matthew 5:48/Luke 6:36.

ΔΙΑΔΟΧΟΥ

ἡμᾶς ἑαυτῷ δι' ἀγάπης καταλλάξαντι· οὐπέρ τις οὐκ ἐπιτεύξεται, εἰ μὴ μὴ πτοεῖσθαι τὴν ἑαυτοῦ ψυχὴν περὶ τὴν τοῦ βίου εὔκολον δόξαν πείσοι.

ε'.

Αὐτεξουσιότης ἐστὶ ψυχῆς λογικῆς θέλησις ἑτοίμως κινουμένη εἰς ὅπερ ἂν καὶ θέλοι· ἥντινα περὶ μόνον τὸ καλὸν ἑτοίμως ἔχειν πείσομεν, ἵνα ἀεὶ ταῖς ἀγαθαῖς ἐννοίαις τὴν μνήμην ἀναλίσκωμεν τοῦ κακοῦ.

ϛ'.

Φῶς ἐστι γνώσεως ἀληθινῆς τὸ διακρίνειν ἀπταίστως τὸ καλὸν ἐκ τοῦ κακοῦ· τότε γὰρ ἡ τῆς δικαιοσύνης ὁδὸς τὸν νοῦν ἀπάγουσα πρὸς τὸν τῆς δικαιοσύνης ἥλιον εἰς ἄπειρον αὐτὸν φωτισμὸν παρεισάγει γνώσεως ὡς μετὰ παρρησίας λοιπὸν τὴν ἀγάπην ζητοῦντα. Δεῖ τοίνυν ἀοργήτῳ θυμῷ ἁρπάζειν τὸ δίκαιον ἐκ τῶν αὐτὸ ἐνυβρίζειν τολμώντων· ὁ γὰρ τῆς εὐσεβείας ζῆλος οὐ μισῶν ἀλλ' ἐλέγχων τὸ νῖκος ἐνδείκνυται.

ζ'.

Ὁ πνευματικὸς λόγος τὴν νοερὰν αἴσθησιν πληροφορεῖ· ἐνεργείᾳ γὰρ ἀγάπης ἐκ τοῦ θεοῦ φέρεται, διόπερ καὶ ἀβασάνιστος ἡμῶν ὁ νοῦς διαμένει ἐν τοῖς τῆς θεολογίας κινήμασιν. Οὐ γὰρ πάσχει τότε πενίαν τὴν μέριμναν φέρουσαν, ἐπειδὴ τοσοῦτον ταῖς θεωρίαις πλατύνεται ὅσον τῆς ἀγάπης ἡ ἐνέργεια θέλει. Καλὸν οὖν ἀεὶ πίστει περιμένειν δι' ἀγάπης ἐνεργουμένῃ τὸν φωτισμὸν τοῦ λέγειν· οὐδὲν γὰρ πτωχότερον διανοίας ἐκτὸς θεοῦ φιλοσοφούσης τὰ τοῦ θεοῦ.

1-2 μὴ μὴ] μὴ Rac ‖ 3 πείσοι] πείσει S ‖ 6 κινουμένη] κινουμένης Ac ‖ 7 καὶ θέλοι] καὶ ἐθέλοι a ‖ 6 πείσομεν ABNc: πείσωμεν M(R)STab ‖ 11 ἀληθινῆς] ἀληθοῦς a ‖ ἐκ] ἀπὸ B ‖ 12 ἀπάγουσα ABMNRSTa: ἀνάγουσα F ‖ 13 ἥλιον AMa: θεὸν BNRST ‖ 15 θυμῷ] τῷ θυμῷ B ‖ τῶν] τοῦ c ‖ αὐτὸ om. Na ‖ ἐνυβρίζειν ABRSTa: ὑβρίζειν MN ‖ 16 τὸ νῖκος] τὴν νίκην FT ‖ 22 πλατύνεται] ἐμπλατύνεται a ‖ 23 οὖν om. b ‖ ἀεὶ] ἂν εἴη a ‖ 24 ἐνεργουμένῃ τὸν φωτισμὸν MN: ἐνεργουμένης τὸν φωτισμὸν ABST ἐνεργούμενον τὸν φωτισμὸν a τὴν ἐνέργειαν R ‖ 25 ἐκτὸς] ἐκ M ‖ pr. θεοῦ] τοῦ θεοῦ AMR ‖ τοῦ] περὶ b.

reconciled us to himself through love.[4] One will not attain this, unless he persuades his own soul not to be excited by the easy glory of this life.

5. Independence is the will of a rational soul moved readily into whatever it may decide; we will persuade it to hold readily only that which is good, so that through good intellectual conceptions we may always eradicate the recollection of that which is bad.

6. Light of true perception is to discern good from bad unerringly; for then the path of righteousness, leading the intellect away to the sun of righteousness,[5] introduces it into a boundless illumination of perception as it then seeks love with boldness. So one must, with a temper free from anger, seize what is righteous from those who have the effrontery to insult it. For the zeal of piety demonstrates victory not by hating but by refuting.

7. Spiritual expression fully convinces the intellectual Sense, for it is borne from God by an activity of love; and so our unaccused intellect stands firm in the movements of divine converse; for then it does not suffer the anxiety which deficiency brings, since it expands in contemplations as much as the activity of love decides. Therefore it is good always to await the illumination to speak, in a faith activated through love.[6] For nothing is more inadequate than reasoning which philosophises outside God about the things of God.

---

[4] See 2 Corinthians 5:19.
[5] Malachi 4:2.
[6] See Galatians 5:6.

ΔΙΑΔΟΧΟΥ

η'.

Οὔτε ἀφώτιστον ὄντα δεῖ ἐπιβάλλειν τοῖς πνευματικοῖς θεωρήμασιν, οὔτε μὴν πλουσίως καταλαμπόμενον ὑπὸ τῆς χρηστότητος τοῦ ἁγίου πνεύματος ἐπὶ τὸ λέγειν ἔρχεσθαι. Ὅπου μὲν γὰρ πενία, φέρει τὴν ἄγνοιαν· ὅπου δὲ πλοῦτος, οὐ συνχωρεῖ τὸ λέγειν. Μεθύουσα γὰρ τότε ἡ ψυχὴ τῇ ἀγάπῃ τοῦ θεοῦ σιγώσῃ φωνῇ θέλει κατατρυφᾶν τῆς δόξης τοῦ κυρίου. Τὴν οὖν μεσότητα δεῖ ἐπιτηροῦντα τῆς ἐνεργείας εἰς λόγους θεηγόρους ἔρχεσθαι. Τοῦτο μὲν γὰρ τὸ μέτρον εἶδός τι λόγων ἐνδόξων χαρίζεται, ἡ δὲ τῆς ἐλλάμψεως πολυτέλεια τὴν πίστιν τρέφει τοῦ λέγοντος ἐν πίστει, ἵνα πρῶτος ὁ διδάσκων τῶν καρπῶν γεύσηται δι' ἀγάπης τῆς γνώσεως. Τὸν κοπιῶντα γάρ, φησίν, γεωργὸν δεῖ πρῶτον τῶν καρπῶν μεταλαμβάνειν.

θ'.

Τοῦ μὲν ἑνὸς ἁγίου πνεύματός ἐστι χαρίσματα ἥ τε σοφία καὶ ἡ γνῶσις ὡς καὶ πάντα τὰ θεῖα χαρίσματα, ἰδίαν δὲ ὥσπερ ἕκαστον τὴν ἐνέργειαν ἔχει. Διόπερ ἄλλῳ μὲν δίδοσθαι σοφίαν, ἄλλῳ δὲ γνῶσιν κατὰ τὸ αὐτὸ πνεῦμα ὁ ἀπόστολος μαρτυρεῖ. Ἡ μὲν γὰρ γνῶσις πείρᾳ τὸν ἄνθρωπον συνάπτει τῷ θεῷ, εἰς λόγους τῶν πραγμάτων τὴν ψυχὴν μὴ κινοῦσα. Διὸ καί τινες τῶν τὸν μονήρη φιλοσοφούντων βίον φωτίζονται μὲν ὑπ' αὐτῆς ἐν αἰσθήσει, εἰς λόγους δὲ θείους οὐκ ἔρχονται. Ἡ δὲ σοφία εἴπερ μετ' αὐτῆς ἐν φόβῳ δοθῇ τινι, σπάνιον δὲ τοῦτο, αὐτὰς τὰς ἐνεργείας φανεροῖ τῆς γνώσεως· ἐπειδὴ ἡ μὲν τῇ ἐνεργείᾳ, ἡ δὲ τῷ λόγῳ φωτίζειν εἴωθεν. Ἀλλὰ τὴν μὲν γνῶσιν εὐχὴ φέρει καὶ πολλὴ ἡσυχία ἐν ἀμεριμνίᾳ παντελεῖ, τὴν δὲ σοφίαν ἀκενόδοξος μελέτη τῶν λογίων τοῦ πνεύματος καὶ πρῶτον ἡ χάρις τοῦ διδόντος θεοῦ.

3 ἁγίου] παναγίου Ta ‖ 4 τὸ] τοῦ b ‖ 6 τῇ ἀγάπῃ] ὑπὸ τῆς ἀγάπης a ‖ 7 τοῦ κυρίου] κυρίου Fb ‖ ἐπιτηροῦντα] ἐπιτηροῦντας Aa ‖ 8 εἶδός τι Aa.c. BMRSTa: εἰδότι Ap.c. ἤδος τι N ‖ λόγων ἐνδόξων] λόγον ἔνδοξον A ‖ 9 χαρίζεται] τῇ ψυχῇ χαρίζεται a ‖ 10 τῶν καρπῶν] τῷ καρπῷ Nb τοῦ καρποῦ S ‖ 12 μεταλαμβάνειν] μεταλαβεῖν N ‖ 15 ἑνὸς om. Mac ‖ ἐστι] εἰσὶ c ‖ χαρίσματα] τὰ χαρίσματα Nb ‖ 15-16 ἡ γνῶσις] γνῶσις Mc γνώσεις b ‖ 16 ὡς om. R ‖ ἕκαστον] ἕκαστον αὐτῶν a ‖ 17 δίδοσθαι] δεδόσθαι c ‖ σοφίαν] λόγον σοφίας a ‖ γνῶσιν] λόγον γνώσεως a ‖ πείρᾳ] τῇ πείρᾳ ARa ‖ 21 θείους] θεηγόρους a ‖ 22 ἐν φόβῳ] ἐμφόβῳ A ἐν φόβῳ θεοῦ a ‖ δοθῇ ABNRc: δοθείη Ta δόθει M δοθέε S ‖ αὐτὰς] αὐτοὺς b ‖ 23 γνώσεως] γνώσεως ἐν ἀγάπῃ a ‖ ἐπειδὴ] ἐπειδὴ ἀγάπῃ A ‖ 25 ἀκενόδοξος] ἡ ἀκενόδοξος RSa ‖ 26 λογίων] λόγων Ab ‖ πνεύματος RSa: θεοῦ ceteri ‖ διδόντος] δόντος M ‖ θεοῦ AMTa: χριστοῦ B om. NRS.

8. One must neither apply oneself to spiritual contemplations while unilluminated nor indeed enter into speaking when shining abundantly from the excellence of the holy Spirit. For where there is deficiency it brings want of perception, but where there is excess it does not allow speech–because then the soul, being intoxicated by the love of God, intends to exult in the glory of the Lord with a silent voice. So one must keep to a middle degree of activity in entering into statements speaking of God, since this degree freely gives any sort of glorious statements; whereas the extravagance of illumining nurtures the faith of the one who speaks in faith, so that he who teaches might be first to taste the fruits through love of perception. For the husbandman who labours, it says, must share in the fruits first.[7]

9. Wisdom and perception, like all divine gifts of grace, are gifts of the one holy Spirit; but each has as it were its own activity. Thus, as the Apostle testifies, wisdom is given to one and perception to another in relation to the same Spirit.[8] Perception binds man to God through evidence, without moving the soul into statements of the facts; and so some of those who philosophise in the solitary life are illuminated by perception in the Sense without entering into divine statements. Even if wisdom *is* given to someone in fear along with perception (and this is seldom) it displays the same activities of perception; since the one habitually illuminates in activity and the other in word. For it is prayer and great stillness which bring perception in absolute freedom from care, while it is freedom from vainglory in attention to the utterances of the Spirit, and primarily the grace of God who gives, which bring wisdom.

---

[7] See 2 Timothy 2:6.
[8] See 1 Corinthians 12:8.

ΔΙΑΔΟΧΟΥ

ι'.

Ὅτε τὸ θυμῶδες τῆς ψυχῆς κινεῖται κατὰ τῶν παθῶν, εἰδέναι δεῖ σιωπῆς εἶναι καιρόν· ὥρα γάρ ἐστι πάλης. Ὅτε δὲ τὴν ἀκαταστασίαν ἐκείνην ἴδοι τις ἢ δι' εὐχῆς ἢ δι' ἐλεημοσύνης εἰς γαλήνην ἐλθοῦσαν, κινείσθω τῷ ἔρωτι τῶν θείων λογίων δεσμῷ τῆς ταπεινοφροσύνης τὰ τοῦ νοῦ διασφαλιζόμενος πτερά. Ἐὰν γὰρ μή τις ἑαυτὸν τῇ ἐξουδενώσει ταπεινώσῃ λίαν, οὐ δύναται περί μεγαλωσύνης θεοῦ διαλέγεσθαι.

ια'.

Ὁ πνευματικὸς λόγος ἀκενόδοξον ἀεὶ τὴν ψυχὴν διατηρεῖ· αἰσθήσει γὰρ φωτὸς ὅλα αὐτῆς τὰ μέρη εὐεργετῶν, τῆς ἐξ ἀνθρώπων αὐτὴν τιμῆς οὐ χρείαν ἔχειν ποιεῖ. Διόπερ καὶ ἀφάνταστον ἀεὶ διαφυλάττει τὴν διάνοιαν ὡς ἀλλοιῶν αὐτὴν ὅλην εἰς τὴν ἀγάπην τοῦ θεοῦ. Ὁ δὲ τῆς τοῦ κόσμου σοφίας λόγος εἰς φιλοδοξίαν ἀεὶ προκαλεῖται τὸν ἄνθρωπον· ἐπειδὴ γὰρ πείρᾳ αἰσθήσεως εὐεργετεῖν οὐ δύναται, ἐπαίνων φιλίαν τοῖς αὐτοῦ ἰδίοις χαρίζεται ὡς πλάσμα ὢν κενοδόξων ἀνθρώπων. Τὴν τοίνυν τοῦ θείου λόγου διάθεσιν ἁπλανῶς ἐπιγνωσόμεθα, ἐὰν ἀμερίμνῳ σιωπῇ τὰς τοῦ μὴ λέγειν ὥρας ἀναλίσκωμεν ἐν θερμῇ μνήμῃ τοῦ θεοῦ.

ιβ'.

Ὁ ἑαυτὸν φιλῶν τὸν θεὸν ἀγαπᾶν οὐ δύναται· ὁ δὲ ἑαυτὸν μὴ φιλῶν ἕνεκεν τοῦ ὑπερβάλλοντος πλούτου τῆς ἀγάπης τοῦ θεοῦ, οὗτος τὸν θεὸν ἀγαπᾷ. Διόπερ οὐ τὴν ἑαυτοῦ ὁ τοιοῦτος ζητεῖ δόξαν ποτέ,

2 ὅτε] ὅτε μὲν M || θυμῶδες] θυμικὸν a || 3 εἶναι om. AMc || 4 pr. ἢ BMNSTa: om. ARc || εἰς γαλήνην om. A || ἐλθοῦσαν] ἀπελθοῦσαν A ἐπανελθοῦσαν a || 5 θείων MNa: om. ABRST || λογίων MNRa: λόγων ABST || τῆς BN: om. AMRSTa || 6-7 τῇ ἐξουδενώσει ταπεινώσῃ RSTc: ἐξουδενώσῃ ABNa τῇ ἐξουδενώσει M || διαλέγεσθαι] διηγήσασθαι c || 11 αὐτὴν] αὐτῆς Mc om. A || 12 ἀφάνταστον] ἀφαντασίαστον a || ἀεὶ om. Mac || 13 διάνοιαν] ἔννοιαν A || ὅλην om. B || τὴν MNRSa: om. ABTb || 14 προκαλεῖται] προσκαλεῖται T || ἄνθρωπον] νοῦν c || 16 αὐτοῦ ABMTb: αὐτοῦ N ἑαυτοῦ RSa || ἰδίοις NRSTa: om. ABM || 17 ἁπλανῶς om. Nb || ἐὰν MRa: εἴπερ BN εἴπερ ἐν T ἵνα AS || 18 τοῦ om. R || 23 οὐ (οὔτε Sac) τὴν ἑαυτοῦ ὁ τοιοῦτος ζητεῖ δόξαν ποτέ MRSac: ὁ τοιοῦτος οὐ τὴν ἑαυτοῦ ζητεῖ δόξαν ποτέ NT οὔτε τὴν ἑαυτοῦ δόξαν ὁ τοιοῦτος ζητεῖ ποτε A ὁ τοιοῦτος οὐ τὴν ἑαυτοῦ δόξαν ζητεῖ B.

20

10. When the entempered part of the soul moves against the passions, one must recognise that it is a time for silence, for it is the hour of struggle. But when one sees that this turbulence has come into calm, either through prayer or through acts of charity, let him be moved by a yearning for divine utterances, firmly securing the wings of the intellect within the bond of humble-mindedness. For unless someone humbles himself utterly by self-abasement, he cannot discuss the grandeur of God.

11. Spiritual expression always keeps the soul free from vainglory; for by a sensation of light working good in all its parts it makes the soul have no need for the honour which is of men; and so it always preserves one's reason free from fantasy, transforming it, whole, into love of God. But the expression of the wisdom of the world always entices man into affection for glory; for since it is not able to confer benefits by the evidence of Sense, it freely gives to its own a liking of flattery, which is the conceit of vainglorious men. Moreover we will recognise the disposition of divine expression unerringly, if we spend occasions of not talking in ardent recollection of God, in a silence free from care.

12. Whoever has affection for himself cannot love God, whereas whoever does not have affection for himself (for the sake of the overflowing abundance[9] of the love of God) he it is who loves God. For this reason such a person does not ever seek his own glory, but rather

---

[9] See Ephesians 2:7.

ΔΙΑΔΟΧΟΥ

ἀλλὰ τὴν τοῦ θεοῦ· ὁ γὰρ ἑαυτὸν φιλῶν τὴν ἑαυτοῦ δόξαν ζητεῖ. Ὁ δὲ τὸν θεὸν φιλῶν τὴν τοῦ ποιήσαντος αὐτὸν δόξαν ἀγαπᾷ· ψυχῆς γὰρ αἰσθητικῆς καὶ θεοφιλοῦς ἴδιον τὴν μὲν δόξαν ἀεὶ ζητεῖν τοῦ θεοῦ ἐν πάσαις αἷς ποιεῖ ἐντολαῖς, ἐπὶ δὲ τῇ ἑαυτῆς ταπεινώσει τέρπεσθαι, ὅτι
5 τῷ θεῷ μὲν δόξα διὰ μεγαλωσύνην πρέπει, ἀνθρώπῳ δὲ ταπείνωσις, ἵνα δι᾽ αὐτῆς οἰκειωθῶμεν θεῷ. Ὅπερ ἐὰν ποιῶμεν, καὶ ἡμεῖς κατὰ τὸν ἅγιον βαπτιστὴν Ἰωάννην χαίροντες τῇ δόξῃ τοῦ κυρίου ἀπαύστως λέγειν ἀρξόμεθα· Ἐκεῖνον δεῖ ὑψοῦσθαι, ἡμᾶς δὲ ἐλαττοῦσθαι.

10 ιγ΄.

Οἶδα ἐγώ τινα τοσοῦτον τὸν θεὸν ἀγαπῶντα καὶ ἔτι πενθοῦντα ὅτι οὐ καθὼς θέλει ἀγαπᾷ, ὥστε ἀπαύστως αὐτοῦ τὴν ψυχὴν ἐν τοιαύτῃ εἶναι τινι θερμῇ ἐπιθυμίᾳ ὥστε τὸν μὲν θεὸν ἐν αὐτῷ δοξάζεσθαι, ἑαυτὸν δὲ ὡς μηδὲ ὄντα εἶναι. Οὗτος δὲ οὐδὲ οἶδεν ὅπερ ἐστὶν οὐδὲ ἐν
15 αὑτοῖς τοῖς ἐπαίνοις τῶν λόγων· τῇ γὰρ πολλῇ ἐπιθυμίᾳ τῆς ταπεινώσεως τὴν ἑαυτοῦ οὐκ ἐννοεῖ ἀξίαν, ἀλλὰ λειτουργεῖ μὲν θεῷ ὡς νόμος ἱερεῦσιν, πολλῇ δέ τινι τῇ τῆς φιλοθεΐας διαθέσει κλέπτει ἑαυτοῦ τὴν μνήμην τῆς ἀξίας ἐν τῷ βάθει που τῆς ἀγάπης τοῦ θεοῦ τὸ ἐκ ταύτης ἐναποκρύπτων καύχημα ἐν πνεύματι ταπεινώσεως, ἵνα παῖς
20 τις ἀχρεῖος παρ᾽ ἑαυτῷ διὰ παντὸς τῇ διανοίᾳ φαίνηται, ὡς ἀλλότριος ὢν τῆς ἑαυτοῦ ἀξίας τῇ ἐπιθυμίᾳ τῆς ταπεινώσεως. Ὅπερ δεῖ καὶ ἡμᾶς ποιοῦντας πᾶσαν τιμὴν ἀποφεύγειν καὶ δόξαν διὰ τὸ ὑπερβάλλον τοῦ πλούτου τῆς ἀγάπης τοῦ οὕτως ἡμᾶς ἀγαπήσαντος κυρίου.

1 ἀλλὰ - ζητεῖ om. B || ζητεῖ] ἐπιζητεῖ F || 2 τὸν om. b || ἀγαπᾷ] ζητεῖ a || 3 καὶ] τε καὶ Mc || 5 μεγαλωσύνην BNR: μεγαλωσύνης AMSTa || ἀνθρώπῳ] ἀνθρώπων B || 6 θεῷ BNRSa: τῷ θεῷ AMT || ἐὰν] ἂν c || 7 ἅγιον om. Ma || τοῦ om. A || κυρίου] χριστοῦ B || 8 ὑψοῦσθαι, ἡμᾶς] αὐξάνειν, ἐμὲ a || 11 τινα] ἄνθρωπον A || τοσοῦτον] τοσούτῳ A || 12 οὐ καθὼς θέλει ἀγαπᾷ BN: οὐκ ἀγαπᾷ ὡς θέλει ARSTac οὐκ ἀγαπᾷ ὡς θέλω M || 13 τινι om. Nb || ὥστε] ὡς AB || αὐτῷ] ἑαυτῷ M || 14 ἑαυτὸν ABSa: αὐτὸν MNRT || pr. δὲ] τε N || μηδὲ Ra: μὴ ASp.c. μήτε BMNSa.c.T || οὗτος] αὐτός Nb || alt. δὲ] τε Nb || pr. οὐδὲ Ra: οὔτε ceteri || alt. οὐδὲ BR: οὔτε ceteri || 16 θεῷ NRa: τῷ θεῷ ABMST || 17 φιλοθεΐας ABM: θεοφιλείας RSTab φιλίας N || 19 ἐναποκρύπτων] ἐναποκρύβων A || 20 διὰ παντὸς om. ac || διανοίᾳ] διανοίᾳ παντὸς c ὑπονοίᾳ BR || ἀλλότριος] ἄλλος N(R) ἄλλως b || 22 τιμὴν ἀποφεύγειν καὶ] ἐκφυγεῖν τιμήν τε καὶ a || 23 ἀγάπης] δόξης A || οὕτως BMRT: ὄντως NSa οὕτως ἁπλῶς A || ἀγαπήσαντος MRab: ἀγαπῶντος BNST ἀγαπῶντας A.

that of God, since he who has affection for himself seeks his own glory, but he who has affection for God loves the glory of his creator. It is characteristic of a soul which is sensitive and has affection for God always to seek the glory of God in all the commandments which it performs, but to delight in its own humbling (since glory befits God because of his greatness, while humility befits man) so that through this we may be closely united to God. If we do this, we also, rejoicing in the glory of the Lord (according to St John the Baptist) will begin to say ceaselessly: 'He must increase, but we must decrease.'[10]

13. I know someone who loves God so much and still mourns that he does not love as he intends; so that his soul is ceaselessly in this ardent desire for God to be glorified in him, and for he himself to be as if he did not exist. This man does not even know what he is, not even when he is actually praised; for in great desire for humility he does not conceive of his own worth. He serves God as is the law for priests, but in a great disposition of affection for God he robs his own recollection of his worth in the profundity of his love for God, covering up the boasting which comes from it, in a spirit of humility–so that he always appears in his own reasoning to be a worthless servant,[11] being estranged from his own worth, in his desire for humility. This is what we too must do: flee from all honour and glory, because of the overflowing of the abundance of that love with which the Lord so loved us.

---

[10] John 3:30.
[11] See Luke 17:10.

ΔΙΑΔΟΧΟΥ

ιδ'.

Ὁ ἐν αἰσθήσει καρδίας ἀγαπῶν τὸν θεὸν ἐκεῖνος ἔγνωσται ὑπ' αὐτοῦ· ὅσον γάρ τις ἐν αἰσθήσει τῆς ψυχῆς παραδέχεται τὴν ἀγάπην τοῦ θεοῦ, τοσοῦτον γίνεται ἐν τῇ ἀγάπῃ τοῦ θεοῦ. Διὸ λοιπὸν τοῦ φωτισμοῦ τῆς γνώσεως ἐν ἔρωτί τινι σφοδρῷ ὁ τοιοῦτος ὀρεγόμενος οὐ παύσεται, ἄχρις ἂν αὐτῆς τῆς τῶν ὀστέων αἰσθήσεως αἴσθηται, οὐκέτι εἰδὼς ἑαυτόν, ἀλλ' ὅλος ὑπὸ τῆς ἀγάπης ἠλλοιωμένος τοῦ θεοῦ. Ὁ τοιοῦτος δὲ καὶ πάρεστιν ἐν τῷ βίῳ καὶ οὐ πάρεστιν· ἔτι γὰρ ἐνδημῶν τῷ ἑαυτοῦ σώματι ἐκδημεῖ διὰ τῆς ἀγάπης τῇ κινήσει τῆς ψυχῆς ἀπαύστως πρὸς τὸν θεόν. Ἀνενδότως γὰρ λοιπὸν διὰ τοῦ πυρὸς τῆς ἀγάπης τὴν καρδίαν καιόμενος ἀνάγκῃ τινὶ πόθου κεκόλληται τῷ θεῷ, ὡς ἐκστὰς ἅπαξ τῆς ἑαυτοῦ φιλίας τῇ ἀγάπῃ τοῦ θεοῦ. Εἴτε γὰρ ἐξέστημεν, φησίν, θεῷ, εἴτε σωφρονοῦμεν, ὑμῖν.

ιε'.

Ὅταν ἄρξηταί τις αἰσθάνεσθαι πλουσίως τῆς ἀγάπης τοῦ θεοῦ, τότε ἄρχεται ἐν αἰσθήσει πνεύματος καὶ τὸν πλησίον ἀγαπᾶν. Αὕτη γάρ ἐστιν ἡ ἀγάπη περὶ ἧς πᾶσαι αἱ γραφαὶ διαλέγονται. Ἡ γὰρ κατὰ σάρκα φιλία εὐχερῶς ἄγαν διαλύεται βραχείας τινὸς εὑρεθείσης αἰτίας· αἰσθήσει γὰρ οὐ δέδεται πνεύματος. Διὰ τοῦτο οὖν, κἂν συμβῇ τινα παροξυσμὸν γενέσθαι ἐπὶ τῆς ἐνεργουμένης ὑπὸ τοῦ θεοῦ ψυχῆς, οὐ λύεται παρ' αὐτῇ ὁ δεσμὸς τῆς ἀγάπης· τῇ γὰρ θέρμῃ τῆς ἀγάπης τοῦ θεοῦ ἀναζωπυροῦσα ἑαυτὴν εὐθέως εἰς τὸ ἀγαθὸν ἐπανακαλεῖται θᾶττον καὶ μετὰ πολλῆς χαρᾶς τὴν τοῦ πλησίου ἀγάπην, κἂν μεγάλως ὑπ'

2 ἔγνωσται] ἔγνωσθαι R ‖ 3 τις] ἄν τις a ‖ τῆς om. ATa ‖ ψυχῆς] καρδίας a om. A ‖ 4 τοῦ θεοῦ] αὐτοῦ a ‖ 5 σφοδρῷ] σφοδρῶ ἑαυτὸν R ‖ ὀρεγόμενος οὐ παύσεται ST: ὀρεγόμενος R ὑπάρχων a ὑπάρχει ceteri ‖ 6 ἂν] ἂν καὶ S om. Rb ‖ αἰσθήσεως] ἰσχύος ἐκδαπαναθείσης ST ‖ εἰδὼς] οἴδεν a ‖ ἀλλ' om. a ‖ 7 ὅλος] ὡς M ‖ δὲ] εἰ Aa ‖ 8 ἐν τῷ βίῳ καὶ οὐ πάρεστιν MRS: ἐν τῷ βίῳ καὶ οὐκ ἔστιν ἐν τῷ (τῷ om. N) βίῳ BN ἐν τῷ βίῳ καὶ οὐκ ἔστιν ἐν αὐτῷ T ἐν τῷ βίῳ A ἐν τῷδε τῷ βίῳ a ‖ ἔτι γὰρ] ἔτι Aa ‖ ἑαυτοῦ om. Aa ‖ 9 τῇ κινήσει τῆς ψυχῆς ἀπαύστως] ἐν ἀπαύστῳ τινὶ τῇ τῆς ψυχῆς κινήσει a ‖ 11 πόθου] πόθῳ AR καὶ πόθω Sa ‖ 12 φησίν om. MSc ‖ 16 ὅταν BNS: ὅτε AMRTa ‖ ἄρξηταί] ἄρξεταί Mac ‖ 17 ἄρχεται] ἔρχεται b ‖ 18 αἱ] αἱ ἅγιαι MTc ‖ 19 ἄγαν διαλύεται] ἀγαπᾶν διαλύεται Aa.c. ἀγαπᾷ διαλύεσθαι Ap.c. ‖ 20 οὖν] γὰρ A om. a ‖ κἂν] καὶ εἰ Aa ‖ 21 τοῦ θεοῦ] θεοῦ T τῆς θείας χάριτος a ‖ 22 αὐτῇ BNS: αὐτῆς AMRTa ‖ ἀγάπης] ἀγάπης τοῦ θεοῦ A ‖ θέρμῃ] θέρμη τῇ M ‖ 22-23 τῆς ἀγάπης τοῦ θεοῦ om. a ‖ 23 ἀναζωπυροῦσα BRSTa: ἀναπυροῦσα AMN ‖ ἑαυτὴν εὐθέως BMST: ἑαυτὴν ANa εὐθέως R ‖ 24 ἀγάπην ABMNR: ἀγάπην ζητεῖ a προσδέχεται ἀγάπην ST.

14. Whoever loves God in the Sense of the heart, this man has been perceived by him;[12] for one comes to live in love for God to the same extent that one receives the love of God in the Sense of the soul. So thereafter such a person will not desist from reaching out for the illumination of perception in excessive yearning, to the point of sensing from that Sense which is of one's bones, no longer aware of himself, but rather being entirely transformed by love for God. Such a person both is and is not present in this life, for while still dwelling in his body he journeys ceaselessly to God through love in the movement of the soul. From then on, his heart being kindled through the fire of love, he unyieldingly clings to God by an imperative of longing, being simply taken up from affection for himself by love for God. For 'if we have been taken up', it says, 'it was for God, but if we are in our right mind, it is for you.'[13]

15. Whenever anyone begins to sense love for God abundantly, then he begins to love his neighbour also by the Sense of the Spirit; for this is the love which all the Scriptures expound. The affection which is according to the flesh is all too easily dissolved when any slight pretext is found, since it has not been bound by the Sense of the Spirit; whereas even if it might happen that some provocation comes upon the soul activated by God, the bond of love is not loosened within it, since immediately rekindling itself in the direction of the good by the ardour of its love for God, it again

---

[12] See 1 Corinthians 8:3.
[13] 2 Corinthians 5:13.

ΔΙΑΔΟΧΟΥ

αὐτοῦ ἢ καθύβρισται ἢ ἐζημίωται. Ἐν γὰρ τῇ γλυκύτητι τοῦ θεοῦ τὸ πικρὸν πάντως ἀναλίσκει τῆς ἔριδος.

ις'.

5   Οὐδείς δύναται μὴ φοβούμενος τὸν θεὸν ἐν αἰσθήσει τῆς καρδίας ἀγαπῆσαι αὐτὸν ἐν ὅλῃ τῇ καρδίᾳ· διὰ γὰρ τῆς ἐνεργείας τοῦ φόβου ἁγνιζομένη καὶ ἀπαλυνομένη ὥσπερ ἡ ψυχὴ εἰς ἀγάπην ἐνεργουμένην ἔρχεται. Οὐκ ἂν δέ τις εἰς φόβον ὅλως ἔλθοι τοῦ θεοῦ τῷ εἰρημένῳ τρόπῳ, εἰ μὴ πασῶν τῶν βιωτικῶν ἔξω γένηται φροντίδων· ὅτε γὰρ ἐν
10 ἡσυχίᾳ πολλῇ καὶ ἀμεριμνίᾳ γένηται ὁ νοῦς, τότε αὐτῷ ὀχλεῖ ὁ φόβος τοῦ θεοῦ καθαρίζων αὐτὸν ἐν αἰσθήσει πολλῇ ἀπὸ πάσης τῆς γεώδους παχύτητος, ἵν᾽ οὕτως αὐτὸν εἰς πολλὴν ἀγάπην ἀγάγοι τῆς ἀγαθότητος τοῦ θεοῦ. Ὥστε ὁ μὲν φόβος τῶν ἔτι καθαριζομένων ἐστὶ μετὰ μεσότητος ἀγάπης· ἡ δὲ ἀγάπη ἡ τελεία τῶν ἤδη καθαρισθέντων ἐστίν,
15 ἐν οἷς οὐκέτι ἐστὶ φόβος. Ἡ γὰρ τελεία, φησίν, ἀγάπη, ἔξω βάλλει τὸν φόβον. Ἀμφότερα δὲ δικαίων ἐστὶ μόνον, οἵτινες ἐνεργείᾳ τοῦ ἁγίου πνεύματος τὰς ἀρετὰς κατεργάζονται. Καὶ διὰ τοῦτο ποῦ μὲν λέγει ἡ θεία γραφή· Φοβήθητε τὸν κύριον πάντες οἱ ἅγιοι αὐτοῦ· ποῦ δέ· Ἀγαπήσατε τὸν κύριον πάντες οἱ ὅσιοι αὐτοῦ, ἵνα μάθωμεν σαφῶς ὅτι
20 τῶν μὲν ἔτι καθαριζομένων δικαίων ὁ φόβος ἐστὶ μετὰ μεσότητος, ὡς εἴρηται, ἀγάπης· τῶν δὲ καθαρισθέντων ἡ τελεία ἀγάπη, ἐν οἷς οὐκέτι ἐστὶν ἔννοια φόβου τινός, ἀλλ᾽ ἔκκαυσις ἄπαυστος καὶ κόλλησις τῆς ψυχῆς πρὸς τὸν θεὸν διὰ τῆς ἐνεργείας τοῦ ἁγίου πνεύματος κατὰ τὸν λέγοντα· Ἐκολλήθη ἡ ψυχή μου ὀπίσω σου, ἐμοῦ δὲ ἀντελάβετο ἡ
25 δεξιά σου.

1 καθύβρισται ABMRSTab: ἢ ὕβρισται N ‖ 2 ἀναλίσκει MNSp.c.Ta: ἀναλίσκεται ABRSa.c. ‖ ἔριδος] ἔριδος καὶ τῆς μαχῆς Β ‖ 5-6 μὴ φοβούμενος τὸν θεὸν ἐν αἰσθήσει τῆς καρδίας ἀγαπῆσαι αὐτὸν ἐν ὅλῃ τῇ καρδίᾳ R: μὴ φοβηθεὶς τὸν θεὸν ἐν αἰσθήσει τῆς (τῆς om. ST) καρδίας ἀγαπῆσαι αὐτὸν ἐν ὅλῃ καρδίᾳ AST ἀγαπῆσαι τὸν θεὸν ἐν αἰσθήσει τῆς (τῆς om. Β) καρδίας (καρδίας αὐτοῦ a) μὴ πρότερον φοβηθεὶς αὐτὸν ἐν ὅλῃ τῇ καρδίᾳ BMNa ‖ 7 ἐνεργουμένην] ἐνεργουμένη Α ‖ 9 γένηται] γένοιτο Μ ‖ 12 αὐτὸν om. Aa ‖ ἀγάγοι] ἀγάγῃ a ‖ 13 καθαριζομένων] καθαριζομένων δικαίων ST ‖ 14 καθαρισθέντων ἐστίν] καθαρθέντων a ‖ 16 μόνον] μόνων Bab ‖ ἁγίου] παναγίου T om. Nb ‖ 17 et 18 ποῦ BNR: πῇ AMSTa ‖ 19 μάθωμεν] μάθομεν Nb ‖ 20 μὲν om. a ‖ φόβος] φόβος τοῦ θεοῦ Τ ‖ 21 καθαρισθέντων] ἤδη καθαρθέντων a ‖ οὐκέτι] οὐκ Aa ‖ 22 ἔκκαυσις] ἔκχυσις S ἔκβασις Τ ‖ 23 τῆς om. a ‖ ἁγίου] παναγίου a ‖ 24 λέγοντα] λέγοντα ἅγιον a ‖ ἀντελάβετο] ἀντιλάβοιτο c.

summons up love of neighbour with great joy, even if it was greatly insulted or injured by him. For the soul activated by God consumes the bitterness of the quarrel absolutely by means of the sweetness of God.

16. No one who doesn't fear God in the Sense of the heart is able to love him in the whole heart; for it is through the activity of fear that the soul is purified and softened, so that it becomes activated into love. But one will not come completely into fear of God in this way unless one comes to be outside all the concerns of this life; for when the intellect comes to be in much stillness and freedom from care, then the fear of God stirs in it, cleansing it from every earthy sediment with a great sensation, so that in this way fear might carry the intellect into great love of the goodness of God. And so fear is characteristic of those still being cleansed, with a middle degree of love; but perfect love is characteristic of those who are already cleansed, in whom there is fear no longer; for 'perfect love,' it says, 'casts out fear.'[14] Both these things are characteristic of the righteous alone–those who perform the virtues by the activity of the holy Spirit; and because of this Scripture says in one place 'fear the Lord all his holy ones',[15] but elsewhere 'love the Lord all his hallowed ones'.[16] Thus we might be clearly instructed that fear is characteristic of the righteous who are still being cleansed, with a middle degree of love, as was said. But perfect love is characteristic of those who have been cleansed, in whom there is no longer an intellectual conception of any fear whatever, but a never-ending inflaming and cleaving of the soul to God through the activity of the holy Spirit, according to the saying: 'My soul clings to you, and your right hand upholds me.'[17]

---

[14] 1 John 4:18.
[15] Psalms 33:10.
[16] Psalms 30:24.
[17] Psalms 62:9.

ΔΙΑΔΟΧΟΥ

ιζ'.

Ὥσπερ τὰ συμβαίνοντα τῷ σώματι τραύματα, ὅταν μὲν κεχερσωκότα ὥσπερ ᾖ καὶ ἀνεπιμέλητα, τοῦ προσαγομένου αὐτοῖς φαρμάκου ὑπὸ τῶν ἰατρῶν οὐκ αἰσθάνεται, καθαρισθέντα δὲ τῆς ἐνεργείας αἰσθάνεται τοῦ φαρμάκου εἰς ἴασιν ταχεῖαν ἐντεῦθεν ἐρχόμενα· οὕτως καὶ ἡ ψυχή, ἕως μὲν ἀνεπιμέλητός ἐστι καὶ ὑπὸ τῆς λέπρας τῆς φιληδονίας ὅλη κεκαλυμμένη, αἰσθάνεσθαι τοῦ φόβου οὐ δύναται τοῦ θεοῦ, κἂν ἀπαύστως αὐτῇ τις τὸ φοβερὸν καὶ δυνατὸν καταγγέλλῃ κριτήριον τοῦ θεοῦ. Ἐπειδὰν δὲ ἄρξηται καθαίρεσθαι διὰ τῆς πολλῆς προσοχῆς, τότε ὡς φαρμάκου τινὸς ὄντος ζωῆς τοῦ θείου φόβου αἰσθάνεται καίοντος αὐτὴν ὥσπερ τῇ ἐνεργείᾳ τῶν ἐλέγχων ἐν πυρὶ ἀπαθείας. Ὅθεν κατὰ μέρος λοιπὸν καθαριζομένη εἰς τὸ τέλειον τοῦ καθαρισμοῦ φθάνει, τοσοῦτον τῇ ἀγάπῃ προστιθεῖσα ὅσον ἐλαττοῦται τῷ φόβῳ, ἵνα οὕτως εἰς τὴν τελείαν καταφθάσῃ ἀγάπην, ἐν ᾗ φόβος, ὡς εἴρηται, οὐκ ἔστιν, ἀλλὰ πᾶσα ἀπάθεια διὰ δόξης ἐνεργουμένη θεοῦ. Ἔστω οὖν ἡμῖν εἰς καύχημα καυχημάτων ἄπαυστον πρῶτον μὲν ὁ φόβος τοῦ θεοῦ, λοιπὸν δὲ ἡ ἀγάπη τὸ πλήρωμα τοῦ νόμου τῆς ἐν Χριστῷ τελειότητος.

ιη'.

Ψυχὴ μὴ τῶν κοσμικῶν ἀπαλλαγεῖσα φροντίδων, οὔτε τὸν θεὸν ἀγαπήσει γνησίως οὔτε τὸν διάβολον βδελύξεται ἀξίως· κάλυμμα γὰρ ἅπαξ ἔχει φορτικὸν τὴν μέριμναν τοῦ βίου. Ὅθεν τὸ ἑαυτοῦ ἐπιγνῶναι ὁ νοῦς ἐπὶ τῶν τοιούτων οὐ δύναται δικαστήριον, ἵνα παρ' ἑαυτῷ δοκιμάζοι ἀπλανῶς τὰς ψήφους τῆς κρίσεως. Διὰ πάντα οὖν ἡ ἀναχώρησις χρήσιμος.

2 ὥσπερ om. Sa || 3 ᾖ] εἴη Mac || προσαγομένου αὐτοῖς (αὐτοῖς om. Aa)] πρὸς αὐτοῖς ἀγομένου R προαγομένου αὐτοῖς c || 4 αἰσθάνεται] ἐπαισθάνεται a || καθαρισθέντα MNRT: καθαρθέντα ABSa || αἰσθάνεται] αἴσθεται Nb || 6 ἐστι BMNRSa.c.: τυγχάνει A τυγχάνῃ Sp.c.Ta || ὅλη om. A || 7 κεκαλυμμένη] κεκάλυπται A || 8 τὸ om. M || καταγγέλλῃ NTc: καταγγέλλει ABMSb καταγγέλλοι a || κριτήριον MRSTa: δικαστήριον A om. BN || 9 ἐπειδὰν] ἐπὰν a || πολλῆς om. a || προσοχῆς] προσευχῆς A || 10 ὡς] ὥσπερ a || ὄντος Sac: ὄντως ABMNT || 12 τὸ om. R || 13 τοσοῦτον] τοῦτον c || προστιθεῖσα BRSp.c.Tac: προστεθεῖσα AMNSa.c. || τῷ φόβῳ BMNR: τοῦ φόβου ASTa || 14 καταφθάσῃ N(R)Tac: καταφθάσει AMS φθάσῃ B || 15 ἔστω-16 δὲ om. a || 15 οὖν] δὲ A || ἡμῖν] ἡμῶν b || 16 καύχημα om. R || ἄπαυστον AMNST: ἀπαύστως Bb || 17 ἡ ἀγάπη] ἐν ᾗ ἀγάπη a || 20-21 οὔτε . . . οὔτε] οὐδὲ . . . οὐδὲ Mc || 22 ἅπαξ om. Mc || φορτικὸν] φροντικὸν R || τοῦ] τοῦδε τοῦ a || 23 δικαστήριον] δικαστηρίων B || 24 δοκιμάζοι] δοκιμάζει N || ἀπλανῶς] ἀπλανὴς A || πάντα] τοῦτο F παντὸς M.

17. The soul responds in just the same way as to wounds sustained by the body, which, when they dry without being treated, do not sense the medications applied to them by doctors, but which, when they are cleaned, sense the activity of the medicine, to the end that they thereby recover speedily. As long as it is untreated and all covered up beneath the scab of affection for pleasure, the soul cannot sense the fear of God, even if one ceaselessly declare to it the fearful and powerful standard of God. But whenever affection for pleasure begins to be subdued through great attention, the soul senses divine fear (which is to life as a medicine) cauterising it in a fire of dispassion by the activity of self-examinations. Then, being cleansed bit by bit, the soul advances into the perfection of cleansing, increasing in love as much as it decreases in fear, so that in this way it may come into perfect love, in which there is no fear (as was said), but all dispassion activated through the glory of God. Therefore let this be our means into never-ending boasting of boastings: first the fear of God, then the love, the fulfilment of the law of perfection in Christ.[18]

18. The soul which is not released from worldly cares will neither love God genuinely nor loathe the devil adequately, since it simply has a cumbersome veil: the anxiety of this life. In the case of such people, the intellect is unable to recognise its own jury, in order to examine the votes of the judgement unerringly within itself. So in every case withdrawal is useful.

---

[18] See Romans 13:10.

ΔΙΑΔΟΧΟΥ

ιθ'.

Ψυχῆς καθαρᾶς ἴδιον λόγος μὲν ἄφθονος, ζῆλος δὲ ἄκακος, ἔρως δὲ ἄπαυστος τοῦ κυρίου τῆς δόξης. Τότε δὴ καὶ τὰς οἰκείας ὁ νοῦς ἀκριβῶς διαρρυθμίζει πλάστιγγας ὡς ἐν καθαρωτάτῳ κριτηρίῳ τῇ ἑαυτοῦ διανοίᾳ ἐμπαρών.

κ'.

Πίστις ἄεργος καὶ ἔργον ἄπιστον τὸν αὐτὸν τρόπον ἀποδοκιμασθήσονται· δεῖ γὰρ τὸν πιστὸν πίστιν ἐπιδεικνυμένην τὰ πράγματα τῷ κυρίῳ προσφέρειν. Οὐδὲ γὰρ τῷ πατρὶ ἡμῶν Ἀβραὰμ εἰς δικαιοσύνην λελόγιστο ἡ πίστις, εἰ μὴ καρπὸν αὐτῆς τὸν παῖδα προσήνεγκεν.

κα'.

Ὁ ἀγαπῶν τὸν θεὸν καὶ πιστεύει γνησίως καὶ τὰ ἔργα τῆς πίστεως ἐπιτελεῖ ὁσίως· ὁ δὲ πιστεύων μόνον καὶ μὴ ὢν ἐν τῇ ἀγάπῃ οὐδὲ αὐτὴν τὴν πίστιν ἣν δοκεῖ ἔχειν ἔχει· ἐλαφρότητι γάρ τινι πιστεύει νοὸς ὡς ὑπὸ τοῦ βάρους τῆς δόξης τῆς ἀγάπης μὴ ἐνεργούμενος. Πίστις οὖν δι' ἀγάπης ἐνεργουμένη τὸ μέγα τῶν ἀρετῶν.

κβ'.

Ὁ τῆς πίστεως βυθὸς ἐρευνώμενος μὲν κυμαίνεται· ἁπλῇ δὲ διαθέσει θεωρούμενος γαληνιᾷ. Λήθης γὰρ κακῶν ὕδωρ ὂν τὸ βάθος τῆς πίστεως οὐ φέρει παρὰ περιέργων ἐννοιῶν θεωρεῖσθαι. Ἁπλότητα οὖν διανοίας τοῖς αὐτῆς ἐμπλέωμεν ὕδασιν, ἵνα εἰς τὸν λιμένα τοῦ θελήματος οὕτω φθάσωμεν τοῦ θεοῦ.

2 ἔρως δὲ BRTa: ἔρος δὲ AN ἔρος b καὶ ἔρως MS || 3 τοῦ κυρίου τῆς δόξης] τῆς δόξης τοῦ κυρίου a || τότε δὴ A: τότε δὲ BNRST τότε γὰρ M τότε δὴ τότε a || οἰκείας] ἰδίας H || ἀκριβῶς AMRTa: ἀπλανῶς BN om. S || 4 κριτηρίῳ] κρατῆρι A || τῇ ἑαυτοῦ διανοίᾳ] τῇ διανοίᾳ αὐτοῦ A τῆς ἑαυτοῦ διανοίας RT || 9 ἐπιδεικνυμένην] ἐπιδεικνύμενον MT || 10 οὐδὲ BR: οὔτε ceteri || 11 καρπὸν MNa: τὸν καρπὸν ABRST || 12 προσήνεγκεν AN: προσήγαγεν BMRSTa || 16 οὐδὲ BNR: οὔτε AMSTa || 17 δοκεῖ ἔχειν] ἔχειν ἐδόκει a || ἔχει] οὐκ ἔχει c || 18 τῆς ἀγάπης] τῆς ἀγάπης κυρίου S om. Nb || ἐνεργούμενος] ἐνεργουμένης B || 19 τὸ μέγα] τὸ μέγα κεφάλαιον T || 23 κακῶν ABMNp.c.RSTb: κακὸν Na.c. om. a || ὃν] ὢν a ὂν c || 24 παρὰ om. c || 25 αὐτῆς ABNSTac: αὐτοῖς MRb || ἐμπλέωμεν BMNRT: ἐνπλέωμεν A ἐπιπλέωμεν S ἐμπλέωμεν a || 26 φθάσωμεν ABNT: καταφθάσωμεν MRSa.

19. It is characteristic of a clean soul that expression is without envy, and zeal without guile: a ceaseless yearning for the Lord of Glory.[19] It is then that the intellect balances its own scales precisely, standing before its own reason as before the most scrupulous tribunal.

20. Faith without works and works without faith will be ruled to be unacceptable[20] in the same way, since the faithful one must offer the Lord a faith that manifests deeds. For faith would not have been reckoned to our father Abraham as righteousness if he had not offered his child as its fruit.[21]

21. Whoever loves God both believes genuinely and fulfils the works of faith devoutly. But whoever believes only and is not in a state of love does not have even that faith which he seems to have; for he believes with levity of intellect, not being activated by the gravity of the glory[22] of love. Therefore faith activated through love[23] is the pinnacle of the virtues.

22. The depth of faith swells when searched, but when contemplated with a simple disposition it is calm; for the depth of faith is a water of oblivion towards bad things–it does not bear being contemplated by inquisitive intellectual conceptions. So let us sail in its waters in simplicity of reason, so that we may in this way arrive in the harbour of the will of God.[24]

---

[19] See 1 Corinthians 2:8.
[20] See Romans 3:27; James 2:17.
[21] See Romans 4; James 2:21.
[22] See 2 Corinthians 4:17.
[23] See Galatians 5:6.
[24] See Psalms 106:30.

ΔΙΑΔΟΧΟΥ

κγ'.

Οὐδεὶς δύναται ἢ ἀγαπᾶν ἢ πιστεύειν γνησίως, εἰ μὴ ἑαυτὸν ἑαυτοῦ μὴ ἔχοι κατήγορον. Ὅταν γὰρ ἡ συνείδησις ἡμῶν ἑαυτὴν τοῖς ἐλέγχοις ταράττῃ, οὐκέτι τῆς ὀσμῆς ὁ νοῦς τῶν ὑπερκοσμίων ἀγαθῶν παραχωρεῖται αἰσθάνεσθαι, ἀλλ' εὐθὺς εἰς ἀμφιβολίαν μερίζεται, θερμῇ μὲν κινήσει διὰ τὴν προλαβοῦσαν πεῖραν τῆς πίστεως ὀρεγόμενος, μηκέτι δὲ αὐτῆς ἐπιλαβέσθαι ἐν αἰσθήσει τῆς καρδίας διὰ τῆς ἀγάπης δυνάμενος διὰ τοὺς πυκνούς, ὡς ἔφην, νυγμοὺς τῆς ἐλεγχούσης συνειδήσεως. Πλὴν καθαρίσαντες ἑαυτοὺς θερμοτέρᾳ προσοχῇ μετὰ πλείονος πείρας ἐν θεῷ τοῦ ποθουμένου τευξόμεθα.

κδ'.

Ὥσπερ πρὸς τὰ φαινόμενα ἡμᾶς καλὰ βιαίως πως αἱ τοῦ σώματος προτρέπονται αἰσθήσεις, οὕτω πρὸς τὰ ἀόρατα ἡμᾶς ἀγαθὰ ἡ τοῦ νοῦ εἴωθε χειραγωγεῖν αἴσθησις, ὅταν τῆς θείας γεύσηται χρηστότητος. Ἕκαστον γὰρ τῆς οἰκείας συγγενείας πάντως ὀρέγεται· ἡ μὲν ψυχὴ ὡς ἀσώματος τῶν οὐρανίων καλῶν, τὸ δὲ σῶμα ὡς χοῦς τῆς ἐπιγείου τροφῆς. Τῆς ἀΰλου οὖν εἰς πεῖραν ἐλευσόμεθα ἀπλανῶς αἰσθήσεως, εἴπερ τὴν ὕλην τοῖς πόνοις λεπτύνομεν.

κε'.

Μίαν μὲν αἴσθησιν εἶναι λογικὴν τῆς ψυχῆς αὐτὴ ἡ τῆς ἁγίας ἡμᾶς γνώσεως ἐκδιδάσκει ἐνέργεια, εἰς δύο λοιπὸν διὰ τὴν παρακοὴν τοῦ Ἀδὰμ διαιρουμένην ἐνεργείας· μίαν δὲ ἁπλῆν τὴν ἐκ τοῦ ἁγίου

---

2 οὐδεὶς] οὐ Mc ‖ pr. ἢ om. ST ‖ 3 μὴ ἔχοι BM(R)STb: μὴ ἔχει Naa.c. μὴ ἔχῃ ap.c. ἔχοι A μὴ ἔχοι τις c ‖ ὅταν] ὅτε S ‖ 4 ταράττῃ a: ταράττοι ABMN ταράττει (R)STb ‖ 5 ἀμφιβολίαν MNRST: ἀμφιβολίας ABa ‖ 6 τῆς πίστεως om. Aa ‖ 7 alt. τῆς om. R ‖ 8 πυκνούς, ὡς ἔφην, νυγμοὺς MRST: νυγμούς, ὡς ἔφην ABNa ‖ ἐλεγχούσης Ap.c.BNRSTa: ἐλέγχου Aa.c.M ‖ 9 προσοχῇ Ap.c.BNRT: τῇ προσοχῇ S προσευχῇ Aa.c.a τῇ προσευχῇ M ‖ 10 ἐν θεῷ] εὐθέως A σὺν θεῷ F ‖ τευξόμεθα AB(R)STa: τευξώμεθα Nc τευξόμενος M ‖ 13 ἡμᾶς MNRSTa: ἡμῖν AB ‖ 14 οὕτω ANR: οὕτως BMST οὕτω καὶ a ‖ 15 ὅταν BMR: ὅτε ANSTa ‖ 16 πάντως om. b ‖ 18 τροφῆς ABNRS: τρυφῆς MTa ‖ ἐλευσόμεθα ABSTab: ἐλευσώμεθα MN ‖ 19 λεπτύνομεν ABMN(R)STa: λεπτύνωμεν bc ‖ 22 αἴσθησιν εἶναι λογικὴν (λογικὴν εἶναι c) τῆς ψυχῆς Rc: εἶναι αἴσθησιν φυσικὴν τῆς ψυχῆς (τῆς ψυχῆς om. T) BNT αἴσθησιν λογικὴν εἶναι τῆς ψυχῆς φυσικὴν M εἶναι αἴσθησιν (αἴσθησιν εἶναι S) λογικὴν τῆς ψυχῆς φυσικὴν AS αἴσθησιν φυσικὴν εἶναι καὶ λογικὴν τῆς ψυχῆς a ‖ ἡμᾶς BNRSTac: ἡμῖν A om. M ‖ 23 γνώσεως] ἐνώσεως RS ‖ δύο] δύο δὲ Ta ‖ τοῦ om. Aaa.c. ‖ 24 διαιρουμένην] διαιρουμένη A ‖ τὴν om. c.

23.   No one can either love or have faith genuinely unless he doesn't have himself as an accuser; for whenever our conscience stirs itself up with self-examinations, the intellect no longer has the capacity to sense the perfume of those good things which are above the world, rather it is immediately divided in doubt. It reaches out in an ardent movement because of the previous evidence of faith, but it can no longer lay hold of it by the Sense of the heart through the power of love, because of the multiplicity of stings (as I said) of an accusing conscience. But when we cleanse ourselves by a more ardent attention, we will obtain what we long for, with greater evidence in God.

24.   Just as the senses of the body propel us violently towards things which appear beautiful, so the Sense of the intellect is wont to lead us by the hand towards those good things which are unseen, whenever it tastes divine excellence.[25] For each thing reaches out completely towards that to which it is itself related; the soul (not being bodily) to heavenly beauties, the body (as being clay) to earthy nourishment. So we will come unerringly into evidence of this immaterial Sense, if we thin down what is material by efforts.

25.   The very activity of holy perception thoroughly teaches us that the rational Sense of the soul is one; it is later divided into two activities because of the disobedience of Adam, but there is one simple Sense

---

[25] See 1 Peter 2:3.

ΔΙΑΔΟΧΟΥ

πνεύματος αὐτῇ ἐγγινομένην, ἥντινα οὐδεὶς δύναται εἰδέναι εἰ μὴ μόνοι οἱ τῶν τοῦ βίου καλῶν διὰ τὴν ἐλπίδα τῶν μελλόντων ἀγαθῶν ἀπαλλαττόμενοι ἡδέως καὶ πᾶσαν τὴν τῶν σωματικῶν αἰσθήσεων διὰ τῆς ἐγκρατείας καταμαραίνοντες ὄρεξιν. Ἐπὶ γὰρ τούτων μόνον εὐρώστως ὁ
5   νοῦς διὰ τὴν ἀμεριμνίαν κινούμενος τῆς θείας ἀρρήτως αἰσθάνεσθαι χρηστότητος δύναται, ὅθεν καὶ τῷ σώματι τότε κατὰ τὸ μέτρον τῆς ἑαυτοῦ προκοπῆς τῆς οἰκείας μεταδίδωσι χαρᾶς ἀπείρῳ τινὶ λόγῳ τῇ ἀγάπῃ τῆς ἐξομολογήσεως ἀγαλλιώμενος. Ἐπ' αὐτῷ γάρ, φησίν, ἤλπισεν ἡ καρδία μου καὶ ἐβοηθήθην καὶ ἀνέθαλεν ἡ σάρξ μου καὶ ἐκ
10 θελήματός μου ἐξομολογήσομαι αὐτῷ. Ἡ γὰρ τότε ὄντως ἐγγινομένη χαρὰ τῇ ψυχῇ καὶ τῷ σώματι ὑπόμνησίς ἐστιν ἀπλανὴς τῆς ἀφθάρτου βιότητος.

κϛ'.

15 Ἀκύμαντον ἀεὶ δεῖ φυλάττειν τοὺς ἀγωνιζομένους τὴν διάνοιαν, ἵνα τοὺς εἰς αὐτὴν διαθέοντας λογισμοὺς ὁ νοῦς διακρίνων τοὺς μὲν καλοὺς καὶ θεοπέμπτους ἐν τοῖς ταμιείοις τῆς μνήμης ἐναποτίθηται, τοὺς δὲ σκαιοὺς καὶ δαιμονιώδεις ἔξω που τῶν ἀποθηκῶν ἀπορρίπτοι τῆς φύσεως. Καὶ γὰρ ἡ θάλασσα γαληνιῶσα μὲν ἄχρις αὐτοῦ αὐτῆς τοῦ
20 βυθίου κινήματος ὑπὸ τῶν τοὺς ἰχθύας ἀγρευόντων καθορᾶται ὡς μηδὲν αὐτοὺς σχεδὸν λανθάνειν τότε τῶν τὰς ἐκεῖσε διαπορευομένων ζῴων τρίβους· ὅτε δὲ ὑπὸ τῶν πνευμάτων ταράττεται, κρύπτει τῇ τῆς ταραχῆς στυγνότητι ἅπερ ἐν τῷ γέλωτι τῆς γαλήνης ὁρᾶσθαι φιλοτιμεῖται. Ὅθεν ἀργὴν οὖσαν τότε τὴν τέχνην ὁρῶμεν τοῖς τοὺς ἁλιευτικοὺς

1 ἐγγινομένην] ἐπιγινομένην Mc ‖ εἰδέναι] γνῶναι B ‖ μόνοι] μόνον a ‖ 2 ἐλπίδα] ἐλπίδα τὴν ἀποκειμένην M ‖ ἀγαθῶν om. a ‖ 3 ἀπαλλαττόμενοι BMRT: ἀπηλλαγμένοι ANSa ‖ ἡδέως] ἰδέων M ‖ πᾶσαν] ἅπασαν M ‖ αἰσθήσεων] ὀρέξεων a ‖ 4 ὄρεξιν] αἴσθησιν a ‖ ἐπὶ] ἐπεὶ B ‖ γὰρ] δὲ A ‖ μόνον AMN(R)S: μόνων BTb καὶ μόνων a ‖ 5 αἰσθάνεσθαι] ἐπαισθάνεσθαι a ‖ 6 τὸ om. A ‖ 7 οἰκείας] ἰδίας a ‖ 7-8 τῇ ἀγάπῃ τῆς] τῆς A τῆς ἀγαπητικῆς a ‖ 9 ἐβοηθήθην] ἐβοηθήθη a ‖ 10 ἐγγινομένη] γινομένη M ‖ 11 χαρὰ] παράκλησις a ‖ 12 βιότητος] ζωῆς Nb βιοτῆς a ‖ 15 ἀεὶ om. A ‖ δεῖ] χρὴ c om. M ‖ φυλάττειν ABRSab: διαφυλάττειν MNT ‖ 17 ἐναποτίθηται RT: ἐναποτιθῆται a ἐναποτίθεται ABMNS ‖ 18 σκαιοὺς] κακοὺς MRSc ‖ 20 ὡς] ὥστε a ‖ 21 σχεδὸν om. RSa ‖ 21-22 τῶν τὰς ἐκεῖσε διαπορευομένων ζῴων τρίβους] τῶν ἐκεῖσε διαπορευομένων ζῴων τὰς τρίβους a τῆς τῶν ἐκεῖσε διαπορευομένων ζῴων τρίβου Mc ‖ 22 ὅτε] ὅταν a ‖ τῶν om. a ‖ ταράττεται] ταράττηται a ‖ τῇ] τὸ R om. a ‖ 24 τότε BMNRSa: om. ATc ‖ τοῖς] τῶν B ‖ τοὺς ἁλιευτικοὺς] τοῦ ἁλιευτικοῦ Mc τὸ ἁλιευτικὸν B.

34

which is engendered in the soul from the holy Spirit. No one is able to know this except those who rejoice to be released from the beautiful things of this life through the hope of the good things which are to come, and who through self-control allow all the appetite of the bodily senses to wither. Among them only is the intellect (moving strongly because of freedom from care) able to sense the divine excellence in a manner beyond telling. The intellect then communicates its own characteristic joy to the body also (according to the measure of the intellect's own progress), rejoicing in love, in a boundless expression of full confession. For 'in him', it says, 'my heart hoped and was helped, and my flesh flourished anew, and of my will I will fully confess it.'[26] The joy which is then truly engendered in the soul and in the body is an unerring reminder of immortal life.

26. Those who contend must always keep the reason undisturbed, so that the intellect, discerning the imaginings which spread into the reason, both lays aside the beautiful imaginings which are sent from God in the treasuries of the recollection, and casts sinister demoniacal imaginings out of the storehouses of its nature. For the sea also, when it is calm, is seen through clearly by those who catch fish, as far as the movements in its depth; so that then virtually none of the living things which make their way along the sea's course escapes their notice. But when it is agitated by the winds, the sea hides in the frown of the turbulence those things which in the smiling of the calm it is eager should be seen. From this we see that at such times skill is futile for those who employ the fishermen's lures.

---

[26] Psalms 27:7.

ΔΙΑΔΟΧΟΥ

μηχανωμένοις δόλους· ὅπερ καὶ τὸν νοῦν πάντως συμβαίνει πάσχειν τὸν θεωρητικόν, ὅταν μάλιστα ἐξ ὀργῆς ἀδίκου ὁ βυθὸς τῆς ψυχῆς ταράττηται.

κζ'.

Ὀλίγων ἐστὶ λίαν πάντα τὰ οἰκεῖα ἀκριβῶς ἐπιγινώσκειν πταίσματα καὶ ὧν οὐδεπώποτε ὁ νοῦς τῆς μνήμης ἐξαρπάζεται τοῦ θεοῦ. Ὃν γὰρ τρόπον οἱ ὀφθαλμοὶ ἡμῶν οἱ σωματικοί, ὅταν μὲν ὑγιαίνωσι, πάντα ὁρᾶν ἄχρι καὶ τῶν διιπταμένων κωνώπων ἢ ἐμπίδων τὸν ἀέρα δύνανται· ὅτε δὲ ὑπὸ θολώσεως ἢ ὑπὸ χυμάτων τινῶν σκεπάζονται, εἰ μέν τι μέγα εἴη τῶν ἀπαντώντων αὐτοῖς, τοῦτο ἀμυδρῶς ὁρῶσι, τῶν δὲ μικρῶν οὐκ αἰσθάνονται τῇ αἰσθήσει τῆς βλέψεως· οὕτω καὶ ἡ ψυχή, ἐὰν μὲν τὴν ἐκ τῆς φιλοκοσμίας αὐτῇ συμβαίνουσαν πήρωσιν τῇ προσοχῇ λεπτύνῃ, καὶ τὰ ἄγαν βραχέα αὐτῆς πταίσματα ὡς μεγάλα ἄγαν ἡγουμένη δάκρυον ἐπὶ δακρύῳ ἐν πολλῇ εὐχαριστίᾳ ἀδιαλείπτως φέρει. Δίκαιοι γάρ, φησίν, ἐξομολογήσονται τῷ ὀνόματί σου. Ἐὰν δὲ τῇ τοῦ κόσμου ἐμμένῃ διαθέσει, εἰ μέν τι φονικὸν ἢ πολλῆς ἄξιον τιμωρίας διαπράξοιτο, τούτου ἠρέμα αἰσθάνεται, τῶν δὲ ἄλλων πταισμάτων οὐδὲ ἐπισημήνασθαι δύναται, ἀλλὰ καὶ ὡς κατορθώματα αὐτὰ πολλάκις ἡγεῖταί τινα· διὸ καὶ ὑπὲρ αὐτῶν θερμῶς λογοποιουμένη ἡ ἀθλία οὐκ αἰσχύνεται.

κη'.

Νοῦν καθαρίσαι μόνου τοῦ ἁγίου πνεύματός ἐστιν· ἐὰν γὰρ μὴ εἰσέλθῃ ὁ δυνατὸς καὶ σκυλεύσῃ τὸν ἅρπαγα, οὐδαμῶς τὸ λάφυρον

1 μηχανωμένοις] μηχανομένους b μηχανωμένων Β || δόλους] δέλος Β || pr. τὸν] τὸν ἡμέτερον ὡς a || 3 ταράττηται BRTa: ταράσσεται A ταράττεται MNS || 6 πάντα NRa: τὸ πάντα BMST ἅπαντα Α || ἀκριβῶς om. ANa || 7 οὐδεπώποτε AMNR: οὐδέποτε BSTa || 8 μὲν om. a || 9 διιπταμένων] ἱπταμένων Β || 9-10 ὅτε δὲ ABN: ὅταν δὲ MSTa ὅταν δὲ ἢ R || ὑπὸ om. a || χυμάτων] ἐπιχυμάτων A || σκεπάζονται] σκέπωνται a || μέν τι] μέντοι Tc || εἴη] ᾖ S || αὐτοῖς om. Aa || 12 αἰσθάνονται] ἐπαισθάνονται a || 13 αὐτῇ om. ANb || συμβαίνουσαν] ἐπισυμβαίνουσαν a || τῇ προσοχῇ] τῇ προσευχῇ Β τῆς προσοχῆς b || 14 ἄγαν ABRS: πάνυ Μ λίαν T om. Na || 15 δακρύῳ] δακρύων BR || 16 τῇ] ἐν τῇ S || 17 ἐμμένῃ M(R)S: ἐμμένει N ἐμμενεῖ Α ἐμμείνῃ BTa || μέν τι] μέντοι b || ἢ] καὶ S || 18 τούτου] τοῦτο MSc || 19 ἐπισημήνασθαι NRSTa: ἐπισημάνασθαι ABM || 20 ἡγεῖτεί τινα· διὸ] ἡγουμένη a || λογοποιουμένη] λογιουμένη Nb || 25 σκυλεύσῃ ABNTac: σκυλεύσει MSb.

This is just what the contemplative intellect comes to experience, most of all whenever the depth of the soul is troubled from unjust anger.

27. It pertains to very few to recognise all their intrinsic failings precisely, and they are those whose intellect is not ever snatched away from the recollection of God. Take the way our bodily eyes, whenever they are healthy, are able to see all things even to the mosquitoes or gnats which fly in the air; but when they are covered over by dirt or by any excretions, if there is something large among those things which encounter them, they see it indistinctly; and of small things they do not sense any by the sense of sight. So it is for the soul also: if, by attentiveness, it thins down the blindness which comes upon it from affection for the world, supposing its very minor failings to be very great it produces tear after tear in great thanksgiving ceaselessly. For 'the righteous', it says, 'will make full confession in your name.'[27] But whenever it remains set in the disposition of the world, if anything murderous or worthy of much retribution comes to pass, the soul senses it vaguely. And of other faults it cannot distinguish any, often supposing them to be successes–and so the wretched soul, not being ashamed of these things, heatedly defends them.

28. It is of the holy Spirit alone to cleanse the intellect; for if he who is strong does not go in and overpower the robber, what has been seized will

---

[27] Psalms 139:14.

ΔΙΑΔΟΧΟΥ

ἐλευθερωθήσεται. Δεῖ οὖν διὰ πάντων πλέον δὲ τῇ εἰρήνῃ τῆς ψυχῆς ἀναπαύειν τὸ πνεῦμα τὸ ἅγιον, ἵνα τὸν λύχνον τῆς γνώσεως ἔχωμεν διὰ παντὸς παρ' ἑαυτοῖς φαίνοντα· ἐξαστράπτοντος γὰρ αὐτοῦ ἀπαύστως ἐν τοῖς ταμιείοις τῆς ψυχῆς οὐ μόνον κατάδηλοι τῷ νοῒ αἱ πικραὶ ἐκεῖναι
5 καὶ σκοτειναὶ τῶν δαιμόνων πᾶσαι γίνονται προσβολαί, ἀλλὰ καὶ ἐξασθενοῦσι λίαν ὑπὸ τοῦ ἁγίου ἐκείνου καὶ ἐνδόξου ἐλεγχόμεναι φωτός. Διὰ τοῦτο ὁ ἀπόστολος λέγει· Τὸ πνεῦμα μὴ σβέννυτε, ἀντὶ τοῦ μὴ κακοεργοῦντες ἢ κακολογιζόμενοι λυπεῖτε τὴν τοῦ ἁγίου πνεύματος ἀγαθότητα, ἵνα μὴ τῆς ὑπερμάχου ἐκείνης στερηθῆτε λαμπάδος. Οὐ γὰρ
10 τὸ ἀΐδιον καὶ ζωοποιὸν σβέννυται, ἀλλ' ἡ ἐκείνου λύπη, τοῦτ' ἔστιν ἡ ἀποστροφή, στυγνὸν καὶ ἀφεγγῆ τὸν νοῦν καταλιμπάνει τῆς γνώσεως.

κθ'.

Μίαν, ὡς ἔφην, αἴσθησιν εἶναι φυσικὴν τῆς ψυχῆς, αἱ γὰρ πέντε
15 ἅπαξ ταῖς τοῦ σώματος ἡμῶν διαφέρουσι χρείαις, τὸ ἅγιον ἡμᾶς καὶ φιλάνθρωπον πνεῦμα διδάσκει τοῦ θεοῦ. Συνδιαιρεῖται δὲ αὐτὴ διὰ τὸν ἐκ τῆς παρακοῆς προσγενόμενον ὄλισθον τῷ νοῒ ταῖς αὐτῆς τῆς ψυχῆς κινήσεσιν· διόπερ τὸ μὲν αὐτῆς τῷ ἐμπαθεῖ συναπάγεται μέρει, ὅθεν τῶν τοῦ βίου καλῶν ἡδέως αἰσθανόμεθα· τὸ δὲ τῷ λογικῷ αὐτῆς καὶ
20 νοερῷ πολλάκις συνήδεται κινήματι, ὅθεν πρὸς τὰ οὐράνια τρέχειν ὁ

---

1 πλέον] πλεῖον c καὶ πλέον RT ‖ δὲ om. a ‖ 2 ἀναπαύειν] διαναπαύειν a ‖ ἔχωμεν AB(R)STabc: ἔχομεν MN ‖ 3 φαίνοντα· ἐξαστράπτοντος] ἐξαστράπτοντα· φαίνοντος Aa ‖ αὐτοῦ] ἑαυτοῦ R om. a ‖ 4 τῷ] ἐν τῷ ATa ‖ νοῒ] νῷ S ‖ 5 καὶ σκοτειναὶ om. a ‖ πᾶσαι om. Ta ‖ 7 λέγει] φησίν Aa ‖ 8 κακολογιζόμενοι AMRTa: κακὰ λογιζόμενοι BNS ‖ 9 λαμπάδος] λαμπρότητος Mc ‖ οὔ] οὔτε a ‖ 10 σβέννυται] ἀποσβέννυται a ‖ pr. ἡ om. A ‖ alt. ἡ om. Nb ‖ στυγνὸν] στυγνόν τινα a ‖ 15 μίαν] μίαν μὲν RSTa ‖ αἱ γὰρ] τὰς δὲ Mc ‖ 15 ταῖς] τῆς B ‖ διαφέρουσι] διαφέρειν Mc ‖ χρείαις] χρείας B ‖ ἅγιον] πανάγιον Ta ‖ ἡμᾶς om. A ‖ 16 πνεῦμα διδάσκει BNRST: διδάσκει πνεῦμα M ἐκδιδάσκει πνεῦμα Aac ‖ τοῦ om. M ‖ αὐτὴ N: αὐτῇ AB αὐταῖς Ma αὕτη ST ‖ 17 προσγενόμενον BNRST: γενόμενον AM ἐγγενόμενον a ‖ τῷ νοῒ BNR: τῷ νῷ T ὁ τόνος AS ὁ νοῦς M om. a ‖ ταῖς αὐτῆς τῆς ABRSp.c.c: ταῖς τῆς N ταῖς τῆς αὐτῆς b ταῖς αὐταῖς τῆς MSa.c.Ta ‖ 18 διόπερ] διὸ Aa ‖ συναπάγεται BRTa: συνάπτεται MNSa.c. συναγάγεται ASp.c. ‖ 19 αἰσθανόμεθα BN(R)T: αἰσθανώμεθα S αἰσθόμεθα A αἰσθάνεται Ma ‖ τὸ δὲ τῷ ABN(R)ST: τῷ δὲ τῷ abc τῷ δὲ M ‖ 20 ὅθεν ASp.c.Ta: καθὸ BMNRSa.c. ‖ τρέχειν AMRSTab: τρέχει BN.

38

never be released. Therefore the holy Spirit must reside continually in the peace of the soul, so that we may have the lamp of perception shining with us at all times; for when it blazes ceaselessly in the treasuries of the soul not only do all these bitter and murky assaults of the demons become manifest to the intellect, but they are also thoroughly weakened, cross-examined by that holy and glorious light. It is for this reason that the apostle says 'Do not extinguish the Spirit',[28] that is to say: Let yourselves not, doing ill and thinking ill, grieve the goodness of the holy Spirit, lest you be deprived of this defending light. For the eternal and life-giving is not extinguished, but when it is grieved, that is, when it utterly abandons us, it leaves behind an intellect which is sullen and unenlightened by perception.

29. As I have said, the natural Sense of the soul is one; the five differentiate for the needs of the body. The holy and benevolent Spirit of God teaches us this. The Sense divides by the movements of the soul itself, because of the slipperiness which comes about in the intellect from disobedience. As a result part of the Sense is led away into the impassioned part, by which we sense the beautiful things of this life pleasantly. Yet often the other part of the Sense is gratified by rational and intelligent movement, whereby our intellect stretches out to run towards

---

[28] 1 Thessalonians 5:19.

ΔΙΑΔΟΧΟΥ

νοῦς ἡμῶν κάλλη, ὅτε σωφρονοῦμεν, ὀρέγεται. Ἐὰν οὖν εἰς ἕξιν ἔλθωμεν τοῦ καταφρονεῖν τῶν ἐν τῷ κόσμῳ καλῶν, δυνησόμεθα καὶ τὴν γεώδη τῆς ψυχῆς ὄρεξιν τῇ λογικῇ αὐτῆς συνάψαι διαθέσει, τῆς κοινωνίας τοῦ ἁγίου πνεύματος τοῦτο οἰκονομούσης εἰς ἡμᾶς. Ἐὰν γὰρ
5 μὴ ἡ αὐτοῦ θεότης ἐνεργητικῶς τὰ τῆς καρδίας ἡμῶν ταμιεῖα καταυγάσῃ, οὐκ ἂν δυνησώμεθα ἐν ἀδιαιρέτῳ τῇ αἰσθήσει, τοῦτ' ἔστιν ἐν ὁλοκλήρῳ διαθέσει, γεύσασθαι τοῦ ἀγαθοῦ.

10 λ'.
Αἴσθησίς ἐστι νοὸς γεῦσις ἀκριβὴς τῶν διακρινομένων. Ὃν γὰρ τρόπον τῇ γευστικῇ ἡμῶν αἰσθήσει τοῦ σώματος τὰ καλὰ ἐκ τῶν φαύλων ἀπλανῶς ἐν τῷ καιρῷ τῆς ὑγιείας διακρίνοντες τῶν χρηστῶν ὀρεγόμεθα, οὕτω καὶ ὁ νοῦς ἡμῶν, ὅταν εὐρώστως καὶ ἐν πολλῇ
15 ἀμεριμνίᾳ κινεῖσθαι ἄρξοιτο, δύναται καὶ τῆς θείας παρακλήσεως πλουσίως αἰσθάνεσθαι καὶ ὑπὸ τῆς ἐναντίας μηδεπώποτε συναρπάζεσθαι. Ὡς γὰρ τὸ σῶμα τῶν γεωδῶν γευόμενον ἡδυσμάτων ἔχει τὴν πεῖραν τῆς αἰσθήσεως ἄπταιστον, οὕτω καὶ ὁ νοῦς, ὅτε ἐπάνω τοῦ τῆς σαρκὸς καυχᾶται φρονήματος, δύναται γεύεσθαι τῆς παρακλήσεως ἀπλανῶς τοῦ
20 ἁγίου πνεύματος (γεύσασθε γάρ, φησίν, καὶ ἴδετε ὅτι χρηστὸς ὁ κύριος) καὶ ἔχειν τὴν μνήμην τῆς γεύσεως διὰ τῆς ἐνεργείας τῆς ἀγάπης ἀνεπίληστον ἐν τῷ δοκιμάζειν ἀπταίστως τὰ διαφέροντα κατὰ τὸν λέγοντα ἅγιον· Καὶ τοῦτο προσεύχομαι, ἵνα ἡ ἀγάπη ὑμῶν ἔτι μᾶλλον καὶ μᾶλλον περισσεύῃ ἐν ἐπιγνώσει καὶ πάσῃ αἰσθήσει εἰς τὸ
25 δοκιμάζειν ὑμᾶς τὰ διαφέροντα.

1 σωφρονοῦμεν] σωφρονῶμεν c ‖ 2 ἔλθωμεν] ἔλθομεν Nb ‖ τῷ om. a ‖ δυνησόμεθα ATac: δυνησώμεθα BMNS ‖ 3 συνάψαι διαθέσει τῆς om. B ‖ 5 θεότης AMRSTb: θειότης BN ἀγαθότης a ‖ καρδίας] ψυχῆς Mc ‖ ἡμῶν om. a ‖ 6 δυνησώμεθα] δυνησόμεθα Aac ‖ τῇ om. A ‖ 6-7 τουτ '- διαθέσει om. Aa ‖ 7 ἐν om. MRSc ‖ διαθέσει om. M ‖ 12 ἐκ] ἀπὸ a ‖ 14 alt. καὶ om. AMc ‖ 15 ἄρξοιτο] ὀρέχοιτο b ἄρξηται FT ‖ καὶ om. a ‖ 16 πλουσίως om. B ‖ μηδεπώποτε ABNR: μηδέποτε MST μηδέπω a ‖ 17 τῆς om. R ‖ 18 νοῦς] νοῦς ἡμῶν a ‖ ὅτε] ὅταν B ‖ 19 γεύεσθαι BNRS: γεύσασθαι AMTa ‖ τῆς] τῆς ἀπλανοῦς Mc ‖ ἀπλανῶς om. Mac ‖ 22 ἀνεπίληστον MRSap.c.: ἄληστον ABNT ἄληκτον aa.c. ‖ δοκιμάζειν] δικάζειν Nb ‖ 23 ἅγιον MNRSa.c.T: ἅγιον ἀπόστολον a ἅγιον ἀπόστολον παῦλον ABSp.c. ‖ 24 μᾶλλον καὶ μᾶλλον MNRST: μᾶλλον ABa.

heavenly beauties–this is when we are reasonable. Therefore if ever we come into a habit of despising the beautiful things in the world, we will also be able to bind the earthy appetite of the soul to its rational disposition, when the fellowship of the holy Spirit regulates this in us. For unless its divinity shines on the treasuries of our hearts actively we will not be able to taste what is good with an undivided Sense, that is with an integrated disposition.

30. The Sense of the intellect is the precise taste of things discerned. For in the way that in times of health we discern the good from the foul unerringly with our body's tasting sense, and reach for the best things, so our intellect, whenever it also begins to be moved strongly in much freedom from care, is able to sense divine consolation abundantly, and never be snatched up by what is the opposite. For as the body (tasting earthy flavours) has the sure evidence of sensation, so also the intellect (when it boasts over and above the mentality of the flesh) is able to taste the consolation of the holy Spirit unerringly (for 'Taste', it says, 'and see that the Lord is excellent'[29]), and able to hold the recollection of the taste through the activity of love unforgettably, in the secure discrimination of things which are superior, according to the holy one who says: 'And this I pray, that your love may abound yet more and more in full perception and a whole Sense that you may discern the things which are superior.'[30]

---

[29] Psalms 33:9.
[30] Philippians 1:9f.

ΔΙΑΔΟΧΟΥ

λα'.

Ὅταν ὁ νοῦς ἡμῶν ἄρξηται τῆς τοῦ ἁγίου πνεύματος αἰσθάνεσθαι παρακλήσεως, τότε καὶ ὁ Σατανᾶς ἐν ἡδυφανεῖ τινι αἰσθήσει ἐν ταῖς νυκτεριναῖς ἡσυχίαις, ὅτε τις ὥσπερ εἰς ὕπνου τινὸς λεπτοτάτου ἔρχεται ῥοπήν, τὴν ψυχὴν παρακαλεῖ. Ἐὰν οὖν εὑρεθῇ ἐν θερμῇ λίαν μνήμῃ κρατῶν ὁ νοῦς τὸ ὄνομα τὸ ἅγιον τοῦ κυρίου Ἰησοῦ καὶ ὥσπερ ὅπλῳ κέχρηται κατὰ τῆς ἀπάτης τῷ ἁγίῳ καὶ ἐνδόξῳ ἐκείνῳ ὀνόματι, ἀναχωρεῖ μὲν ὁ πλάνος τοῦ δόλου, εἰς πόλεμον δὲ λοιπὸν ἐνυπόστατον ἐξάπτεται τῆς ψυχῆς. Ὅθεν ἐπιγινώσκων ὁ νοῦς τὴν ἀπάτην ἀκριβῶς τοῦ πονηροῦ πλέον εἰς τὴν πεῖραν προκόπτει τῆς διακρίσεως.

λβ'.

Ἡ ἀγαθὴ παράκλησις ἐγρηγορότος τοῦ σώματος γίνεται ἢ καὶ εἰς ὕπνου τινὸς μέλλοντος ἔρχεσθαι ἔμφασιν, ὅτε τις ἐν θερμῇ μνήμῃ τοῦ θεοῦ τῇ αὐτοῦ ὥσπερ κεκόλληται ἀγάπῃ· ἡ δὲ τῆς πλάνης εἰς λεπτόν τινα ἀεί, ὡς εἶπον, ὕπνον ἐλθόντος τοῦ ἀγωνιστοῦ μετὰ μέσης μνήμης τοῦ θεοῦ· ἡ μὲν γὰρ ὡς ἐκ θεοῦ οὖσα φανερῶς τὰς ψυχὰς τῶν τῆς εὐσεβείας ἀγωνιστῶν ἐν ἐκχύσει πολλῇ τῆς ψυχῆς παρακαλεῖν πρὸς τὴν ἀγάπην θέλει· ἡ δέ, ἐπειδὴ ἐν ἀνέμῳ τινὶ πλάνης ῥιπίζειν τὴν ψυχὴν εἴωθεν, κλέπτειν διὰ τοῦ ὕπνου τοῦ σώματος τὴν πεῖραν τῆς αἰσθήσεως τοῦ ὑγιαίνοντος νοῦ περὶ τὴν μνήμην τοῦ θεοῦ ἐπιχειρεῖ. Ἐὰν οὖν εὑρεθῇ ὁ νοῦς, ὡς εἶπον, μεμνημένος προσεχῶς τοῦ κυρίου, σκορπίζει μὲν τὴν αὔραν ἐκείνην τὴν ἡδυφανῆ τοῦ ἐχθροῦ, χαίρων δὲ εἰς τὸν κατ' αὐτοῦ κινεῖται πόλεμον ὡς ὅπλον ἔχων δεύτερον μετὰ τὴν χάριν τὸ ἐκ τῆς πείρας καύχημα.

---

4 ὕπνου] ὕπνον c || τινὸς λεπτοτάτου] λεπτότητα a || 5 ῥοπήν] ῥοπῇ A om. a || ἐὰν] εἰ R || 5-6 εὑρεθῇ ἐν θερμῇ λίαν μνήμῃ MR: εὑρεθῇ λίαν μνήμῃ c || 6 τὸ ἅγιον om. Mc || 8 ὁ πλάνος] ἀπλανῶς A || 9 ἀκριβῶς om. Aa || 10 πλέον] πλεῖον Aa || τὴν om. BN || προκόπτει] προκόπτοι Nb || 13 ἐγρηγορότος] ἢ ἐγρηγορότος Ta || καὶ om. a || 14 ὕπνου] ὕπνον ac || ὅτε] ὅταν Mac || 16 ἀεί om. STa || μέσης] μεσότητος RS || 19 ἐν om. a || 20 εἴωθεν] εἰώθει B ὅθεν A || 22 προσεχῶς] συνεχῶς a || κυρίου RS: κυρίου Ἰησοῦ χριστοῦ M κυρίου Ἰησοῦ ceteri || 24 ὅπλον om. a || δεύτερον AaSp.c.: λοιπὸν δεύτερον B δεξιὸν Sa.c. λοιπὸν δεξιὸν MNRT.

31. Whenever our intellect begins to sense the consolation of the holy Spirit, then Satan consoles the soul with apparent sweetness, by one of the senses, in nocturnal stillnesses when one comes to the verge of a very light sleep. But if ever the intellect is found in exceedingly ardent recollection, holding fast the holy name of the Lord Jesus and using that holy and glorified name as a weapon against the deception, the impostor of deception withdraws, and then fastens onto the soul in substantive war. And so the intellect, recognising the deception of the evil one precisely, advances further into the evidence of discernment.

32. The good consolation comes about when the body is wakeful, or when it is about to enter into a state that resembles sleep–when one is in ardent recollection of God, indeed cleaving to his love; but the consolation of deception always comes (as I have said) when he who contends is coming into a light sleep, with a middling recollection of God. That which is clearly from God wants to summon to love the souls of those who contend for piety, in a great outpouring of the soul; the other, since it is accustomed to enflame the soul in a breeze of error, attempts to steal the evidence of the healthy intellect's Sense concerning the recollection of God, through the sleep of the body. Therefore if ever the intellect is found to have recollected the Lord attentively (as I have said) it disperses that apparently pleasant fanning of the Enemy, and rejoicing it moves into battle against him, having a second weapon after grace: the boasting which comes from evidence.

ΔΙΑΔΟΧΟΥ

λγ'.

Ἐὰν ἀναμφιβόλῳ καὶ ἀφαντάστῳ κινήσει ἡ ψυχὴ πρὸς τὴν ἀγάπην ἐξάπτηται τοῦ θεοῦ ἕλκουσα ὥσπερ καὶ τὸ σῶμα εἰς τὸ βάθος τῆς ἀγάπης ἐκείνης τῆς ἀρρήτου ἢ ἐγρηγορότος ἢ ᾧ εἴρηκα τρόπῳ εἰς ὕπνον ἐρχομένου τοῦ ὑπὸ τῆς ἁγίας χάριτος ἐνεργουμένου, μηδὲν ἄλλο τότε ὅλως ἐννοῦσα ἢ τοῦτο μόνον εἰς ὅπερ κινεῖται, εἰδέναι δεῖ τοῦ ἁγίου πνεύματος εἶναι τὴν ἐνέργειαν. Ἡδυνομένη γὰρ ὅλη ὑπ' ἐκείνης τῆς ἀφράστου γλυκύτητος οὐδὲν ἕτερον δύναται τότε ἐννοεῖν, ἐπειδὴ ἀνενδότῳ τινὶ εὐφραίνεται χαρᾷ. Ἐὰν δὲ ἀμφιβολίαν ὅλως ἢ ῥυπαράν τινα ἔννοιαν ὁ νοῦς ἐν τῷ ἐνεργεῖσθαι συλλάβῃ, εἰ καὶ τῷ ἁγίῳ κέχρηται ὀνόματι πρὸς ἄμυναν τοῦ κακοῦ καὶ οὐχὶ δὴ μᾶλλον πρὸς ἀγάπην μόνον τοῦ θεοῦ, δεῖ νοεῖν ὅτι ἐκ τοῦ ἀπατεῶνός ἐστιν ἐκείνη ἡ παράκλησις χαρᾶς ἐμφάσει· ἡ δὲ χαρὰ ἐκείνη ἄποιός ἐστι καὶ ἀδιάθετος ὅλη μοιχεύεσθαι θέλοντος τοῦ ἐχθροῦ τὴν ψυχήν. Ὅταν γὰρ ἴδῃ τὸν νοῦν τῇ πείρᾳ τῆς ἑαυτοῦ αἰσθήσεως ἀκριβῶς καυχώμενον, τότε παρακλήσεσί τισιν, ὡς ἔφην, χρηστοφανέσι προσκαλεῖται τὴν ψυχήν, ἵνα διαφορουμένης αὐτῆς ὑπὸ τῆς χαύνης ἐκείνης καὶ καθύγρου ἡδύτητος ἀγνώριστος αὐτῇ γένοιτο ἡ μίξις τοῦ δολίου. Ἐκ τούτου οὖν γνωσόμεθα τὸ πνεῦμα τῆς ἀληθείας καὶ τὸ πνεῦμα τῆς πλάνης. Ἀδύνατον μέντοι ἢ τῆς θείας χρηστότητος ἐν αἰσθήσει γεύσασθαί τινα ἢ τῆς τῶν δαιμόνων πικρίας αἰσθητῶς πειραθῆναι, εἰ μή τις ἑαυτὸν πληροφορήσῃ τὴν μὲν χάριν εἰς τὸ βάθος τοῦ νοῦ κατεσκηνωκέναι, τὰ

2 ἀναμφιβόλῳ] ἀμφιβόλῳ B ἐν ἀμφιβόλῳ M ‖ 3 ἐξάπτηται MRST: ἐξάπτεται AN ἐξίσταται Ba ‖ τὸ βάθος] τὸν βυθὸν a ‖ 4 ἀγάπης] ἀγαθότητος a ‖ ἀρρήτου] ἀφράστου MRSc ‖ pr. ἢ ABTa: om. MNRS ‖ ἐγρηγορότος] ἐγρηγορότως c ἐγρηγοροῦντος Nb ‖ ἢ ᾧ εἴρηκα τρόπῳ ABMRST: ἢ ὃν εἴρηκα τρόπον N ἢ ὧν εἴρηκα τρόπων b τοῦ σώματος ὥσπερ εἴρηκα τρόπῳ ἢ a ‖ 5 ἁγίας ANRST: θείας Ma om. B ‖ 6 ὅλως om. ARSa ‖ κινεῖται MNRST: κεκίνηται Aac καὶ κινεῖται B ‖ 7 ὅλη] ὥσπερ ὅλη a ‖ 9 ἀνενδότῳ τινὶ MRST: ἀνενδότῳ ABNa ‖ εὐφραίνεται ANRTa: ἐνευφραίνεται BMS ‖ 10 συλλάβῃ M: συλλάβοι ceteri ‖ εἰ Ma: ἢ BN(R)ST ἡ A ‖ 11 οὐχὶ δὴ μᾶλλον R: οὐχὶ μᾶλλον ABSTa οὐχὶ δὴ N οὐκ ἤδη M ‖ 12 μόνον τοῦ om. A ‖ νοεῖν ABNT: ἐννοεῖν MRSa ‖ ὅτι] ὅτι ὡς T ‖ 14 τοῦ εχθροῦ MRSTa: om. ABN ‖ ἴδῃ] εὔρῃ A ‖ 15 τῇ πείρᾳ MRSTa: τὴν πεῖραν ABN ‖ ἑαυτοῦ] αὐτοῦ a ‖ ἀκριβῶς om. Aa ‖ 16 ὡς ἔφην om. a ‖ χριστοφανέσι] ἡδυφανέσι a ‖ προσκαλεῖται ABNRST: προκαλεῖται Ma ‖ 18 γένοιτο] γένηται S ‖ ἐκ τούτου] ἐν τούτῳ a ‖ 19 τῆς ἀληθείας καὶ τὸ πνεῦμα om. A ‖ 21 αἰσθητῶς] ἀναισθήτως Nb ‖ πειραθῆναι MRS: πειρασθῆναι ABNTa ‖ 22 πληροφορήσῃ] πληροφορήσει b.

44

33. If the soul fastens onto the love of God in an unambivalent and unfantasising movement, drawing (as it were) the body also into the depth of that unutterable love, whoever is either wakeful or coming into sleep in the way I have described is activated by holy grace; then, when the soul conceives of nothing other than that alone into which it moves, one must know it to be the activity of the holy Spirit. For when the whole of it is gladdened by this indescribable sweetness, the soul can conceive of nothing else–since it is cheered by an unwavering joy. But if ever the intellect takes part in some altogether ambivalent or sordid intellectual conception while being activated, even if (as defence from what is bad and not rather for the love of God alone) it had made use of the holy name, it must reckon that this consolation is from the deceiver in the appearance of joy; but this joy (when the Enemy wants to debauch the soul) is without quality, and wholly confused. For whenever he sees the intellect boasting precisely in the evidence of its own Sense, then he entices the soul by consolations which (as I have said) appear excellent; so that, dispersed by this shifting and indistinct pleasure, the mingling of deceit might become indistinguishable to it. And so from this we will perceive the spirit of truth and the spirit of error.[31] Indeed it is impossible for anyone to taste the divine excellence in the Sense or for the bitterness of the demons to be evidenced sensibly, unless one fully convinces oneself that grace has settled in the depth of the intellect, whereas the evil spirits loiter around

---

[31] See 1 John 4:6.

ΔΙΑΔΟΧΟΥ

δὲ πονηρὰ πνεύματα περὶ τὰ μέλη τῆς καρδίας ἐνδιατρίβειν· ὅπερ οὐδέποτε θέλουσι παρὰ ἀνθρώποις πιστευθῆναι οἱ δαίμονες, ἵνα μὴ ὁ νοῦς τοῦτο αὐτὸ εἰδὼς ἀκριβῶς τῇ μνήμῃ τοῦ θεοῦ κατ᾽ αὐτῶν ὁπλίζηται.

λδ'.

Ἄλλη ἐστὶν ἡ ἀγάπη τῆς ψυχῆς ἡ φυσικὴ καὶ ἄλλη ἡ ἐκ τοῦ ἁγίου πνεύματος αὐτῇ προσγινομένη. Ἡ μὲν γὰρ ἐκ τῆς ἡμετέρας, ὅτε θέλομεν, συμμέτρως κινεῖται θελήσεως· διόπερ καὶ εὐχερῶς ὑπὸ τῶν πονηρῶν πνευμάτων, ἡνίκα μὴ βίᾳ κρατῶμεν τῆς ἑαυτῶν προαιρέσεως, διαρπάζεται. Ἡ δὲ τοσοῦτον ἐκκαίει τὴν ψυχὴν πρὸς τὴν ἀγάπην τοῦ θεοῦ ὥστε πάντα τὰ τῆς ψυχῆς τότε μέρη τῇ τοῦ θείου πόθου ἀλαλήτως ἐγκολλᾶσθαι χρηστότητι ἐν ἀπείρῳ τινὶ ἁπλότητι διαθέσεως. Ἐγκύμων γὰρ ὥσπερ ὁ νοῦς τότε ὑπὸ τῆς πνευματικῆς ἐνεργείας γινόμενος πηγήν τινα ἀγάπης ἀναβλύζει καὶ χαρᾶς.

λε'.

Ὥσπερ ἡ θάλασσα τῷ ἐπιχεομένῳ αὐτῇ ἐλαίῳ, ὅταν ταράττηται, φύσιν ἔχει τοῦ εἴκειν ὑπὸ τῆς αὐτοῦ πιότητος νικωμένης τῆς ζάλης, οὕτω καὶ ἡ ψυχὴ ἡμῶν, ὅταν ὑπὸ τῆς χρηστότητος πιαίνηται τοῦ ἁγίου πνεύματος, ἡδέως γαληνιᾷ. Χαίρουσα γὰρ ἡττᾶται κατὰ τὸν λέγοντα ἅγιον· Πλὴν τῷ θεῷ ὑποτάγηθι ἡ ψυχή μου, τῇ ἐπισκιαζούσῃ αὐτῇ ἐκείνῃ ἀπαθεῖ καὶ ἀρρήτῳ χρηστότητι. Διὰ τοῦτο οὖν κἂν ὁπόσοι

---

1 ἐνδιατρίβειν] διατρίβειν NTb ‖ 2 μὴ om. R ‖ 3 τοῦτο αὐτὸ: ABRSTa: τοῦτο MN ‖ 4 ὁπλίζηται BRST: ὁπλίζεται Νc ὁπλίζοιτο A ἐξοπλίζοιτο a ὡπλίζετο M ‖ 7 ἄλλη ἡ] ἄλλη A ‖ 8 προσγινομένη] ἐγγινομένη a ‖ γὰρ] γὰρ καὶ S ‖ 9 θέλομεν] θέλωμεν Nb ‖ κινεῖται θελήσεως] προαιρέσεώς ἐστι a ‖ καὶ om. Mc ‖ ὑπὸ] ἐκ Αa ‖ 11 διαρπάζεται] ἁρπάζεται a ‖ ἐκκαίει ABMRSTa: ἐκχέει Nc ‖ 12 τὰ τῆς ψυχῆς τότε (τότε om. M) μέρη] αὐτῆς τότε τὰ μέρη τοῦ σώματος a ‖ ἀλαλήτως] ἀλαλήτῳ S ‖ 13 ἐγκολλᾶσθαι] συγκολλᾶσθαι R ‖ ἐν om. a ‖ 14 γινόμενος] γενόμενος MTc ‖ 15 ἀναβλύζει MNRST: ἀναβλύει AB ἀναδύει a ‖ 18 αὐτῇ] αὐτὴν a ‖ ταράττηται BRSTac: ταράττεται AMN ‖ 19 νικωμένης AR: νεκρουμένης Μa νικωμένη BNST ‖ τῆς ζάλης ΑΜa: τὴν ζάλην BNST τῆς ζάλην R ‖ 20 ἡμῶν om. AS ‖ χρηστότητος] χάριτος MRTc ‖ πιαίνηται] πιαίνεται MNb ‖ 21 ἡττᾶται] ἡττᾶται τῇ αὐτοῦ χάριτι a ‖ λέγοντα] λέγοντα αὐτῷ Mc ‖ 22 τῇ] καὶ τῇ R ‖ 23 ἀπαθεῖ M(R)S: ἀπαθὴ b ἀγαθῇ ABNTa ‖ ὁπόσοι] πόσοι ANb.

the parts of the heart; and this is what the demons never want to be believed among men lest the intellect, knowing this very thing precisely, arm itself against them by recollection of God.

34. The natural love of the soul is one thing, and that which comes to it from the holy Spirit is another. For the former moves proportionately from our will, when we will; and so it is easily seized as plunder by the evil spirits when we do not hold fast to our chosen course by force. But the latter sort so kindles the soul to the love of God that then all the parts of the soul cling to the excellence of divine longing in boundless simplicity of disposition, in a manner beyond telling; for then the intellect, becoming as it were pregnant by spiritual activity, sends forth a fountain of love and joy.

35. Just as the sea in having oil poured upon it whenever it is troubled has a nature to subside, due to the sea-spray being overcome by the oiliness, so our soul also is pleasantly calmed whenever it is swollen by the excellence of the holy Spirit; for it is subdued, rejoicing (according to the holy one who says: 'Be very obedient to God, O my soul'[32]), when that dispassionate and unutterable excellence overshadows[33] it. And so as

---

[32] Psalms 61:6.
[33] See Luke 1:35.

ΔΙΑΔΟΧΟΥ

τότε παροξυσμοὶ ὑπὸ τῶν δαιμόνων ἐπιτηδεύωνται κατὰ τῆς ψυχῆς, ἀόργητός τε διαμένει καὶ πάσης ἔμπλεως χαρᾶς. Εἰς ὅπερ τις ἔρχεται ἢ μένει, εἰ τῷ φόβῳ τοῦ θεοῦ τὴν ἑαυτοῦ ψυχὴν ἀπαύστως καθηδύνει. Τοῖς γὰρ ἀγωνιζομένοις εἶδός τι φέρει ἁγνισμοῦ ὁ φόβος· ὁ γὰρ φόβος,
5 φησίν, τοῦ κυρίου ἁγνὸς διαμένων εἰς αἰῶνα αἰῶνος.

λς'.

Μηδεὶς ἀκούων αἴσθησιν νοὸς ὁρατῶς αὐτῷ τὴν δόξαν τοῦ θεοῦ ὀφθῆναι ἐλπιζέτω. Αἰσθάνεσθαι μὲν γάρ φαμεν, ὅταν καθαρεύῃ τὴν
10 ψυχήν, ἐν ἀρρήτῳ τινὶ γεύσει τῆς θείας παρακλήσεως, οὐ φαίνεσθαι δὲ αὐτῇ τι τῶν ἀοράτων, ἐπειδὴ νῦν διὰ πίστεως καὶ οὐ διὰ εἴδους, ὡς ὁ μακάριος λέγει Παῦλος, περιπατοῦμεν. Ἐὰν οὖν ὀφθῇ τινι τῶν ἀγωνιζομένων ἢ φῶς ἢ σχῆμά τι πυροειδές, μηδαμῶς καταδεξάσθω τὸ τοιοῦτον ὅραμα. Ἀπάτη γάρ ἐστι φανερὰ τοῦ ἐχθροῦ· ὅπερ πολλοὶ
15 παθόντες ἐξ ἀγνοίας ἐξετράπησαν τῆς ὁδοῦ τῆς ἀληθείας. Ἡμεῖς δὲ ἴσμεν ὅτι, ἐφ᾽ ὅσον ἐνδημοῦμεν ἐν τῷ φθαρτῷ τούτῳ σώματι, ἐκδημοῦμεν ἀπὸ τοῦ θεοῦ, τοῦτ᾽ ἔστιν ὁρατῶς ἢ αὐτὸν ἤ τι τῶν ἐπουρανίων αὐτοῦ θαυμάτων ὁρᾶν οὐ δυνάμεθα.

---

1 τότε om. RSc ‖ ἐπιτηδεύωνται AB(R)ST: ἐπιτηδεύονται MNa ‖ 2 τε om. ATa ‖ διαμένει] μένει a ‖ ἔμπλεως] ἔμπλεος NTb ἔμπλεω a ‖ ὅπερ τις] ὅνπερ A ὃν γὰρ a ‖ ἔρχεται BMNR: εἰσέρχεται Aa οὐκ ἔρχεται T ἐὰν ἄρξηται S ‖ 2-3 ἢ μένει, εἰ MNR: ἢ μένει, εἰ μὴ T παραμένει Aa παραμένειν B ἐμμένειν S ‖ ἑαυτοῦ] αὐτοῦ a ‖ καθηδύνει N(R)S: καθηδύνοι BMT καθηδύνουσα Aa ‖ 4 τι φέρει] διαφέρει A ‖ pr. φόβος R: φόβος τοῦ κυρίου MSc φόβος τοῦ κυρίου ἡμῶν Ἰησοῦ χριστοῦ B φόβος τοῦ κυρίου Ἰησοῦ ceteri ‖ 5 φησίν, τοῦ R: φησί BNS om. AMTa ‖ 8 ὁρατῶς] ἀοράτως A ‖ 9 μὲν om. M ‖ ὅταν καθαρεύῃ] ὅτε καθαρεύει NRb ‖ 11 ἀοράτων] ὁρατῶν a ‖ νῦν] νῦν μὲν a ‖ 12 μακάριος λέγει Παῦλος] ἀπόστολός φησι a ‖ οὖν om. M ‖ 13 ἢ φῶς ἢ σχῆμά τι πυροειδές BMNR et (+ ἢ φωνή) T: πυροειδές τι σχῆμα ἢ φωνή Aa ἢ φωνὴ ἢ σχῆμά τι πυροειδές S πυροειδές τι σχῆμα ἢ φῶς ἢ φωνή P ‖ καταδεξάσθω] καταδεξώμεθα Aa ‖ 14 ἐχθροῦ] πονηροῦ a ‖ 15 ἐξ ἀγνοίας ABMS: ὡς ἐξ ἀγνοίας T ὡς ἔγνων NR ἐν ἀγνοίᾳ a ‖ τῆς ὁδοῦ om. a ‖ ἀληθείας BMNRSa.c.T: εὐθείας AaSp.c. ‖ 16 ἐφ᾽ om. Aa ‖ ἐν om. ac ‖ τούτῳ om. A ‖ 17 ἀπὸ BMRSa: om. ANT ‖ θεοῦ] κυρίου A ‖ 18 ἐπουρανίων] οὐρανίων a ‖ ὁρᾶν] ἰδεῖν a.

48

many provocations as are then invented by the demons against the soul, it remains free from anger and full of all joy. One comes into or remains in this state if he gladdens his soul continually with the fear of God. For to those who contend fear brings a form of purification, since, it says, 'the fear of the Lord remains pure unto the age of ages'.[34]

36. Let no one, hearing about the Sense of the intellect, hope that the glory of God will be seen by him visibly. For we say the soul 'senses' whenever it is cleansed with an inexpressible taste of divine consolation—not that one of those things which are unseen appears to it; for now it is through faith and not through form that we walk, as the blessed Paul says.[35] Therefore if ever either light or any shape in the form of fire is seen by one of those who contend, let him in no way accept such a vision, for the deception of the Enemy is evident; it is due to this that many who suffer from lack of perception have turned from the path of truth. But we know that, to the extent to which we dwell in this mortal body, we dwell away from God;[36] that is, we are able to see visibly neither Him nor any one of his heavenly wonders.

---

[34] Psalms 18:10.
[35] 2 Corinthians 5:7.
[36] 2 Corinthians 5:6.

ΔΙΑΔΟΧΟΥ

λζ'.

Οἱ ἐν τῇ ἀγάπῃ τοῦ θεοῦ ἐμφαινόμενοι τῇ ψυχῇ ὄνειροι ὑγιαινούσης ψυχῆς πώς εἰσιν ἀπλανεῖς κατήγοροι. Διόπερ οὔτε ἀπὸ ἑτέρου σχήματος εἰς ἕτερόν τι σχῆμα μεταβάλλονται, οὔτε μὴν πτοοῦσι τὴν αἴσθησιν οὔτε γελῶσιν ἢ στυγνάζουσιν ἀθρόως· ἀλλὰ μετὰ πάσης ἐπιεικείας τῇ ψυχῇ προσεγγίζουσι πνευματικῆς αὐτὴν καταγεμίζοντες θυμηδίας. Ὅθεν καὶ μετὰ τὸ διυπνισθῆναι τὸ σῶμα πολλῷ τῷ πόθῳ ζητεῖ ἡ ψυχὴ τὴν χαρὰν τοῦ ὀνείρου. Αἱ δὲ τῶν δαιμόνων φαντασίαι διὰ πάντων ἐναντίως ἔχουσιν· οὔτε γὰρ ἐν τῷ αὐτῷ μένουσι σχήματι οὔτε μορφὴν ἐπὶ πολὺ ἀτάραχον ἐπιδείκνυνται. Ὃ γὰρ ἐκ προαιρέσεως μὲν οὐκ ἔχουσιν, ἐκ δὲ τῆς οἰκείας κιχρῶνται μόνον πλάνης, ἀρκεῖν αὐτοῖς ἐπὶ πλεῖστον οὐ δύναται, ἀλλὰ καὶ μεγάλα λέγουσι καὶ ἀπειλοῦσι δὲ πλεῖστα εἰς στρατιωτῶν εἶδος ἑαυτοὺς πολλάκις σχηματίζοντες· ποτὲ δὲ καὶ προσψάλλουσι μετὰ κραυγῆς τῇ ψυχῇ. Ὅθεν ἐπιγινώσκων αὐτοὺς ὁ νοῦς, ὅτε καθαρεύει, πεφαντασμένως διυπνίζει τὸ σῶμα· ἔστι δὲ ὅτε καὶ χαίρει ὡς τὸν δόλον αὐτῶν ἐπιγνῶναι δυνηθείς. Διόπερ ἐν αὐτῷ τῷ ὀνείρῳ πλειστάκις ἐλέγχων αὐτοὺς εἰς ὀργὴν αὐτοὺς μεγάλην κινεῖ. Πλὴν ἔστιν ὅτε καὶ τὰ χρηστὰ ἐνύπνια χαρὰν μὲν οὐ φέρουσι τῇ ψυχῇ, λύπην δὲ αὐτῇ ἡδεῖαν ἐμποιοῦσι καὶ ἀνάλγητον δάκρυον. Τοῦτο δὲ γίνεται ἐπὶ τῶν εἰς πολλὴν ταπεινοφροσύνην προκοπτόντων.

---

2 ἀγάπῃ] ἀγαθότητι Mc || 3 πώς om. Aa || διόπερ] διότι A διὸ a || 4 τι om. STa || σχῆμα om. Sa || μεταβάλλονται] μετακινοῦσιν S || 5 ἢ] οὔτε Aa || ἀθρόως] ἀθρόως ἢ μεταβάλλονται a || πάσης om. a || 6 αὐτὴν] αὐτῇ a || καταγεμίζοντες] πληροῦντες Aa || 7 τῷ ABNTa: om. MRSb || ζητεῖ ABNRT: ἐπιζητεῖ MS (post ὀνείρου) et a || 9 οὔτε] οὐδὲ a || αὐτῷ om. c || μένουσι] μένουσι διὰ παντός a || 10 μὲν om. Mac || 11 κιχρῶνται μόνον BNR: κέχρηνται μόνον T μόνον κιχρῶνται A καὶ μόνον κιχρῶνται a μόνης κιχρῶνται MS || ἀρκεῖν] ἐπαρκεῖν a || πλεῖστον] πλεῖον A || 12 δὲ om. M || 15 ὅτε καθαρεύει] ὅταν καθαρεύῃ MSc || πεφαντασμένως om. a || 16 αὐτῶν] αὐτὸν B || τῷ om. M || 17 ἐλέγχων] διελέγχων a || αὐτοὺς MNRST: om. ABa || 18 τὰ om. M || 19 δὲ AMRSTa: τε BN || ἡδεῖαν FGMP(R)SV: ἰδίαν ABNTa || ἐμποιοῦσι] ἐμποιεῖ a || ἀνάλγητον FPRSTc: om. ABMNa || 20 ταπεινοφροσύνην] ταπείνωσιν Nab.

37. Those dreams which are made to appear to the soul in the love of God are unerring accusers of a soul which is in any way healthy. So they do not change from one shape into another shape, nor do they excite the Sense, nor laugh, nor are they suddenly threatening; they rather draw near to the soul with all reasonableness, loading it down with spiritual gladness; so that after the body wakens, the soul seeks the joy of the dream with much longing. But the fantasies of the demons always behave oppositely; for they neither remain in the same shape nor do they display an unwavering posture for long, since what they do not hold from choice but only borrow out of their inherent deceit cannot satisfy them for very long. Often they pattern themselves on the form of soldiers, speaking loudly and threatening very many things; and sometimes they pluck at the soul with shrieking. So when the intellect in a dreaming state (being clean) recognises them, it wakens the body; but there are also times when the intellect rejoices as it is able to recognise their deception, and so it most often cross-examines them in the dream itself, moving them into great anger. However there are also times when excellent dreams do not bring joy to the soul, but create a pleasant grief in it, and painless weeping; but this comes about for those who are progressing into great humble-mindedness.

ΔΙΑΔΟΧΟΥ

λη'.

Εἰρήκαμεν μὲν ἡμεῖς, ὡς παρὰ τῶν ἐν πείρᾳ γεγονότων ἠκούσαμεν, καλῶν τε καὶ φαύλων ὀνείρων διάκρισιν· ἀρκείτω δὲ ἡμῖν πρὸς ἀρετὴν μεγάλην τὸ μηδεμιᾷ ὅλως πείθεσθαι φαντασίᾳ. Οἱ γὰρ ὄνειροι οὐδὲν ἕτερον ὡς ἐπὶ τὸ πλεῖστόν εἰσιν ἀλλ' ἢ εἴδωλα λογισμῶν πλανωμένων ἢ πάλιν, ὡς ἔφην, δαιμόνων ἐμπαίγματα. Ὁπότε κἂν ἐκ τῆς τοῦ θεοῦ ἀγαθότητος καταπεμφθῇ ἡμῖν ὅραμα πώποτε καὶ μὴ αὐτὸ καταδεξώμεθα, οὐκ ἂν ἡμῖν ὁ πολυπόθητος ἡμῶν κύριος ὀργισθῇ διὰ τοῦτο· οἶδε γὰρ ὅτι διὰ τοὺς δόλους τῶν δαιμόνων ἐπὶ τοῦτο ἐρχόμεθα. Ἡ μὲν γὰρ προειρημένη διάκρισις ἀκριβής ἐστιν, συμβαίνει δὲ ἐκ συναρπαγῆς τινος ἀνεπαισθήτου ῥυπωθεῖσαν τὴν ψυχήν, οὗπερ ἐκτὸς οὐδείς, ὡς οἶμαι, εὑρίσκεται, ἀπολέσαι τὸ ἴχνος τῆς ἀκριβοῦς διαγνώσεως καὶ πιστεῦσαι ὡς καλοῖς τοῖς μὴ καλοῖς.

λθ'.

Ἤτω πρὸς ὑπόδειγμα ἡμῖν τοῦ πράγματος δοῦλος ὑπὸ δεσπότου νύκτωρ καὶ μετὰ πολλὴν ἀποδημίαν πρὸ τῶν περιβόλων τῆς οἰκίας καλούμενος. ᾯτινι τὴν ἄνοιξιν τῶν θυρῶν δι' ὅλου ὁ οἰκέτης ἠρνήσατο· ἐδεδίει γὰρ μὴ ὁμοιότης αὐτὸν φωνῆς συναρπάσασα προδότην παρασκευάσῃ γενέσθαι ὧνπερ παρ' αὐτοῦ πεπίστευτο πραγμάτων. ᾯτινι οὐ μόνον οὐκ ὠργίσθη ἡμέρας γενομένης ὁ κύριος αὐτοῦ, ἀλλὰ καὶ πολλῶν ἐπαίνων αὐτὸν ἠξίωσεν, ὅτι καὶ τὴν τοῦ δεσπότου φωνὴν πλάνην εἶναι ἐνόμισεν μὴ θέλων τι τῶν αὐτοῦ ἀπολέσαι χρημάτων.

2 μὲν om. RSa ǁ ἠκούσαμεν BMRST: ἐγνώκαμεν ANa ǁ 3 πρὸς] ὡς πρὸς M ǁ 4 μηδεμιᾷ] μηδὲ a ǁ φαντασίᾳ] φαντασίᾳ τινί a ǁ 5 ἕτερον ὡς ἐπὶ τὸ πλεῖστόν εἰσιν] ἕτερόν εἰσιν ἐπὶ τὸ πλεῖστον Mc ǁ ἢ ABNS: om. MRTa ǁ 6 κἂν] οὖν κἂν S οὖν T ǁ 7 καταπεμφθῇ] καταπεμφθείη a ǁ πώποτε ABMRT: πώσποτε N om. Sa ǁ μὴ] μηδαμῶς S ǁ καταδεξώμεθα A(R)Sa: καταδεξόμεθα BNT δεξώμεθα M ǁ 8 ἡμῶν om. Mac ǁ κύριος MRSa: κύριος Ἰησοῦς ABNT ǁ ὀργισθῇ] ὀργίσθη A ὀργισθείη B ǁ 9 διὰ τοὺς] διαυτοὺς A ǁ ἐπὶ] εἰς Aa ǁ 10 προειρημένη] εἰρημένη a ǁ ἀκριβής] ἀληθής a ǁ 11 ἀνεπαισθήτου BMNRS: ἀνεπαισθήτως ATa ǁ οὗπερ] ὅπερ Nb ǁ οὐδείς om. Nb ǁ 12 διαγνώσεως ABNT: διακρίσεως MRSa ǁ 17 πρὸ τῶν] πρῶτον A ǁ 19 μὴ BMb: μὴ ἡ ANTa μή πως ἡ S μή τις R ǁ ὁμοιότης] ὁμοία τις c ǁ αὐτὸν] αὐτὸ R ǁ φωνῆς BMb: τῆς φωνῆς NRSTa φωνὴ Ac om. T ǁ συναρπάσασα] συναρπάξασα A ǁ 20 παρασκευάσῃ (R)STa: παρασκευάσει BN παρασκευάσοι AM ǁ πεπίστευτο] ἐπιπίστευτο a πεπίστευται S ǁ αὐτοῦ om. a ǁ 22 αὐτὸν ABMS: om. NRTa ǁ 23 χρημάτων MNRS: πραγμάτων ABTa.

38. We have spoken of discernment of good and of worthless dreams, as we have heard from those who have had evidence; let it be sufficient for us, in respect of great virtue, to obey no fantasy whatever. For dreams are nothing other for the most part than either phantoms of erroneous imaginings or else (as I have said) delusions of the demons. And whenever a vision is sent to us from the goodness of God, and we do not accept it, our much-longed-for Lord will not be angry with us because of it; for he knows that we come to this pass because of the deceptions of the demons. For the discernment spoken of above is accurate; but when the soul is soiled from some imperceptible beguilement (from which no one is found to be exempt, I should think), it correspondingly comes to lose the track of precise distinction, and believes that those things which are good are not good.

39. Take as an example of this a servant who is called at night by his master after a long absence, in front of the enclosure of the house. The household servant denied the entry of the doors to him altogether; for he dreaded lest a similarity of voice beguile him and make him be a traitor to those things with which he had been entrusted by his master. Not only was his lord not angry with him when day came, but he rather thought him worthy of much praise, since he had thought the voice of his master was a deception, and did not want to lose any of his possessions.

ΔΙΑΔΟΧΟΥ

μ'.

Ὅτι μὲν ὁ νοῦς, ὅταν ἄρξηται πυκνῶς ὑπὸ τοῦ θείου φωτὸς ἐνεργεῖσθαι, διαφανής τις ὅλος γίνεται, ὥστε τὸ ἑαυτοῦ φῶς αὐτὸν πλουσίως ὁρᾶν, οὐ δεῖ ἀμφιβάλλειν. Τοῦτο γὰρ λόγος γίνεσθαι, ὅταν ἡ δύναμις τῆς ψυχῆς κατακυριεύσῃ τῶν παθῶν. Ὅτι δὲ πᾶν τὸ ἐν σχήματι αὐτῷ φαινόμενον, εἴτε ὡς φῶς, εἴτε ὡς πῦρ, ἐκ τῆς τοῦ ἐχθροῦ κακοτεχνίας γίνεται, ὁ θεσπέσιος ἡμᾶς Παῦλος σαφῶς διδάσκει, εἰς ἄγγελον αὐτὸν φωτὸς λέγων μετασχηματίζεσθαι. Οὐ δεῖ οὖν ἐπὶ ταύτῃ τῇ ἐλπίδι τινὰ τὸν ἀσκητικὸν μετιέναι βίον, ἵνα μὴ ὁ Σατανᾶς ἕτοιμον εὕρῃ τὴν ψυχὴν ἐντεῦθεν εἰς συναρπαγήν, ἀλλ' ἵνα φθάσωμεν μόνον ἐν πάσῃ αἰσθήσει καὶ πληροφορίᾳ τῆς καρδίας ἀγαπῆσαι τὸν θεόν, ὅπερ ἐστὶν ἐν ὅλῃ τῇ καρδίᾳ καὶ ἐν ὅλῃ τῇ ψυχῇ καὶ ἐν ὅλῃ τῇ διανοίᾳ. Ὁ γὰρ εἰς τοῦτο ὑπὸ τῆς χάριτος ἐνεργούμενος τοῦ θεοῦ ἀποδημεῖ τοῦ κόσμου, κἂν ἐν τῷ κόσμῳ παρῇ.

μα'.

Ἡ ὑπακοὴ πρῶτον ἐν πάσαις ταῖς εἰσαγωγοῖς ἀρεταῖς ὑπάρχειν ἔγνωσται καλόν· ἀθετεῖ γὰρ τέως τὴν οἴησιν, τίκτει δὲ ἡμῖν τὴν ταπεινοφρωσύνην. Ὅθεν εἴσοδος καὶ θύρα γίνεται τοῖς αὐτῆς ἀνεχομένοις ἡδέως τῆς εἰς τὸν θεὸν ἀγάπης. Ταύτην ἀθετήσας ὁ Ἀδὰμ εἰς τὸν βύθιον ἀπωλίσθησεν τάρταρον· ταύτης ἐρασθεὶς ὁ κύριος τῷ τῆς οἰκονομίας λόγῳ ἄχρι σταυροῦ καὶ θανάτου ὑπήκουσε τῷ ἑαυτοῦ πατρὶ καὶ ταῦτα ἐν οὐδενὶ ὢν ἥττων τῆς αὐτοῦ μεγαλωσύνης, ἵνα τὸ τῆς ἀνθρωπείας παρακοῆς ἔγκλημα διὰ τῆς ἑαυτοῦ ἐκλύσας ὑπακοῆς εἰς

2 ὅτι μὲν MRSTa: ὅτι ABN ‖ νοῦς] νοῦς ἡμῶν a ‖ ὅταν] ὅτε a ‖ 3 τις om. ANb ‖ ὅλος BN(R)Ta: ὅλως AM καὶ λαμπρὸς ὅλως S ‖ 4 λόγος γίνεσθαι ABMN: ὡς λόγος γίνεσθαι πέφυκεν a ὁ λόγος γίνεται Τ ὅλως γίνεσθαι δύναται S ὅλως γίνεται FR ‖ 6 αὐτῷ] αὐτῇ a om. S ‖ ὡς (bis) om. Mc ‖ 7 σαφῶς om. Nab ‖ διδάσκει] ἐκδιδάσκει a ‖ 9 ἕτοιμον] ἑτοίμην Sc ‖ συναρπαγὴν MNRSa.c.T: ἁρπαγὴν ABSp.c.a ‖ μόνον om. c ‖ τῆς καρδίας BNRST: καρδίας AMa ‖ 12 pr. καὶ om. A ‖ καρδίᾳ . . . ψυχῇ . . . διανοίᾳ MRS: ψυχῇ . . . καρδίᾳ . . . διανοίᾳ BNT καρδίᾳ . . . διανοίᾳ . . . ψυχῇ Aa ‖ 13 εἰς τοῦτο om. a ‖ 14 κἂν] καὶ Μ ‖ παρῇ] εἴη a ‖ 17 εἰσαγωγοῖς] εἰσαγωγίμοις Β ‖ 19 εἴσοδος καὶ θύρα γίνεται RST: καὶ θύρα γίνεται καὶ εἴσοδος Mc καὶ θύρα γίνεται ceteri ‖ 20 τὸν ANRST: om. BMa ‖ ὁ om. Τ ‖ 21 ἀπωλίσθησεν ABNT: ὠλίσθησεν MRSa ‖ 22 ἑαυτοῦ] ἰδίῳ a ‖ 23 ἐν οὐδενὶ] κατ' οὐδὲν a ‖ ἥττων AN(R)STa: ἥττον Mb ἥττω Β ‖ 24 ἑαυτοῦ NRSb: αὐτοῦ ceteri ‖ ἐκλύσας] ἑλκύσας Β ἑλκύσῃ a ‖ εἰς] καὶ εἰς a.

40. One must not doubt that when the intellect begins to be activated constantly by the divine light it becomes a transparent whole, so that it sees its own light abundantly; for this comes to be expressed whenever the power of the soul masters the passions. But the inspired Paul clearly teaches us that everything which appears to it in a shape, either as light, or as fire, comes about from the evil art of the Enemy–saying that he changed his shape into an angel of light.[37] So one must not turn to the ascetic life in this hope: that thereby Satan won't find the soul ready for beguilement; but rather so that we might succeed in loving God alone with a whole Sense and complete assurance of heart, which is in the whole heart and in the whole soul and in the whole reasoning.[38] For whoever is activated to this by the grace of God is away from the world, even if he is present in the world.[39]

41. Obedience is recognised to be the first good among all introductory virtues, for it sets aside presumption and instead engenders humble-mindedness in us; and thus for those who sustain it gladly, obedience also becomes an entrance and door of love for God. Setting obedience aside, Adam slipped away into deep Tartaros: yearning for obedience, the Lord was obedient to his own Father in the expression of Providence to the point of the cross and death[40] (and this while not being inferior in any aspect of His majesty) so that, putting an end to the accusation of human disobedience through his own obedience, he might lead those who live in

---

[37] 2 Corinthians 11:14.
[38] Luke 10:27.
[39] See John 17:11ff.
[40] See Philippians 2:8.

ΔΙΑΔΟΧΟΥ

τὴν μακαρίαν καὶ διαιωνίζουσαν τοὺς ἐν ὑπακοῇ ζήσαντας ἐπαναγάγοι ζωήν. Πρῶτον οὖν τούτου ἐπιμελεῖσθαι δεῖ τοὺς πρὸς τὴν οἴησιν τοῦ διαβόλου ἀναδεχομένους πάλην· δείξει γὰρ ἡμῖν αὕτη προϊοῦσι πάσας ἀπλανῶς τὰς τρίβους τῶν ἀρετῶν.

μβ΄.

Ἡ ἐγκράτεια κοινόν ἐστι πασῶν τῶν ἀρετῶν ἐπώνυμον· δεῖ οὖν τὸν ἐγκρατευόμενον πάντα ἐγκρατεύεσθαι. Ὥσπερ γὰρ ἀνθρώπου οἱονδήποτε τῶν λεπτοτάτων ἀφαιρεθὲν μελῶν τὸ πᾶν τοῦ ἀνθρώπου, κἂν βραχὺ ᾖ τὸ λεῖπον τοῦ σχήματος, ἄμορφον ἀπεργάζεται, οὕτω καὶ ὁ μιᾶς παραμελῶν ἀρετῆς, ὅλην, ὡς οὐκ οἶδεν, τὴν τῆς ἐγκρατείας ἀφανίζει εὐπρέπειαν. Ἐχρῆν οὖν μὴ μόνον τὰς σωματικὰς φιλοπονεῖν ἀρετάς, ἀλλὰ καὶ τὰς τὸν ἔνδον ἡμῶν ἄνθρωπον καθαίρειν δυναμένας. Ποῖον γὰρ ὄφελος ἔσται τῷ τὸ σῶμα παρθένον τηρήσαντι, εἰ τὴν ψυχὴν ὑπὸ τοῦ τῆς παρακοῆς μεμοίχευται δαίμονος; ἢ πῶς στεφανωθήσεται ὁ γαστριμαργίας μὲν καὶ πάσης σωματικῆς ἐπιθυμίας φεισάμενος, οἰήσεως δὲ καὶ φιλοδοξίας μὴ ἐπιμελησάμενος μήτε βραχείας ἀνεχόμενος θλίψεως, τῆς τὸ φῶς τῆς δικαιοσύνης μελλούσης ἀντισταθμίζειν πλάστιγγος τοῖς τὰ ἔργα τῆς δικαιοσύνης ἐν πνεύματι διαπραξαμένοις ταπεινώσεως.

1 τοὺς ἐν ὑπακοῇ ζήσαντας om. a || 2 πρῶτον BRSp.c.b: πρώτου AMNSa.c.T πρώτης a || τούτου ἐπιμελεῖσθαι δεῖ] ταύτης ἐπιμελητέον a || τοὺς] τοὺς τὴν BR || 3 ἀναδεχομένους] ἀναδεδεγμένους a ἀναδεξαμένους R || πάλην ABNRa: τὴν πάλην MST || αὕτη] αὐτὴ c || προϊοῦσι MNRS: προσιοῦσιν ABT προϊοῦσα a || πάσας] ἀπάσας MRSc || 4 ἀπλανῶς] σαφῶς a || 8 ἐγκρατευόμενον ABNRTa: ἀγωνιζόμενον MS || οἱονδήποτε] τὸ οἱονδήποτε a || 9 τῶν λεπτοτάτων ἀφαιρεθὲν μελῶν AMRSTa: τῶν μελῶν τῶν λεπτοτάτων ἀφαιρεθὲν BN || ἀνθρώπου] ἀνθρωπείου Α ἀνθρωπίνου Nb || βραχὺ] βραχεῖ Nb || 9-10 τὸ λεῖπον τοῦ σχήματος Ν: τὸ λειπόμενον τοῦ σχήματος MTa τὸ λεῖπον σχήματος ΑΒ τὸ λεῖπον σχῆμα RS || 10 παραμελῶν] παραμελήσας Mac || 11 ὡς οὐκ οἶδεν om. A || 12 ἐχρῆν ABNa: χρὴ MRST || 12-13 τὰς σωματικὰς . . . ἀρετὰς . . . τὰς . . . δυναμένας] τὴν σωματικὴν . . . ἀρετὴν . . . τὴν . . . δυναμένην Aa || 13 ἔνδον] ἔσω BNb || ἔσται] ἐστι BNb || 14 τῷ om. R || σῶμα] σῶμα μὲν a || 15 πῶς] ποῦ a || στεφανωθήσεται] στήσεται Aa || 15-16 γαστριμαργίας μὲν καὶ πάσης σωματικῆς ἐπιθυμίας] πάσης ἐπιθυμίας καὶ γαστριμαργίας Α πάσης μὲν ἐπιθυμίας a || 17 βραχείας] μίας NRb || ἀνεχόμενος ἀνεχομένης BMc || θλίψεως] λήψεως B.

obedience back into blessed and everlasting life. So those who undertake the fight with the presumption of the devil must first of all attend to obedience; for as we progress it will show us all the paths of the virtues unerringly.

42. Self-control is given as a name common to all the virtues, and so whoever exercises self-control must do so in everything.[41] For just as the loss of any one of the least of a man's members makes all of him deformed (even if what is missing from his form is small) so also whoever disregards one of the virtues, in a way he does not know, does away with the whole comeliness of self-control. So one must be attached not only to the bodily virtues, but also to those which are able to cleanse our inner man.[42] For what profit will it be to him who has kept the body virgin, if he commits adultery in his soul with the demon of disobedience? Or how, since the scales are going to balance the light of justice for those who have accomplished the works of justice in a spirit of humility, will he who has refrained from gluttony and every bodily desire be crowned, when he has not concerned himself about presumption and affection for glory, or doesn't bear up under a little tribulation?

---

[41] See 1 Corinthians 9:25.
[42] See Ephesians 3:16.

ΔΙΑΔΟΧΟΥ

μγ´.

Πάσας μὲν τὰς ἀλόγους ἐπιθυμίας οὕτω δεῖ μελετᾶν μισεῖν τοὺς ἀγωνιζομένους, ὥστε εἰς ἕξιν τὸ πρὸς αὐτὰς μῖσος κτήσασθαι, τὴν δὲ ἐπὶ τῶν βρωμάτων ἐγκράτειαν οὕτως ἐχρῆν διατηρεῖν, ἵνα μὴ εἰς
5   βδέλυξίν τινος αὐτῶν ἔλθῃ τίς ποτε· τοῦτο γὰρ καὶ ἐπικατάρατόν ἐστι καὶ δαιμονιῶδες ὅλον. Οὐ γὰρ ὡς φαύλων αὐτῶν, μὴ γένοιτο, ἀπεχόμεθα, ἀλλ᾽ ἵνα τῶν πολλῶν καὶ χρηστῶν τροφῶν ἑαυτοὺς ἀποσπῶντες τὰ φλεγμαίνοντα μέρη τῆς σαρκὸς συμμέτρως κολάζωμεν, λοιπὸν δὲ ἵνα καὶ τὸ ἡμέτερον περίσσευμα εἰς οἰκονομίαν ἀρκοῦσαν τοῖς πτωχεύουσι
10 γένηται, ὅπερ ἐστὶν ἀγάπης εἰλικρινοῦς γνώρισμα.

μδ´.

Τὸ ἀπὸ πάντων τῶν παρατιθεμένων ἢ κιρνωμένων ἐσθίειν καὶ πίνειν εὐχαριστοῦντας τῷ θεῷ οὐδαμῶς τῷ κανόνι τῆς γνώσεως μάχεται· πάντα
15 γὰρ καλὰ λίαν. Τὸ δὲ τῶν ἡδέων καὶ πολλῶν ἡδέως ἀπέχεσθαι καὶ διακριτικώτατον ὑπάρχει καὶ γνωστικώτερον· οὐκ ἂν δὲ τῶν παρόντων ἡδέων ἡδέως καταφρονήσωμεν, εἰ μὴ τῆς τοῦ θεοῦ γλυκύτητος ἐν πάσῃ αἰσθήσει καὶ πληροφορίᾳ γευσώμεθα.

με´.

Ὃν τρόπον ὑπὸ πλήθους βρωμάτων βαρούμενον τὸ σῶμα δειλόν τινα καὶ δυσκίνητον τὸν νοῦν ἀπεργάζεται, οὕτως καὶ ἐξατονοῦν ὑπὸ πολλῆς ἐγκρατείας στυγνόν τι καὶ ἀφιλόλογον τὸ θεωρητικὸν τῆς ψυχῆς ἀποτελεῖ μέρος. Δεῖ οὖν πρὸς τὰς τοῦ σώματος κινήσεις καὶ τὰς τροφὰς εὐτρεπίζεσθαι, ἵνα, ὅτε μὲν ὑγιαίνει, κολάζοιτο πρεπόντως, ὅτε δὲ

2 ἐπιθυμίας] ἡδονὰς a || μελετᾶν ANac: om. BMRST || μισεῖν] μισῆσαι S om. c || 5 ἔλθῃ BN: ἔλθοι AM(R)STa || 6 ἀπεχόμεθα] ἀπεχώμεθα B || 7 χρηστῶν] χρηστοτέρων a || τροφῶν] τρυφῶν AB || ἀποσπῶντες] ἀφιστῶντες T || 8 μέρη] μέλη Ta || κολάζωμεν AM(R)Ta: κολάζομεν S κολάζοιμεν BN || 9 ἡμέτερον AMa: ἡμῶν BNRT ὑμῶν S || 10 γένηται] γένοιτο AR γίνοιτο T || 13 ἀπὸ] ἐκ a om. Nb || πάντων] ἁπάντων Nb || 14 εὐχαριστοῦντας] εὐχαριστοῦντα A || pr. τῷ om. b || μάχεται] ἀπομάχεται a || 15 alt. καὶ om. R || 16 διακριτικώτατον] διακρικωτάτων B || γνωστικώτερον AMNT: γνωστικώτατον RSa γνωστικωτάτων B || 17 ἡδέων om. Nb || 18 γευσώμεθα BM(R)STb: γευσόμεθα ANa || 21 βαρούμενον] βαρυνόμενον Ta || δειλόν] δῆλόν Nb || 22 ἀπεργάζεται] ἀπεργάζεται τὸν ἡμέτερον a || ἐξατονοῦν AMRSTa: ἐξασθενοῦν BN || 23 τι ABNRa: τε MST om. c || 25 pr. ὅτε ABNT: ὅταν MRSa || ὑγιαίνει AMN: ὑγιαίνῃ B(R)Sa ὑγιαίνοι T || πρεπόντως] μετρίως a || alt. ὅτε] ὅταν RSc.

DIADOCHOS

43. Those who contend must so attend to hating all the irrational desires, as to acquire the habit of hating them; so one must maintain self-control in matters of foodstuffs, so that one never comes to abominate any of them–which is both accursed and completely demoniacal. For we do not abstain from them as being despicable–heaven forbid!–but so that drawing ourselves away from various and fine foods, we might discipline the burning members of the flesh in due measure; and so that then our superfluity might become an economy for those who beg, which is the mark of unalloyed love.

44. To eat and drink of all that is served or poured out, while giving thanks to God, in no way contradicts the rule of perception–for everything is very good;[43] but to abstain from pleasant things and from many things pleasantly is really most discerning and more perceptive. However we will not pleasantly despise the pleasant things which are at hand if we do not taste the sweetness of God with a whole Sense and complete assurance.

45. In the same way that the body makes the intellect reluctant and sluggish when weighed down under a multitude of foods, so it also renders the contemplative part of the soul sullen and uninterested in discourse when it is exhausted by great self-control. So one must prepare foods for oneself for the movements of the body, so that it might be disciplined suitably when healthy, but when weak it might be indulged moderately.

---

[43] Genesis 1:31.

ΔΙΑΔΟΧΟΥ

ἀσθενεῖ, πιαίνοιτο μετρίως. Οὐ γὰρ ἀτονεῖν δεῖ τῷ σώματι τὸν ἀγωνιζόμενον, ἀλλ' ὅσον ἀρκεῖν πρὸς τὸν ἀγῶνα δύνασθαι, ἵνα κἂν τοῖς πόνοις τοῦ σώματος ἡ ψυχὴ πρεπόντως καθαίροιτο.

μϛ'.

Ὅταν ἡ κενοδοξία μεγάλα φλεγμαίνῃ καθ' ἡμῶν τὴν ἀδελφῶν τινων ἐπιδημίαν ἢ οἰωνδήποτε ξένων εἰς πρόφασιν τῆς οἰκείας κακίας εὑρίσκουσα, καλὸν τὸ σύμμετρον ἐπιτρέπειν σχολὴν τῇ συνήθει διαίτῃ. Καὶ γὰρ τὸν δαίμονα ἄπρακτον καὶ μᾶλλον πενθοῦντα τὴν ἐπιχείρησιν ἀποπεμψόμεθα καὶ τὸν θεσμὸν τῆς ἀγάπης ἐγκρίτως πληρώσομεν καὶ τὸ μυστήριον τῆς ἐγκρατείας ἀνεπίδεικτον διὰ τῆς συγκαταβάσεως φυλάξομεν.

μζ'.

Ἡ νηστεία ἔχει μὲν καθ' ἑαυτὴν καύχημα, ἀλλ' οὐ πρὸς θεόν· ἐργαλεῖον γάρ ἐστιν ὥσπερ εἰς σωφροσύνην ῥυθμίζον τοὺς θέλοντας. Οὐ δεῖ οὖν ἐπ' αὐτῇ μεγάλα φρονεῖν τοὺς τῆς εὐσεβείας ἀγωνιστάς, ἐκδέχεσθαι δὲ μόνον ἐν πίστει τοῦ θεοῦ τὸ πέρας ἡμῶν τοῦ σκοποῦ· οὐδὲ γὰρ οἱ τῶν οἰωνδήποτε τεχνῶν ἐπιστήμονες ἐκ τῶν ἐργαλείων τὸ τοῦ ἐπαγγέλματος ἀποτέλεσμα καυχῶνταί ποτε, ἀλλὰ περιμένει τούτων ἕκαστος τὸ εἶδος τοῦ ἐγχειρήματος, ἵνα ἐξ ἐκείνου τὸ ἀκριβὲς τῆς τέχνης ἐνδείξηται.

---

1 ἀσθενεῖ BN(R)Ta: ἀσθενῇ AMS || 1-2 τῷ σώματι τὸν ἀγωνιζόμενον] τὸ σῶμα τῶν ἀγωνιζωμένων Nb || 2 ἀρκεῖν] ἀρκεῖ b || 2-3 κἂν τοῖς πόνοις FT: ἐν τοῖς πόνοις ANR τοῖς πόνοις S κἂν τοῖς τόνοις Ma καὶ τοῖς τόνοις B || 3 πρεπόντως] δεόντως BNb || 6 φλεγμαίνῃ] φλεγμαίνει Nb φλεγμαίνοι Mc || 7 οἰκείας] ἰδίας Mac || 8 καλὸν] καλὸν τότε T || 9 καὶ γὰρ] οὕτως γὰρ B καὶ γὰρ καὶ c || 10 ἀποπεμψόμεθα BN(R)T: ἀποπεμψώμεθα MS ἀποπέμψομεν a ἀποπέμψωμεν A || πληρώσομεν AB(R)Ta: πληρώσωμεν MNS || 12 φυλάξομεν AB(R)Ta: φυλάξωμεν MNS || 15 μὲν om. Aa || θεόν ABNRS: τὸν θεὸν MTa || 16-17 τοὺς θέλοντας - φρονεῖν om. b || θέλοντας] ἐθέλοντας a || 17 αὐτῇ] ταύτῃ a || μεγάλα φρονεῖν ANR: μεγαλοφρονεῖν B μέγα φρονεῖν MSTa || 18 ἐκδέχεσθαι] εἰσδέχεσθαι a || μόνον] μᾶλλον a || ἐν] τῇ Aa || πίστει] πίστει τῇ Mc || 19 οὐδὲ BRa: οὔτε AMNST || οἰωνδήποτε AMTa: οἰωνδηποτοῦν BN δηποτοῦν RS || τεχνῶν] χρειῶν A.

DIADOCHOS

For one who contends must not exhaust the body but be capable of whatever is sufficient for the contest, so that, by the labours of the body, the soul might be cleansed as is fitting.

46. It is good to permit moderate relaxation of normal practice whenever vainglory flares up greatly against us, finding the visit of some brothers or other guests a pretext for its own wickedness. For we will banish the demon, unsuccessful and mourning the attempt all the more, and will fulfil the precept of love acceptably; and by making accommodation we will preserve the mystery of self-control unvaunted.

47. Fasting has a boasting according to itself, but not in relation to God; for it is a tool which trains those who so decide into prudence. So pious contenders must not have high opinions of themselves on its account, but simply await our attainment of the goal in faith in God. For those who are versed in any skills whatever never boast that the result of their craft comes from the tools; each of them rather awaits the final form of the undertaking, so that the accuracy of skill might be demonstrated from that.

ΔΙΑΔΟΧΟΥ

μη'.

"Ον τρόπον ἡ γῆ συμμέτρως μὲν ἀρδευομένη καθαρὸν τὸ καταβαλλόμενον εἰς αὐτὴν σπέρμα μετὰ πλείστης προσθήκης ἀνίησιν, ὑπὸ πολλῶν δὲ μεθυσκομένη ὄμβρων ἀκάνθας φέρει μόνον καὶ τριβόλους, οὕτω καὶ ἡ γῆ τῆς καρδίας, ἐὰν μὲν συμμέτρῳ οἴνῳ χρώμεθα, καθαρὰ τὰ φυσικὰ αὐτῆς ἀναδίδωσι σπέρματα καὶ τὰ ἀπὸ τοῦ ἁγίου πνεύματος εἰς αὐτὴν σπειρόμενα εὐθαλῆ λίαν ἀναφέρει καὶ πολύκαρπα, ἐὰν δὲ διάβροχος ὑπὸ τῆς πολυποσίας γένηται, ἀκάνθας ὄντως φέρει τοὺς ἅπαντας αὐτῆς λογισμοὺς καὶ τριβόλους.

μθ'.

"Οταν ὁ νοῦς ἡμῶν τῷ τῆς πολυποσίας ἐννήχηται κύματι, οὐ μόνον τοῖς ὑπὸ τῶν δαιμόνων ἐν τῷ ὕπνῳ σχηματιζομένοις ἐμπαθῶς εἰδώλοις ἐνορᾷ, ἀλλὰ καὶ ἐν ἑαυτῷ ὄψεις τινὰς ἀναπλάττων εὐπρεπεῖς ταῖς ἑαυτοῦ φαντασίαις ὡς ἐρωμέναις τισὶ κέχρηται διαπύρως. Θερμαινομένων γὰρ τῶν συνουσιαστικῶν ὀργάνων ὑπὸ τῆς τοῦ οἴνου ζέσεως ἀνάγκη πᾶσα παριστᾶν ἑαυτῷ τὸν νοῦν σκιὰν τοῦ πάθους ἐνήδονον. Ἐχρῆν οὖν τῇ συμμετρίᾳ ἡμᾶς κεχρημένους τὴν ἐκ τοῦ πλεονάζοντος διαφεύγειν βλάβην. Ὅταν γὰρ οὐκ ἔχῃ τὴν ὑποσύρουσαν αὐτὸν ὁ νοῦς ἡδονὴν πρὸς τὴν ζωγραφίαν τῆς ἁμαρτίας, ἀφάνταστος ὅλος διαμένει καὶ τὸ κρεῖττον ἀθήλυντος.

2 ἡ om. A ‖ μὲν om. A ‖ ἀδρευομένη] ἀδρομένη a ‖ 3 πλείστης] πολλῆς Β πολλῆς τῆς a ‖ 4 μόνον om. A ‖ 5 συμμέτρῳ οἴνῳ] συμμέτρως Mc ‖ 6 ἀναδίδωσι BNRST: ἀναδείκνυσι a ἀναδεικνῦσα A ἀναδεικνύσουσα M ‖ ἁγίου] ἁγίου δὲ Rb ‖ 7 σπειρόμενα] ἐνσπειρόμενα Sa ἐπισπειρόμενα T ‖ ἀναφέρει] φέρει a ‖ καὶ - 8 φέρει om. M ‖ 8 τῆς om. a ‖ γένηται] γένοιτο c γίνοιτο T ‖ φέρει] ἀναφέρει Β ‖ 9 ἅπαντας] πάντας Mac ‖ 12 ἐννήχηται a: ἐννήχεται BMN(R)ST ἐνήχεται A ‖ 13 ὑπὸ] ἀπὸ Mc ‖ ἐν τῷ BMNRST: ἐν a τῷ A ‖ 14 ἐν ἑαυτῷ] ἐν αὐτῷ MRc ἑαυτῷ a ‖ εὐπρεπεῖς] εὐτρεπεῖς c ‖ 15 ἑαυτοῦ] ἀεὶ αὐτοῦ c ‖ ἐρωμέναις MRST: ἐρρωμέναις AB ὁρωμέναις a ἐν ὁρωμέναις N ‖ 16 ὑπὸ] διὰ Nb ‖ 17 παριστᾶν] παριστάναι Β ‖ ἑαυτῷ] αὐτῷ Β ‖ σκιὰν] σκιάν τινα S ‖ 18 ἐνήδονον] ἀνήδονον b ‖ ἐχρῆν] χρὴ Mc ‖ τῇ συμμετρίᾳ] τὴν συμμετρίαν A ‖ κεχρημένους ABNRST: χρωμένους M κεχρῆσθαι a ‖ 18-19 τοῦ πλειονάζοντος] τῆς ἀμετρίας a ‖ 19 διαφεύγειν] διαφεύγοντας a ‖ ὅταν] ὅτε Ta ‖ ἔχῃ Β: ἔχει ceteri ‖ ὑποσύρουσαν] ὑποπυροῦσαν M ὑπὸ πυρᾶσαν c ‖ 20 τῆς ἁμαρτίας] τοῦ πάθους a ‖ 21 ὅλος] ὅλως BMT ‖ κρεῖττον] κριτικὸν Mc ‖ ἀθήλυντος] ἀθήλυντον c.

62

48. In the same way that the earth when watered moderately sends up the pure seed scattered upon it greatly multiplied, whereas soaked by many rain-storms it bears only thorns and burrs, so the earth of the heart also sends forth its pure natural seed if we use a moderate amount of wine, and bears very flourishingly and very fruitfully that which the holy Spirit sows in it; but if it ever becomes saturated by over-drinking, it bears all its imaginings veritably as thorns and burrs.

49. Whenever our intellect swims in the swell of over-drinking, not only does it see passionately the forms shaped by the demons in sleep, but it also, inventing attractive visions in itself, indulges its own fantasies as being feverishly yearned for. For when the organs of intercourse are warmed by the heat of wine, it is altogether inevitable that the intellect represent to itself a delightful shadow of passion. Therefore we must use wine in moderation, to escape the damage which comes from excess. For whenever the intellect does not hold to the pleasure which draws it towards the depiction of sin, it remains entirely free from fantasy and, what is best, uneffeminate.

ΔΙΑΔΟΧΟΥ

ν'.

Πάντα τὰ κατασκευαστὰ πόματα, ἃ δὴ προπόματα καλοῦσιν οἱ ταύτης τεχνῖται τῆς ἐπινοίας, ὡς ἔοικεν διὰ τὸ ὁδηγεῖν εἰς γαστέρα τὸ πλῆθος τῶν βρωμάτων, οὐ δεῖ μεταδιώκειν τοὺς θέλοντας τὰ οἰδαίνοντα μέρη κολάζειν τοῦ σώματος· οὐ γὰρ μόνον ἡ ποιότης αὐτῶν ἐπιβλαβὴς τοῖς ἀγωνιζομένοις σώμασι γίνεται, ἀλλὰ καὶ αὐτὴ ἡ παράλογος αὐτῶν σύγκρασις πλήττει λίαν τὴν θεοφόρον συνείδησιν. Τί γὰρ ἄρα τὸ λεῖπον τῇ τοῦ οἴνου φύσει, ἵνα διαφόρων ἡδυσμάτων ἐπιμιξίᾳ ἡ τούτου στερρότης θηλύνοιτο;

να'.

Ὁ κύριος ἡμῶν καὶ ταύτης τῆς ἱερᾶς πολιτείας διδάσκαλος Ἰησοῦς Χριστὸς ὄξος ἐν τῷ πάθει παρὰ τῶν ὑπουργούντων τοῖς διαβολικοῖς ἐπιτάγμασι πεπότισται, ἵν' ὑπογραμμὸν ἡμῖν, ἐμοὶ δοκεῖ, ἐναργῆ καταλείποι τῆς τῶν ἱερῶν ἀγώνων διαθέσεως. Οὐ δεῖ γάρ, φησίν, τοῖς ἡδύνουσι κεχρῆσθαι πόμασιν ἢ βρώμασι τοὺς ἀγωνιζομένους κατὰ τῆς ἁμαρτίας, ἀλλὰ μᾶλλον τοῦ πικροῦ τῆς μάχης μετὰ καρτερίας ἀνέχεσθαι. Προστεθήτω δὲ καὶ ὕσσωπον τῷ σπόγγῳ τῆς ὕβρεως, ὅπως ἂν τελείως ἐμφέροιτο τῷ ὑποδείγματι τὸ σχῆμα τῆς ἡμῶν καθάρσεως. Τὸ μὲν γὰρ δριμὺ τῶν ἀγώνων ἴδιον, τὸ δὲ καθαριστικὸν πάντως τῆς τελειώσεως.

νβ'.

Τὸ λουτρῷ παραβάλλειν οὐκ ἄν τις ἁμαρτωλὸν ἢ παράλογον ἀποφαίνοιτο· τὸ δὲ δι' ἐγκράτειαν καὶ τούτου ἀπέχεσθαι καὶ ἀνδρεῖον λέγω καὶ σωφρονέστατον. Οὔτε γὰρ τὸ σῶμα ἡμῶν ἐκθηλύνει ἡ ἐνήδονος ἐκείνη ὑγρασία οὔτε μὴν εἰς ὑπόμνησιν τῆς γυμνότητος τοῦ

---

3 εἰς γαστέρα om. a ‖ 4 θέλοντας] ἐθέλοντας a ‖ 5 μέρη MNRST: μέλη ABa ‖ μόνον AMNRT: δὴ μόνον BSa ‖ ἡ] ἡ παράλογος a ‖ 6 σώμασι om. A ‖ γίνεται] τυγχάνει a ‖ 7 θεοφόρον AMRSp.c.a: θεόφοβον BNSa.c.T ‖ ἄρα] ἃ Nb ‖ 8 ἐπιμιξίᾳ] ἐπιμελείᾳ ANb ‖ 13 χριστὸς BMNRT: ὁ χριστὸς AS om. a ‖ 14 ἡμῖν om. Ta ‖ δοκεῖ] δοκεῖν A ‖ 15 καταλείποι] καταλίποι S ‖ 18 προστεθήτω] προστέθηται Nb ‖ καὶ ὕσσωπον om. Nb ‖ ὕβρεως] βρώσεως Aa ‖ 19 ἂν] ὢν b ‖ τὸ μὲν] τότε A ‖ 20 δὲ] τε M ‖ καθαριστικὸν] καθαρτικὸν a ‖ 23 τὸ AB(R)Sa: τῷ BMT ‖ 24 ἀποφαίνοιτο] ἀποφήνοιτο STa ‖ τὸ] δεῖ a ‖ ἀπέχεσθαι] ἀνέχεσθαι A ‖ 25 λέγω] γὰρ τοῦτο a ‖ οὔτε] οὐδὲ Nb ‖ 26 γυμνότητος] γυμνώσεως b.

50. Those who want to discipline the swelling members of the body must not run after any artificial drinks–which those who make these concoctions call pre-dinner drinks (apparently because they guide the plethora of foods into the stomach). For not only is their quality harmful to contending bodies, but their unreasonable blending strikes the God-bearing conscience very hard. For what then is wanting in the nature of wine, that by mixing in various spices its roughness should be softened?

51. Our Lord and teacher of the sacred manner of living, Jesus Christ, was given vinegar to drink during the Passion by those who obeyed diabolical commands, in order (it seems to me) that he might leave behind a palpable model for us of the disposition of sacred contests. For it says, those who contend against sin must not make use of gratifying drinks or food, but rather hold out against the bitterness of the fight, with patience. But let hyssop be applied to the sponge of insolence, so that the form of our cleansing might be brought perfectly into the pattern. For that which is bitter is characteristic of contests, and that which cleanses is altogether characteristic of perfection.

52. No one can demonstrate that to have a bath is sinful or unreasonable; but to abstain from this out of self-control is, I say, manly and very prudent. For then neither does this delightful wetness soften our body, nor do we enter into a reminder of the inglorious nakedness of

ΔΙΑΔΟΧΟΥ

Ἀδὰμ τῆς ἀδόξου ἐρχόμεθα, ἵνα καὶ τῶν ἐκείνου φύλλων εἰς τὸ σκεπάσαι τὴν δευτέραν τῆς αἰσχύνης φροντίζωμεν πρόφασιν, οἵ γε μάλιστα ἀπὸ τῆς τοῦ βίου πρὸ βραχέως ἐκπηδήσαντες ἐξωλείας ἁγνείᾳ τοῦ ἑαυτῶν σώματος τῷ κάλλει τῆς σωφροσύνης ἑνωθῆναι ὀφείλομεν.

νγ'.

Ἰατροὺς μετακαλεῖσθαι ἐν τῷ καιρῷ τῶν νόσων οὐδὲν τὸ κωλύον. Ἐπειδὴ γὰρ ἔμελλεν ὑπὸ τῆς ἀνθρωπίνης πείρας ποτὲ συλλέγεσθαι ἡ τέχνη, διὰ τοῦτο καὶ προϋπῆρχε τὰ φάρμακα. Πλὴν οὐκ ἐχρῆν εἰς αὐτοὺς τὴν ἐλπίδα ἔχειν τῆς ἰάσεως, ἀλλ᾽ εἰς τὸν ἀληθινὸν ἡμῶν σωτῆρα καὶ ἰατρὸν Ἰησοῦν Χριστόν. Ταῦτα δὲ λέγω τοῖς ἐν κοινοβίοις ἢ ἐν πόλεσι τὸν σκοπὸν τῆς ἐγκρατείας κατορθοῦσι διὰ τὸ μὴ δύνασθαι αὐτοὺς ἐκ τῶν συμβαινουσῶν περιστάσεων ἄπαυστον ἔχειν διὰ τῆς ἀγάπης τὴν ἐνέργειαν τῆς πίστεως, ἄλλως τε καὶ διὰ τὸ μὴ εἰς κενοδοξίαν αὐτοὺς καὶ πειρασμὸν ἐμπίπτειν τοῦ διαβόλου. Ἐξ ὧν τινες αὐτῶν ἰατρῶν μὴ χρῄζειν ἐπὶ πολλῶν ἐπαγγέλλονται. Εἰ δέ τις τὸν ἀναχωρητικὸν βίον ἐν ἐρημοτέροις μεταξὺ δύο ἢ τριῶν ὁμοτρόπων ἀδελφῶν κατορθοῖ τόποις, μόνῳ τῷ κυρίῳ ἑαυτὸν τῷ ἰωμένῳ ἡμῶν πᾶσαν νόσον καὶ πᾶσαν μαλακίαν ἐν πίστει προσαγέτω, κἄν ὁποίοις ἂν περιπίπτοι πάθεσιν. Ἔχει γὰρ τῶν νόσων ἱκανὴν μετὰ τὸν κύριον τὴν ἐρημίαν παρήγορον. Ὅθεν οὔτε τῆς ἐνεργείας ὁ τοιοῦτος πένεταί ποτε τῆς πίστεως, ἐπειδὴ μάλιστα οὔτε που ἐνδείξασθαι τὴν ἐκ τῆς ὑπομονῆς εὑρίσκει ἀρετὴν καλῷ τῇ ἐρημίᾳ κεχρημένος παραπετάσματι· διὰ τοῦτο γὰρ ὁ κύριος κατοικίζει μονοτρόπους ἐν οἴκῳ.

1 καὶ] διὰ A ‖ 2 τῆς] ὡς Aa ‖ φροντίζωμεν Bb: φροντίζομεν AN(R)T φροντίσωμεν MS ‖ πρόφασιν] γύμνωσιν Sa.c. ‖ 3 ἀπὸ τῆς] ἀπὸ S τοῖς a ‖ ἐξωλείας ἁγνείᾳ] ἐξωλείας ἀγνοίᾳ c ἐξωλείας ἁγνείας R ἐξορίας ἁγνείας S ‖ 4 ὀφείλομεν] ὀφείλοντες a ‖ 8 ἔμελλεν] ἔμελλέ ποτε ab ἤμελλεν A ‖ ἀνθρωπίνης MNS: ἀνθρωπείου ABRT(a) ἀνθρωπείας b ‖ ποτὲ om. ab ‖ 9 καὶ om. B ‖ 10 ἡμῶν om. b ‖ 11 Ἰησοῦν χριστόν] τὸν κυρίον Ἰησοῦν χριστόν A Ἰησοῦν τὸν κύριον a ‖ 12 ἢ ἐν] ἢ Sb ‖ σκοπὸν τῆς ἐγκρατείας] ἀσκητικὸν βίον a ‖ 13 συμβαινουσῶν] συμβαινουσῶν αὐτοῖς STa ‖ 14 τε] τε δὲ B ‖ 15 πειρασμὸν] πειρασμοὺς a ‖ 15-16 ἐξ - ἐπαγγέλλονται om. A ‖ τινες αὐτῶν om. B ‖ 16 ἰατρῶν] ἰατροῦ a ‖ 17 ἀναχωρητικὸν] μονήρη a ‖ ἐρημοτέροις] ἐρημικωτέροις ST ‖ δύο AMa: μόνον δύο BN δύο μόνον RST ‖ 18 μόνῳ om. Mc ‖ τῷ ἰωμένῳ] τῷ καὶ ἰωμένῳ BNRb ‖ ἡμῶν om. Aa ‖ 20 περιπίπτοι ABM(R)S: περιπίπτῃ a περιπίπτει NT ‖ 21 παρήγορον] κατήγορον a ‖ τῆς ἐνεργείας] τὴν ἐνεργείαν a τῇ ἐνεργείᾳ R ‖ 22 οὔτε που] οὐδέπου Mac ‖ 23 καλῷ τῇ ἐρημίᾳ] καλὸν τῆς ἐρημίας R ‖ κεχρημένος] κεκτημένος a ‖ 24 γὰρ ὁ BRTc: γὰρ AMNS γὰρ καὶ a.

Adam–so that we might consider it a second occasion of shame to cover with his leaves; we especially who, having just escaped from the ruin of this life, ought by the purity of our bodies to be united to the beauty of prudence.

53. There is nothing to prevent doctors being called in, in times of illness. For medicines already existed for this reason, since the skill was going to be devised by human experimentation. However, one must not place one's hope of healing in them, but in our true Saviour and Healer, Jesus Christ. I say these things to those who attain the goal of self-control in communities or cities, because of their not being able (due to contingent circumstances) to hold constantly to the activity of faith through love,[44] and likewise for the sake of their not falling into vainglory or the temptation of the devil.[45] It is due to these that some of them profess, in the presence of many, not to need doctors. But if anyone achieves the withdrawn life in very desert places, in the midst of two or three brothers of similar habits, let him in faith approach the Lord who alone heals all our illness and weakness,[46] whatever kind of suffering he falls into. For he has after the Lord the desert as a sufficient soother for illnesses. Thus such a one never lacks time for the activity of faith, especially since he finds nowhere to vaunt the virtue of steadfastness, using the desert as a good veil. It is for this reason that 'the Lord lodges solitaries in his house.'[47]

---

[44] See Galatians 5:6.
[45] See 1 Timothy 3:6.
[46] See Matthew 4:23.
[47] Psalms 67:7.

ΔΙΑΔΟΧΟΥ

νδ'.

Ὅταν πρὸς τὰς συμβαινούσας ἡμῖν σωματικὰς ἀνωμαλίας λίαν ἀπεχθανώμεθα, εἰδέναι δεῖ ὅτι ἡ ψυχὴ ἡμῶν ἔτι δεδούλωται ταῖς ἐπιθυμίαις τοῦ σώματος· διόπερ τὰς ὑλώδεις ποθοῦσα εὐπραγίας οὔτε ἀναχωρῆσαι τῶν καλῶν τοῦ βίου βούλεται, ἀλλὰ καὶ ἀσχολίαν μεγάλην ἡγεῖται τὸ μὴ δύνασθαι διὰ τὰς νόσους κεχρῆσθαι τοῖς τοῦ βίου ὡραίοις. Ἐὰν δὲ εὐχαρίστως τὰς ἐκ τῶν νόσων προσδέχεται ἀνίας, οὐ μακρὰν οὖσα τῶν τῆς ἀπαθείας ὅρων γνωρίζεται· ὅθεν καὶ τὸν θάνατον ὡς πρόφασιν ὄντως ὄντα ζωῆς μᾶλλον ἀληθινῆς τότε μετὰ χαρᾶς ἀπεκδέχεται.

νε'.

Οὐκ ἂν ἐπιθυμήσῃ ἡ ψυχὴ χωρισθῆναι τοῦ σώματος, εἰ μὴ ἄποιος αὐτῇ ἡ πρὸς τὸν ἀέρα τοῦτον διάθεσις γένοιτο. Πᾶσαι γὰρ αἱ αἰσθήσεις τοῦ σώματος τῇ πίστει ἀντίκεινται· ἐπειδὴ αἱ μὲν τῶν παρόντων γίνονται, ἡ δὲ τὴν τῶν μελλόντων μόνον ἀγαθῶν ἐπαγγέλλεται πολυτέλειαν. Προσήκει οὖν τὸν ἀγωνιζόμενον μὴ περὶ δένδρων τινῶν εὐκλώνων ἢ συσκίων ἢ πηγῶν καλλιρρόων ἢ λειμώνων ποικίλων ἢ οἴκων εὐπρεπῶν ἢ καὶ περὶ συγγενικῶν συνδιατριβῶν ἐνθυμεῖσθαι πώποτε, μήτε δὲ τῶν πανηγυρικῶν, εἰ τύχοι, μεμνῆσθαι φιλοτιμιῶν, ἀλλὰ κεχρῆσθαι μὲν τοῖς ἀναγκαίοις εὐχαρίστως, ὁδὸν δέ τινα ξένην ἡγεῖσθαι τὸν βίον πάσης σαρκικῆς διαθέσεως ἔρημον. Οὕτω γὰρ ἂν μόνον στενώσαντες ἡμῶν τὴν διάνοιαν εἰς τὸ ἴχνος αὐτὴν ὅλην τῆς αἰωνίου ἐπιστρέψωμεν ὁδοῦ.

3 ὅτι BNRST: ὡς AMa ‖ δεδούλωται] δουλοῦται b ‖ 4 διόπερ] διόπερ καὶ Aa ‖ ὑλώδεις] ὑλικὰς a ‖ 6 τὸ] τοῦ B ‖ διὰ τὰς νόσους] εἰς τὰς νόσους A ἐν ταῖς νόσοις a ‖ 7 τῶν νόσων] τῆς νόσου BNb ‖ 9 ὄντως ὄντα R: ὄντα ceteri ‖ τότε om. a ‖ 10 ἀπεκδέχεται] ἀποδέχεται R ‖ 13 ἐπιθυμήσῃ BM(R)ST: ἐπιθυμήσει ANac ‖ ἡ om. AMc ‖ 16 γίνονται] γίνωνται ab ‖ ἡ δὲ τὴν] ἡ δὲ Aa διὰ ἡ τὴν R ‖ μελλόντων] ὄντως S om. R ‖ μόνον BMNR: om. ASTac ‖ ἀγαθῶν om. a ‖ 17 τινῶν om. c ‖ 18 ποικίλων] ποικίλων καὶ εὐανθῶν T ‖ 19 συγγενικῶν] συγγενῶν AMc ‖ συνδιατριβῶν BN: ἠδιατρίβων A διατριβῶν RST om. Ma ‖ 19-20 ἐνθυμεῖσθαι - πανηγυρικῶν om. a ‖ 20 μήτε δὲ] μηδὲ Nb ‖ 22 τὸν] τὸν τῆδε a ‖ μόνον om. a ‖ 23 αἰωνίου] αἰωνίου ζωῆς Ba ‖ 24 ἐπιστρέψωμεν] ἐπιστρέψομεν ST ‖ ὁδοῦ om. a.

54. Whenever we are too incensed against contingent bodily disorders, we must know that our soul is still enslaved to the desires of the body; since, longing for material success, it does not intend to withdraw from the good things of this life, but deems it a great trouble not to be able to make use of the burgeoning things of this life due to illnesses. But if our soul accepts with thanksgiving annoyances which come from illnesses, it discovers that it is not far from the boundaries of dispassion; so then it also awaits death with joy as really being rather an occasion of true life.

55. The soul will not desire to be separated from the body unless its disposition towards this air comes to be devoid of quality. For all the senses of the body are opposed to faith, since they pertain to transient things, while faith only proclaims the great value of the good things to come. So it is seemly for the one who contends never to take thought of any flourishing or thickly shaded trees, or beautifully flowing springs, or dappled meadows, or attractive houses, or even with spending time with relatives, nor (if it should arise) be mindful of flattering honours; rather it is seemly to make use of constraints with thanksgiving, and destitute of all fleshly disposition, to think of this life as an alien road. For thus alone, confining our reason, will we turn it round, complete, into the track of the road which is eternal.

ΔΙΑΔΟΧΟΥ

νς'.

Ὅτι ἡ βλέψις καὶ ἡ γεῦσις καὶ αἱ λοιπαὶ αἰσθήσεις διαφοροῦσι τὴν μνήμην τῆς καρδίας, ὅταν αὐταῖς ὑπὲρ τὸ μέτρον κεχρήμεθα, πρώτη ἡ Εὔα ἡμῖν ὁμιλεῖ τό τοιοῦτο· ἕως μὲν γὰρ ὅτε οὐκ ἀπεῖδεν ἐκείνη εἰς τὸ δένδρον τῆς παραγγελίας ἡδέως, ἐμέμνητο τοῦ θείου ἐπιμελῶς προστάγματος. Διόπερ καὶ ταῖς πτέρυξιν ἔτι τοῦ θείου ὥσπερ ἐσκέπετο ἔρωτος, ἐντεῦθεν τὴν ἑαυτῆς ἀγνοοῦσα γυμνότητα. Ἐπειδὴ δὲ εἶδε τὸ ξύλον ἡδέως καὶ μετὰ πολλῆς αὐτοῦ ἐπιθυμίας ἥψατο καὶ λοιπὸν τοῦ ἐξ αὐτοῦ καρποῦ μετὰ ἐνεργοῦς τινος ἐγεύσατο ἡδονῆς, εὐθὺς μὲν διηδύνθη πρὸς σωματικὴν συμπλοκὴν ὡς γυμνὴ τῷ πάθει συνάψασα· ὅλην δὲ αὐτῆς τὴν ἐπιθυμίαν εἰς τὴν τῶν παρόντων ἀπόλαυσιν ἔδωκεν, μίξασα διὰ τὸ τοῦ καρποῦ ἡδυθανὲς τῷ ἑαυτῆς καὶ τὸν Ἀδὰμ πταίσματι· ὅθεν δυσχερῶς λοιπὸν ὁ ἀνθρώπινος νοῦς μεμνῆσθαι τοῦ θεοῦ δύναται ἢ τῶν αὐτοῦ ἐντολῶν. Ἡμεῖς οὖν εἰς τὸ βάθος ἀεὶ τῆς καρδίας ἡμῶν ἀφορῶντες μετὰ μνήμης ἀπαύστου τοῦ θεοῦ ὡς πηροὶ τὰς ὄψεις τῷ φιλαπατεῶνι τούτῳ ἐνδιάγωμεν βίῳ. Φιλοσοφίας γὰρ ὄντως πνευματικῆς ἴδιον ἄπτερον ἀεὶ τὸν ἔρωτα διαφυλάττειν τῶν ὄψεων. Τοῦτο δὲ καὶ ὁ πολυπειρότατος Ἰὼβ διδάσκει ἡμᾶς λέγων· Εἰ δὲ καὶ τῷ ὀφθαλμῷ μου ἐπηκολούθησεν ἡ καρδία μου. Οὕτως ἀκροτάτης ἐγκρατείας ὑπάρχει ἡ ὑπόθεσις γνώρισμα.

νζ'.

Ὁ ἐνδημῶν ἀεὶ τῇ ἑαυτοῦ καρδίᾳ ἐκδημεῖ πάντως τῶν ὡραίων τοῦ βίου· πνεύματι γὰρ περιπατῶν τὰς τῆς σαρκὸς ἐπιθυμίας εἰδέναι οὐ δύναται. Ἐπειδὴ λοιπὸν ἐν τῷ φρουρίῳ τῶν ἀρετῶν τοὺς περιπάτους ὁ

2 διαφοροῦσι] διαφέρουσι Nb διαφθείρουσιν R || 3 ὑπὲρ τὸ μέτρον] ἀμέτρως a || ἡ NRc: om. ABMSTa || 4 τοιοῦτο AMNRS: τοιοῦτον BTa || ὅτε om. Nb || 5 ἡδέως om. B || 6 ὥσπερ om. A || ἐσκέπετο MSa: ἐπεσκέπετο NT ἐσκεπάζετο A ἐσκέπαστο BR || 7 ἀγνοοῦσα] διαγνοῦσα Ab || γυμνότητα] γύμνωσιν a || ἐπειδὴ δὲ BNRTa: ἐπειδὴ AM ἐπεὶ δὲ S || εἶδε] εἶδέν τε Mc οἶδεν b || τὸ] τότε τὸ R || 8 ἐπιθυμίας] τῆς ἐπιθυμίας STa || alt. καὶ BNRST: om. AMa || 9 καρποῦ] καρποῦ καὶ Mc || 10 δὲ om. AB || ἔδωκεν ABRSTa: δέδωκεν MN || 12 διὰ om. R || τὸ om. b || τῷ] τὸ Nb || τὸν] τῷ A || 13 λοιπὸν om. a || 14 ἡμῶν om. a || 15 θεοῦ] κυρίου Ἰησοῦ a || ὡς] ὥσπερ a || 16 ἐνδιάγωμεν] ἐσδιάγωμεν N || 17 ἴδιον ἄπτερον] ἴδιον τοῦτο ἄπτερον R || δὲ καὶ] γὰρ καὶ c γὰρ M || 18 διδάσκει] ἐκδιδάσκει a || 19 οὕτως M(R)ST: οὗτος BN ὄντως a || ἡ MRSTa: om. BN || 20 γνώρισμα] καὶ γνωρίσμα B || 24 περιπατῶν] περιπατῶν ὁ τοιοῦτος B.

70

56. Eve first acquaints us with this: that sight and taste and the rest of the senses disperse the heart's recollection, whenever we make use of them beyond measure. For as long as she didn't look with pleasure at the tree of prohibition, she carefully recollected the ordinance of God; so she was also still covered (as it were) by the wings of yearning for God, and in consequence did not perceive her own nakedness. But as soon as she looked with pleasure at the wood and took hold of it with much desire, and then tasted its fruit with an active pleasure, she immediately slipped into a bodily embrace, as, naked, she united in passion. She gave the whole of her desire to the enjoyment of those things which were at hand, involving (because of the gratifying appearance of the fruit) Adam also in her downfall; and as a result the human intellect was hardly able to recollect God or his commandments. So, always looking back into the depth of our heart with ceaseless recollection of God, we dwell in this deceit-ridden life as if our eyes were dimmed. For truly it is characteristic of spiritual philosophy to keep the yearning for visible things flightless at all times. And this is what the much-tested Job teaches us, saying, 'If my heart followed my eye . . .'[48] So this principle is the mark of the highest self-control.

57. He who always dwells in his own heart dwells completely apart from the burgeoning things of this life[49]–for walking in spirit[50] he cannot know the desires of the flesh. From then on such a man makes his rounds

---

[48] Job 31:7.
[49] See 2 Corinthians 5:8.
[50] See Galatians 5:25.

ΔΙΑΔΟΧΟΥ

τοιοῦτος ποιεῖται, αὐτὰς ὥσπερ τὰς ἀρετὰς πυλωροὺς ἔχων τοῦ τῆς ἁγνείας πολίσματος· διὸ δὴ καὶ ἄπρακτοι λοιπὸν αἱ τῶν δαιμόνων τότε ἐπ' αὐτῷ γίνονται μηχαναί, κἂν ἄχρι τῶν θυρίδων τῆς φύσεως τὰ τοῦ πανδήμου ἔρωτος καταφθάσωσί πως βέλη.

νη'.

Ὅταν μηκέτι τῶν τῆς γῆς ὡραίων ἄρξηται ἐπιθυμεῖν ἡμῶν ἡ ψυχή, τότε ἀκηδιαστής τις τὰ πολλὰ νοῦς αὐτὴν ὑπεισέρχεται μήτε τῇ διακονίᾳ τοῦ λόγου αὐτὴν συγχωρῶν ἡδέως ὑπηρετεῖν μήτε μὴν τρανὴν ἐπιθυμίαν τῶν μελλόντων αὐτῇ καταλιμπάνων ἀγαθῶν, ἀλλὰ καὶ τὴν πρόσκαιρον ταύτην ὑπερβαλλόντως ἐξαχρειῶν ζωὴν ὡς οὐκ ἔχουσαν ἔργον ἀρετῆς ἄξιον καὶ αὐτὴν δὲ τὴν γνῶσιν ἐξουδενῶν ἢ ὡς καὶ ἄλλοις ἤδη πολλοῖς παρασχεθεῖσαν ἢ μηδὲν τέλειον ἐπαγγελλομένῃ σημαίνειν ἡμῖν. Τοῦτο δὲ τὸ χλιαρὸν καὶ νωθροποιὸν ἐκφευξόμεθα πάθος, εἰ στενοὺς ἄγαν ὅρους ἐπιστήσομεν ἡμῶν τῇ διανοίᾳ πρὸς μόνην τὴν μνήμην τοῦ θεοῦ ἀφορῶντες· οὕτω γὰρ ἂν μόνον εἰς τὴν ἑαυτοῦ ὁ νοῦς ἐπαναδραμὼν θέρμην τῆς διαφορήσεως ἐκείνης ἀναχωρῆσαι τῆς ἀλόγου δυνήσεται.

νθ'.

Ἀπαιτεῖ ἡμᾶς πάντως ὁ νοῦς, ὅταν αὐτοῦ πάσας τὰς διεξόδους τῇ μνήμῃ ἀποφράξωμεν τοῦ θεοῦ, ἔργον ὀφεῖλον αὐτοῦ πληροφορεῖν τὴν ἐντρέχειαν. Δεῖ οὖν αὐτῷ διδόναι τὸ κύριε Ἰησοῦ μόνον εἰς ὁλόκληρον

2 πολίσματος] πολιτεύματος Nb κλείσματος a || λοιπὸν BNT: om. MRSa || 3 ἐπ' BNRST: παρ' Ma || γίνονται μηχαναί] πᾶσαι γίνονται αἱ μηχαναὶ a || κἂν] καὶ c || 4 καταφθάσωσί N: καταφθάσῃ T καταφθάνῃ RS καταφθάνουσι BMa || πως NRST: om. BMa || 8 τὰ] ὡς τὰ T || νοῦς] ὁ νοῦς R || αὐτὴν] αὐτῇ BT || ὑπεισέρχεται] ἐπεισέρχεται Nb || μήτε] μηδὲ Mc || 9 αὐτὴν BMRS: om. NTa || μὴν] δὲ S || τρανὴν] τρανὴν τὴν Mc || 10 αὐτῇ] αὐτὴν Mc || 12 ἢ - 13 παρασχεθεῖσαν om. M (ἢ om. a ἤδη om. c) || 12 ὡς καὶ NRSac: καὶ ὡς BT || 13 μηδὲν Ma: μηδέν τι BNRST || ἐπαγγελλομένην MRSa: ἐπαγγελλομένης BNT || σημαίνειν Nac: om. BMRST || 14 ἡμῖν om. Nb || τὸ] τὸ καὶ b || εἰ a: εἰς M εἴ γε εἰς BNRST || ὅρους] πόρους c || ἐπιστήσομεν (R)Sab: ἐπιστήσωμεν BMNT || τῇ διανοίᾳ MRa: τὴν διάνοιαν BNST || 16 τοῦ] τὴν τοῦ Nb || ἀφορῶντες BNT: om. MRSa || μόνον] μόνον πάλιν a || 17 ἐπαναδραμὼν] ἀναδραμὼν a || θέρμην] θερμότητα S || τῆς ἀλόγου NRSTa: τῆς λοιμώδους B ἀλύπως M || 18 δυνήσεται] οὐ δυνήσεται B || 22 ἀποφράξωμεν] ἀποφράξομεν N.

72

in the citadel of the virtues, as having the virtues themselves as warders of the city walls of purity. And so the contrivances of the demons become ineffective against him, even if the missiles of vulgar yearning reach as far as the windows of his nature.

58. Whenever our soul begins no longer to desire the burgeoning things of the earth, then in many instances a restless intellect creeps into it, neither allowing it to serve with pleasure in the ministry of the word, nor leaving in it a clear desire for the good things to come, but vilifying this transient life excessively as not having work worthy of virtue, and setting at naught perception itself, either as having been offered already to many others or as promising to show us nothing perfect. But we will escape from this tepid and sloth-inducing passion if, setting very narrow boundaries for our reason, we look back to the recollection of God alone; for only in this way will the intellect, running back to its own ardour, be able to withdraw from this irrational fragmentation.

59. The intellect demands us back absolutely whenever we block up all its exits by the recollection of God—which is the work which ought fully to occupy its industry. So one must give it the 'Lord Jesus' alone for a

ΔΙΑΔΟΧΟΥ

πραγματείαν τοῦ σκοποῦ. Οὐδεὶς γάρ, φησίν, λέγει κύριος Ἰησοῦς, εἰ μὴ ἐν πνεύματι ἁγίῳ. Ἀλλ' οὕτω στενῶς τὸ ῥητὸν διὰ παντὸς ἐν τοῖς ἑαυτοῦ ταμιείοις θεωρείτω, ἵνα μὴ εἰς φαντασίας ἐκτρέποιτό τινας. Ὅσοι γὰρ τοῦτο τὸ ἅγιον καὶ ἔνδοξον ὄνομα ἐν τῷ βάθει αὐτῶν
5 μελετῶσιν ἀπαύστως τῆς καρδίας, οὗτοι καὶ τὸ φῶς αὐτῶν τοῦ νοῦ δύνανται ὁρᾶν ποτε. Στενῇ γὰρ μερίμνῃ ὑπὸ τῆς διανοίας κρατούμενον πάντα τὸν ἐπιπολάζοντα ῥύπον ἐν τῇ ψυχῇ ἐν αἰσθήσει ἱκανῇ καταφλέγει· καὶ γάρ· Ὁ θεὸς ἡμῶν, φησίν, πῦρ καταναλίσκον. Ὅθεν εἰς ἀγάπην λοιπὸν πολλὴν τὴν ψυχὴν τῆς ἑαυτοῦ δόξης προσκαλεῖται ὁ
10 κύριος. Ἐγχρονίζον γὰρ τὸ ἔνδοξον ἐκεῖνο καὶ πολυπόθητον ὄνομα διὰ τῆς μνήμης τοῦ νοῦ τῇ θέρμῃ τῆς καρδίας, ἕξιν ἡμῖν πάντως τοῦ ἀγαπᾶν τὴν αὐτοῦ ἀγαθότητα μηδενὸς ὄντος λοιπὸν τοῦ ἐμποδίζοντος ἐμποιεῖ. Οὗτος γάρ ἐστιν ὁ μαργαρίτης ὁ πολύτιμος, ὅντινα πωλήσας τὴν περιουσίαν αὐτοῦ πᾶσάν τις κτήσασθαι δύναται καὶ ἔχειν
15 ἀνεκλάλητον ἐπὶ τῇ αὐτοῦ εὑρέσει χαράν.

ξ'.

Ἄλλη ἐστὶν ἡ εἰσαγωγὸς χαρὰ καὶ ἄλλη ἡ τελειοποιός· ἡ μὲν γὰρ φαντασίας οὐχ ὑπάρχει ἄμοιρος, ἡ δὲ ταπεινοφροσύνης ἔχει τὴν
20 δύναμιν· μέσον δὲ τούτων ἐστὶ λύπη θεοφιλὴς καὶ ἀνάλγητον δάκρυον. Ἐν γὰρ πλήθει ὄντως σοφίας πλῆθος γνώσεως καὶ ὁ προστιθεὶς γνῶσιν προστίθησιν ἄλγημα. Διὰ τοῦτο οὖν δεῖ πρῶτον τῇ εἰσαγωγῷ χαρᾷ πρὸς τοὺς ἀγῶνας προσκληθῆναι τὴν ψυχήν, ἐλεγχθῆναι δὲ αὐτὴν καὶ δοκιμασθῆναι λοιπὸν ὑπὸ τῆς ἀληθείας τοῦ ἁγίου πνεύματος, περί τε ὧν
25 ἔπραξε κακῶν ἢ καὶ ὧν ἔτι πράττει μετεωρισμῶν. Ἐν ἐλεγμοῖς

1 κύριος Ἰησοῦς] κύριον Ἰησοῦν ST || 2 οὕτω] οὕτω αὐτὸ Nb || ῥητὸν] ῥῆμα Mac || 3 ἑαυτοῦ] αὐτοῦ MSc || 4 αὐτῶν] που a om. M || 5 ἀπαύστως om. a || οὗτοι] αὐτοὶ Nb || αὐτῶν om. a || νοῦ] οἰκείου νοὸς a || 6 ποτε om. a || μερίμνῃ] τῇ μνήμῃ a || 7 τὸν om. Mc || pr. ἐν MN: om. BRSTa || ἱκανῇ] πολλῇ a || 8 καταναλίσκον] καταναλίσκον τὴν μοχθηρίαν T || 9 εἰς] καὶ εἰς R || λοιπὸν om. Nb || πολλὴν om. M || ἑαυτοῦ] αὐτοῦ Mac || 11 ἡμῖν] ἡμῖν ποιεῖ Mc || πάντως om. S || τοῦ] εἰς τὸ T || 12 μηδενὸς - ἐμποδίζοντος om. a || 13 ἐμποιεῖ om. Mc || γάρ] γάρ, φησίν a || 14 αὐτοῦ om. Nb || πᾶσάν] ἅπασάν T || τις om. a || 15 ἀνεκλάλητον] ἀνεκλάλητον καὶ ἀνέκλειπτον M ἀνέκλειπτον Sc || 19 ταπεινοφροσύνης MTa: ταπεινοφροσύνην BNRS || τὴν om. Mac || 20 ἀνάλγητον] ἐνεργὲς τὸ Mc || 21 ἐν γὰρ] ἐν μὲν γὰρ R || 22 προστίθησιν] προσθήσει Mc || οὖν om. a || δεῖ MNRST: χρὴ Ba || πρῶτον] πρῶτον μὲν c πρώτῳ μὲν M || εἰσαγωγῷ] εἰσαγωγικῇ a || 23 προσκληθῆναι] κληθῆναι a παρακληθῆναι F || δὲ BMRST: τε Na || 24 ἁγίου] παναγίου a || 25 ἢ om. Mc || καὶ om. R.

74

perfect undertaking of this end; for it says, 'No one says "Lord Jesus" except in the holy Spirit.'[51] Let one constantly contemplate this phrase carefully in his own treasuries in this way, lest he turn aside into any fantasies. As many as attend to this holy and glorious name ceaselessly in the depth of their heart are always able to see the light of their intellect– since governed by reason with a strict solicitude, it burns up the sordidness which prevails in the soul, with a strong sensation; for it also says, 'Our God is a consuming fire.'[52] As a result the Lord then invites the soul into great affection for his own glory; for when this glorified and much-longed-for name tarries in the ardour of the heart through the recollection of the intellect, it produces in us a habit of loving its excellence completely, there being nothing to hinder it. And this is the pearl of great price which, selling all that one has, one can acquire, to have inexpressible joy in one's finding of it.[53]

60. Initial joy is one thing, and that which perfects is another; for the one is not really free of fantasy, while the other has the power of humble-mindedness; and in between them is godly grief[54] and painless tears. For truly, 'In fullness of wisdom is fullness of perception,' and 'he who increases perception increases pain.'[55] So for this reason the soul must first be invited to contests by initial joy, and then be cross-examined and tested by the truth of the holy Spirit concerning the bad things it has done (or again the haughty things it is still doing). For 'by cross-examinations

---

[51] 1 Corinthians 12:3.
[52] Deuteronomy 4:24.
[53] Matthew 13:46.
[54] See 2 Corinthians 7:10.
[55] Ecclesiastes 1:18.

ΔΙΑΔΟΧΟΥ

γάρ, φησίν, ὑπὲρ ἀνομίας ἐπαίδευσας ἄνθρωπον καὶ ἐξέτηξας ὡς ἀράχνην τὴν ψυχὴν αὐτοῦ, ἵνα τῆς θείας αὐτὴν ἐλέγξεως ὥσπερ ἐν χωνευτηρίῳ δοκιμασάσης οὕτως τὴν ἐνέργειαν λάβοι τῆς ἀφαντάστου χαρᾶς ἐν θερμῇ μνήμῃ τοῦ θεοῦ.

ξα΄.

Ὅταν ὑπὸ ὀργῆς ἡ ψυχὴ ταράττηται ἢ ὑπὸ κραιπάλης θολοῦται ἢ ὑπὸ χαλεπῆς δυσθυμίας ὀχλῆται, οὐ δύναται ὁ νοῦς ἐγκρατής, κἂν ὅπως αὐτόν τις βιάζοιτο, γενέσθαι τῆς τοῦ κυρίου Ἰησοῦ μνήμης. Ἐσκοτωμένος γὰρ ὅλος ὑπὸ τῆς δεινότητος τῶν παθῶν ἀλλότριος τῆς οἰκείας γίνεται πάντως αἰσθήσεως· διόπερ οὐκ ἔχει ποῦ ἡ ἐπιθυμία τὴν ἑαυτῆς ἐκτυπώσει σφραγίδα ἵνα φέρῃ ἄληστον ὁ νοῦς τὸ εἶδος τῆς μελέτης, σκληρᾶς τῆς μνήμης τῆς διανοίας ἐκ τῆς τῶν παθῶν γινομένης ὠμότητος. Εἰ δὲ τούτων ἐκτὸς ᾖ, κἂν βραχὺ ὑπὸ τῆς λήθης ὑποκλαπῇ τὸ ποθούμενον, εὐθέως πάλιν ὁ νοῦς τῇ οἰκείᾳ ἐντρεχείᾳ χρησάμενος θερμῶς ἐπιλαμβάνεται τοῦ πολυποθήτου ἐκείνου καὶ σωτηρίου θηράματος. Ἔχει γὰρ αὐτὴν τὴν χάριν τότε καὶ συμμελετῶσαν αὐτῇ ἡ ψυχὴ καὶ συγκράζουσαν τὸ κύριε Ἰησοῦ, καθὼς ἂν μήτηρ διδάσκοι καὶ πάλιν συμμελετᾷ τῷ ἑαυτῆς κνωδάλῳ τὸ πάτερ ὄνομα, ἄχρις οὗ εἰς ἕξιν αὐτὸ ἀγάγοι τοῦ ἀντ᾽ ἄλλης οἱασδηποτοῦν βρεφοπρεποῦς ὁμιλίας τρανῶς τὸν πατέρα, κἂν ὑπνοῖ, καλεῖν. Διὰ τοῦτο ὁ ἀπόστολος λέγει· Ὡσαύτως δὲ καὶ τὸ πνεῦμα συναντιλαμβάνεται τῇ ἀσθενείᾳ ἡμῶν· τὸ γὰρ τί προσευξόμεθα, καθ᾽ ὃ δεῖ, οὐκ οἴδαμεν, ἀλλ᾽ αὐτὸ τὸ πνεῦμα ὑπερεντυγχάνει ὑπὲρ ἡμῶν στεναγμοῖς ἀλαλήτοις. Ἐπειδὴ γὰρ ἡμεῖς

2 αὐτὴν] αὐτὸν a || 3 ἐνέργειαν] ἐνέργειαν εἰ θέλοι a || 4 τοῦ om. RSc || 7 ταράττηται B(R)Tac: ταράττεται MNS || ὑπὸ κραιπάλης] πικρίας a || 8 ὀχλῆται a : ὀχλεῖται BMN(R)ST || 8-9 ὅπως αὐτόν τις βιάζοιτο MS: ὅπως οὖν αὐτόν τις βιάζοιτο a ὅπως ἄν τις αὐτὸν βιάζοιτο B ὅπως ἑαυτὸν βιάζοιτο RT ὅπως ἑαυτὸν βιάζεται N || κυρίου Ἰησοῦ] θεοῦ NTb || 10 ἐσκοτωμένος γὰρ] ἀλλ᾽ ἐσκοτωμένος Mc ἀλλ᾽ ἐσκοτισμένος a || τῶν] ὧν τῶν a || 12 ἐκτυπώσει MRT: ἐκτυπῶσαι BNSa ἣν R || φέρῃ] φέρει Nb || τῆς μνήμης BNRT: om. MSa || 14 ᾖ MN: εἰ BT εἴη Sa || βραχὺ] βραχύ τι a || 15 ὑποκλαπῇ BMNRST: κλαπῇ ac || 15 ποθούμενον] πρόθυμον Mc || 16 πολυποθήτου] ποθουμένου R || 17 θηράματος] θησαυρίσματος Nb || 17-18 αὐτῇ ἡ ψυχὴ NR: αὐτῇ τῇ ψυχῇ B τῇ ψυχῇ ST τὴν ψυχὴν M αὐτῆς ἡ ψυχὴ a || 18 συγκράζουσαν Ta: συγκρατοῦσαν BNRS συγκροτοῦσαν M || διδάσκοι M(R)Sa et (οι s. ει) Tp.c.: διδάσκει BNTa.c. || 19 συμμελετᾷ MNRST: συμμελετᾶν B συμμελετῶσαν a || πάτερ BRT: πατὴρ NSa πάτριον M || οὗ BNRS: ἂν Ma οὖν T || 20 αὐτὸ] αὐτὸν Mc || τοῦ] τὸ Nb || οἱασδηποτοῦν] οἱασδήποτε MRc τινος S.

for iniquity,' it says, 'you instruct man, and melt his soul like a spider,'[56] so that when the divine cross-examination tests it (as in a smelting furnace) the soul might receive as a result the activity of that joy which is free from fantasy, in ardent recollection of God.

61. Whenever the soul is stirred up by anger or rendered dull by a hangover or troubled by grievous despair, the self-controlled intellect is not able to come into the recollection of the Lord Jesus even if one forces it. For being wholly darkened by the severity of the passion, it becomes altogether estranged from its inherent Sense; since when the recollection of one's reason becomes hardened from the fierceness of the passions, desire for recollection has no place to print its seal, that the intellect might ceaselessly bear the form of attentiveness. But if the intellect is free from these things, even if what is longed for is stolen away by forgetfulness for a short time it immediately lays hold again ardently of that much-longed-for and salvific prize, making use of its inherent industry. For then the intellect has grace itself which attends with the very soul and calls out the 'Lord Jesus' with it, just as a mother might teach and practise over again with her inarticulate child the name 'Father,' to the point where she brings it into the habit of calling 'Father'[57] distinctly instead of any sort of other childish babbling, even in sleep. For this reason the Apostle says, 'Likewise also the Spirit participates in our weakness; for what it is that we pray (in terms of what is necessary) we do not know, but the Spirit itself intercedes for us with unutterable sighs'.[58] For since we are

---

[56] Psalms 38:12.
[57] See Galatians 4:6.
[58] Romans 8:26.

ΔΙΑΔΟΧΟΥ

νηπιάζομεν προς το της αρετής τέλειον, της αυτού πάντως χρήζομεν βοηθείας, ίνα υπό της αυτού ανεκλαλήτου γλυκύτητος των λογισμών ημών πάντων συνεχομένων τε και καθηδυνομένων εξ όλης διαθέσεως προς την του θεού και πατρός ημών κινηθώμεν μνήμην τε και αγάπην.
5 Διόπερ εν αυτώ, ως αυτός πάλιν ο θεσπέσιος Παύλος λέγει, κράζομεν, ότε υπ' αυτού θεόν πατέρα ρυθμιζόμεθα καλείν ακαταπαύστως· Αββά ο πατήρ.

ξβ'.
10 Ὁ θυμὸς πλέον τῶν ἄλλων παθῶν ταράττειν εἴωθε καὶ συγχέειν τὴν ψυχήν· ἔστι δ' ὅτε καὶ τὰ μέγιστα αὐτὴν ὠφελεῖ. Ἡνίκα γὰρ κατὰ τῶν ἀσεβούντων ἢ ὁπωσδήποτε ἀσελγαινόντων αὐτῷ ἀταράχως, ἵνα ἢ σωθῶσιν ἢ καταισχυνθῶσιν, κεχρήμεθα, προσθήκην αὐτῇ προξενοῦμεν πραΰτητος· τῷ γὰρ σκοπῷ πάντως τῆς δικαιοσύνης καὶ τῆς ἀγαθότητος
15 συντρέχομεν τοῦ θεοῦ, ἀλλὰ καὶ τὸ θηλυδριῶδες αὐτῆς βαρέως ὀργισθέντες κατὰ τῆς ἁμαρτίας ἀπαρρενοῦμεν πολλάκις. Ὅτι δὲ καὶ αὐτῷ τῷ τῆς φθορᾶς πνευματικῶς ἐμβριμώμενοι, ὅταν ἐν πολλῇ ὦμεν ἀθυμίᾳ, δαίμονι ἐπάνω τῆς τοῦ θανάτου φρονοῦμεν καυχήσεως, οὐ δεῖ ἀμφιβάλλειν. Ὅπερ ἵνα διδάξῃ ἡμᾶς ὁ κύριος δὶς ἐν τῷ πνεύματι τῷ
20 Ἅιδῃ ἐμβριμησάμενος καὶ ταράξας ἑαυτόν, καίτοιγε ἀταράχως βουλήσει μόνῃ πάντα ὅσα θέλει ποιῶν, οὕτω τὴν Λαζάρου ψυχὴν ἀπέδωκε τῷ σώματι, ὥστε μοι δοκεῖν εἰς ὅπλον μᾶλλον δικαιοσύνης τῇ φύσει ἡμῶν τὸν σώφρονα θυμὸν παρὰ τοῦ κτίσαντος ἡμᾶς παρασχεθῆναι θεοῦ.

1 ἀρετῆς BMNRST: εὐκτικῆς ἀρετῆς a || πάντως] πάντοτε M || 3 ἡμῶν BMSTa: om. NRc || 4 πατρὸς BMTa: σωτῆρος NRS || κινηθῶμεν Ma: om. BNRST (sed, post ἀγάπην, hab. ἐρχώμεθα RS, ἐλθεῖν δυνηθῶμεν BNT) || 5 ὡς om. Mc || αὐτὸς] αὔτως Nb ὁ αὐτὸς a || 6 ὑπ' αὐτοῦ om. N || 10 συγχέειν BN(R)c: συγχεῖν STa συγχαίειν Mb || 11 ὅτε] ὅταν BR || καὶ om. Nbc || τὰ om. a || αὐτὴν om. Mac || γὰρ] ἂν a || 12 δήποτε] οὖν a || αὐτῷ BTb: αὐτὸν NR om. MSa || 13 καταισχυνθῶσιν] κατακριθῶσι T || αὐτῇ] αὐτῷ RS om. a || 14 πραΰτητος] πραότητος Mc || 15 θηλυδριῶδες BMNRa: θηλυδρῶδες STc || 16 ἀπαρρενοῦμεν BNRSc: παρανοῦμεν Ma ἀπαρνοῦμεν T || 17 πνευματικῶς BNRSp.c.: πνεύματι MSa.c.Ta || 18 δαίμονι BN: om. MSTa || δεῖ] χρὴ Mc || 19 ἵνα διδάξῃ M(R)S: ἵνα διδάξει NT ἐδίδαξεν B καὶ διδάσκων a || 20 καίτοιγε] καίτοι a || ἀταράχως BR: ἀταράχῳ NST om. Ma || 21 μόνῃ Bc: μόνον M καὶ μόνη a om. NRST || ὅσα θέλει om. Mac || 22 δοκεῖν BNRS: δοκεῖ MTa || εἰς] ὡς b || μᾶλλον δικαιοσύνης RST: μᾶλλον BMa om. N || ἡμῶν om. a || 23 παρασχεθῆναι] παρεσχῆσθαι BR.

ourselves like children in terms of the perfection of this virtue, we need the Spirit's help completely, that by its unutterable sweetness, all our imaginings being constrained and gladdened from a complete disposition, we might be moved towards the recollection and love of our God and Father. And so we call out in the Spirit (as again the divine Paul says) when we are trained by it to call on God the Father ceaselessly: 'Abba, Father'.[59]

62. Temper is wont to stir up and confound the soul more than the other passions; but there are times when it benefits the soul greatly. For when we make use of temper calmly against those who are profane or in any way licentious (so that they are either saved or shamed) we procure a supplement of gentleness for the soul, since we run absolutely straight to the goal of the justice and excellence of God; and often when we are angered impatiently against sin we make manly that which is effeminate in the soul. So we must not doubt that we reckon beyond the boasting of Death when we make rebukes spiritually at the very demon of perdition whenever we are in great despair. And this is why the Lord made rebukes and stirred himself up twice in spirit at Death, and restored the soul of Lazaros to the body, doing calmly (with a single intention) everything which he willed:[60] this was in order that he might teach us. And so it seems to me that prudent temper was supplied to our nature by the God who created us, to be a tool of righteousness instead. If Eve had made use

---

[59] Romans 8:15f.
[60] John 11:33-44.

ΔΙΑΔΟΧΟΥ

Ὥιπερ εἰ κατὰ τοῦ ὄφεως ἐχρήσατο ἡ Εὔα, οὐκ ἂν ὑπ' ἐκείνης τῆς ἐμπαθοῦς ἐνήργητο ἡδονῆς. Ὥστε μοι φαίνεσθαι ὅτι ὁ διὰ ζῆλον τῆς εὐσεβείας τῷ θυμῷ σωφρόνως κεχρημένος δοκιμώτερος πάντως παρὰ τῇ τῶν ἀνταποδόσεων εὑρεθήσεται πλάστιγγι τοῦ οὐδ' ὅλως διὰ
5 δυσκινησίαν νοῦ εἰς θυμὸν κινουμένου· ὁ μὲν γὰρ ἀγύμναστον τὸν τῶν ἀνθρωπίνων φρενῶν ἡνίοχον ἔχων φαίνεται, ὁ δὲ ἀεὶ ἐπὶ τῶν ἵππων τῆς ἀρετῆς ἐναγώνιος γίνεται καὶ φέρεται ἐν μέσῳ τῆς τῶν δαιμόνων παρατάξεως τὸ τῆς ἐγκρατείας καταγυμνάζων ἐν φόβῳ θεοῦ τέθριππον. Ὅπερ ἅρμα Ἰσραὴλ ἐν τῇ ἀναλήψει τοῦ θεσπεσίου Ἠλίου παρὰ τῇ
10 γραφῇ εἰρημένον εὑρίσκομεν, ἐπειδὴ πρώτοις τοῖς Ἰουδαίοις περὶ τῶν τεσσάρων ἀρετῶν διαφόρως φαίνεται ὁμιλήσας ὁ θεός. Διόπερ ὅλως καὶ ἐπὶ ἅρματος πυρὸς ἀνελήφθη ὁ τοσοῦτος τῆς σοφίας τρόφιμος, ὡς ἵπποις ταῖς οἰκείαις ἐμοὶ δοκεῖν ὁ σώφρων χρησάμενος ἀρεταῖς ἐν τῷ ἁρπάξαντι αὐτὸν ἐν αὔρᾳ πυρὸς πνεύματι.
15
ξγ'.

Ὁ γνώσεως μετασχὼν ἁγίας καὶ γλυκύτητος θεοῦ γευσάμενος οὔτε δικάζειν ὀφείλει οὔτε δίκην ὅλως κινεῖν πρός τινα, κἂν αὐτὰ ἅπερ ἠμφίασται ἀφέληταί τις. Ἡ γὰρ τῶν ἀρχόντων τοῦ κόσμου τούτου
20 δικαιοσύνη ἥττηται πάντως τῇ δικαιοσύνῃ τοῦ θεοῦ, μᾶλλον δὲ οὐδέν ἐστι πρὸς τὸ δίκαιον τοῦ θεοῦ. Ἐπεὶ ποία διαφορὰ μεταξὺ τῶν τροφίμων τοῦ θεοῦ καὶ τῶν τοῦ αἰῶνος τούτου ἀνθρώπων, εἰ μὴ τὸ

1 ᾧπερ RST: ὅνπερ BN ὥσπερ b ὡς Ma ‖ ἐχρήσατο ἡ Εὔα] ἡ Εὔα ἐχρήσατο τούτῳ Mc ‖ 2 ἐνήργητο B(R): ἐνηργεῖτο STac ἐνεργεῖτο MN ‖ φαίνεσθαι] δοκεῖ a ‖ ὁ om. b ‖ 4 οὐδ'] μηδὲ B ‖ 5 εἰς BNRST: πρὸς Ma ‖ ὁ μὲν γὰρ Ma: ἐπειδὴ ὁ μὲν BNRST ‖ 6 ὁ] ὁ ὡς R ‖ 7 ἐναγώνιος γίνεται καὶ φέρεται R: γίνεται καὶ φέρεται T ἐναγώνιος φέρεται ceteri ‖ τῆς Ma: τῇ B om. NRST ‖ 7-8 δαιμόνων παρατάξεως BMa: δαιμονικῶν παρατάξεων NRST ‖ 8 τὸ] τὸν B ‖ ἐγκρατείας BNT: ἐγκρατείας ἀεὶ MRSa ‖ καταγυμνάζων] καταγυμναζόμενος N ‖ 9 θεσπεσίου] θεσβίτου a ‖ τῇ] τῇ θείᾳ a ‖ 10 εὑρίσκομεν] εὑρήκαμεν S ‖ τοῖς Rb: om. ceteri ‖ 11 διαφόρως MRSTa: om. BN ‖ 12 ἐπὶ MRSa: ὑπὸ BNT ‖ τοσοῦτος] τοσοῦτος καὶ τηλικοῦτος T ‖ ἵπποις] ἵπποις οἶμαι a ‖ 13 ἐμοὶ δοκεῖν] ἐμοὶ δοκεῖ T om. a ‖ ὁ σώφρων om. a ‖ ἐν τῷ ἁρπάξαντι NRT: ἐν τῷ ἁρπάσαντι Bb ἁρπάξαντι MS ἁρπάξαντος c ἁρπάξασιν a ‖ 14 πνεύματι BNRST: πνεύματος Ma ‖ 18 ὀφείλει] ὀφείλει ποτὲ RST ‖ 19 ἠμφίασται BNRSc: ἠμφίεσται MTa ‖ κόσμου] αἰῶνος Mc ‖ 20 ἥττηται] ἡττᾶται Mac.

of this against the serpent, she would not have been activated by that pleasurable passion. So it appears to me that whoever makes use of temper prudently because of zeal for piety will be found altogether more approved on the scale of recompenses than the intellect not moved into temper simply because of being inflexible. For the latter intellect clearly has an untrained charioteer of human wits, whereas the former is always contending; he is borne by the horses of virtue and carried into the midst of the ranks of the demons, training the four chariot horses of self-control in fear of God. This is why we find a chariot of Israel spoken of by Scripture in the ascension of the divine Elijah (for it is clear that God expounded distinctly on the four virtues to the Jews first); and so such a child of wisdom was taken up completely on a chariot of fire; being prudent he made use of the inherent virtues as horses, it seems to me, in being snatched up by the Spirit in a gust of fire.[61]

63. Whoever shares in holy perception and tastes the sweetness of God ought neither to judge nor to initiate judgement on anyone at all, even if someone takes away the clothes on his back. For the justice of the rulers of this world is altogether inferior to the justice of God; or rather it is nothing next to the judgement of God–since what sort of distinction is there between the children of God and the men of this age, except that their

---

[61] 2 Kings 2:11.

ΔΙΑΔΟΧΟΥ

τούτων δίκαιον ἀτελὲς πρὸς τὴν ἐκείνων δικαιοσύνην φαίνοιτο, ὥστε τὸ μὲν λέγεσθαι ἀνθρώπινον δίκαιον, τὸ δὲ θείαν δικαιοσύνην; Οὕτως οὖν ὁ μὲν κύριος ἡμῶν οὔτε λοιδορούμενος ἀντελοιδόρει οὔτε πάσχων ἠπείλει, ἀλλὰ καὶ τὴν ἀφαίρεσιν τῆς ἐσθῆτος σιωπῶν ὑπέμεινεν καὶ ὑπὲρ τῆς
5 σωτηρίας δέ, ἵνα τὸ μεῖζον εἴπω, τῶν κακούργων τὸν πατέρα ἠξίου. Οἱ δὲ τοῦ κόσμου ἄνθρωποι οὐκ ἂν τοῦ δικάζεσθαι παύσονται, εἰ μὴ μετὰ προσθήκης ἐνίοτε τὰ τῶν ἐναγωγῶν ἀπολάβωσι πράγματα, ὅταν μάλιστα πρὸ τοῦ χρέους τοὺς τόκους κομίζωνται, ὥστε αὐτῶν γενέσθαι τὸ δίκαιον ἀρχὴν πολλάκις ἀδικίας μεγάλης.
10
ξδ'.

Οὐ δεῖ, φησίν, ἤκουσά τινων λεγόντων εὐλαβῶν, παραχωρεῖν τοῖς τυχοῦσι διαρπάζειν ἅπερ πρὸς τὴν ἑαυτῶν διοίκησιν ἢ καὶ πρὸς τὴν τῶν πενήτων ἀνάπαυσιν ἔχομεν, μάλιστα εἰ παρὰ Χριστιανῶν τοῦτο
15 πάσχομεν, ἵνα μὴ ἁμαρτίας πρόξενοι τοῖς ἀδικοῦσιν ἡμᾶς, δι' ὧν ἀνεξικακοῦμεν, γινώμεθα. Τοῦτο δὲ οὐδὲν ἕτερόν ἐστιν ἢ θέλειν τὰ ἑαυτοῦ ὑπὲρ ἑαυτὸν μετὰ ἀλόγου προφάσεως. Εἰ γὰρ καταλιπὼν τὸ εὔχεσθαι καὶ προσέχειν τῇ ἐμαυτοῦ καρδίᾳ δίκας ἀγορεύειν πρὸς τοὺς θέλοντάς με ἐπηρεάζειν κατὰ μικρὸν ἄρξομαι καὶ δικαστηρίων
20 παρεδρεύειν προαυλίοις, δῆλον ὅτι τὰ ἐκδικούμενα κρείττονα τῆς ἐμαυτοῦ ἡγοῦμαι σωτηρίας, ἵνα μὴ εἴπω καὶ αὐτοῦ τοῦ σωτηρίου ἐντάλματος. Πῶς γὰρ ἂν ὅλως τῷ εὐαγγελικῷ ἀκολουθήσω προστάγματι

1 ἀτελὲς] ἀτελὲς ὂν MRT ἀτέλεστον c ‖ ἐκείνων] ἐκείνου NRb ‖ 3 κύριος ἡμῶν RT: κύριος ἡμῶν Ἰησοῦς BMa κύριος ἡμῶν Ἰησοῦς χριστὸς N κύριος ἡμῶν Ἰησοῦς ὁ χριστὸς S ‖ 4 ὑπέμεινεν] ὑπέμενεν BMc ‖ 5 σωτηρίας δέ, ἵνα τὸ μεῖζον εἴπω, τῶν (ὑπὲρ τῶν Nb) κακούργων] ἡμῶν σωτηρίας ὠδυνᾶτο καί, τὸ μεῖζον, ὑπὲρ τῶν κακουργούντων RST ‖ 6 κόσμου] κόσμου τούτου a ‖ παύσονται MN(R)T: παύσωνται Sc παύσοιντο Ba ‖ 7 ὅταν] ὁπόταν T ‖ 8 κομίζωνται] κομίζονται NTb ‖ αὐτῶν] αὐτοῖς Mc ‖ γενέσθαι BMRSa: γίνεσθαι NTc ‖ 12 ἤκουσά] ἤκουσα παρὰ B ‖ 13 διαρπάζειν] ἁρπάζειν R ‖ ἢ om. R ‖ alt. τὴν BMRSa: om. NT ‖ τῶν BRSa: om. MNT ‖ 14 ἔχομεν] επχωμεν NTb ‖ 14-15 μάλιστα - πάσχομεν post 15 ἡμᾶς R, post 16 ἀνεξικακοῦμεν S ‖ 15 πάσχομεν] πάσχωμεν B ‖ ἡμᾶς om. a ‖ 16 γινώμεθα] γενόμεθα Nb ‖ θέλειν] τὸ θέλειν N ‖ 17 μετὰ ἀλόγου BNRT: ὦ ἀλόγου MS ὦ ἀλογίστου a ‖ καταλιπὼν BM(R)Sa: καταλείπων NTc ‖ 18 εὔχεσθαι] προσεύχεσθαι a ‖ καὶ om. R ‖ τῇ ἐμαυτοῦ καρδίᾳ BMNRS: τῇ ἑαυτοῦ καρδίᾳ Tc ἑαυτῷ a ‖ 19 θέλοντάς] ἐθέλοντάς a ‖ ἄρξομαι] ἄρξωμαι B ‖ 20 παρεδρεύειν BNT: προσεδρεύειν MRSa ‖ 21 καὶ] κατ' a ‖ 22 γὰρ ἂν BNRST: γὰρ a δὲ M ‖ ἀκολουθήσω] ἐξακολουθήσω a.

judgement appears imperfect next to the justice of the children of God; and so that which is human is spoken of as 'judgement', but that which is divine 'justice'? And so our Lord 'being reviled, neither reviled in return nor when he suffered did he make threats';[62] rather he remained silent when his clothes were taken and what is more I say, he made a claim on the Father for the salvation of the evil-doers. But the men of this world will not stop 'judging', except at the times they recover the sums brought before the court, with interest–especially when they gather the interest before the debt; thus their judgement often becomes the beginning of great injustice.

64. I have heard certain pious men who say, 'We must not allow chance acquaintances to plunder what pertains to our expenditure or even what we have for the relief of the poor, especially if we suffer this from Christians; lest through the things we forbear we become the assistants of sin to those who do us injustice.' This is nothing else than to want one's things in preference to one's self, by means of an unreasoning pretext. For if, forsaking prayer and the care of my heart, I begin little by little to speak in public to those who want to injure me, and to be always near the vestibules of law courts, it is clear that I suppose acts of vengeance to be better than my own salvation–not to mention the very commandment of salvation. For how shall I wholly follow the evangelical ordinance which

---

[62] 1 Peter 2:23.

ΔΙΑΔΟΧΟΥ

τῷ κελεύοντί μοι· Καὶ ἀπὸ τοῦ αἴροντος τὰ σὰ μὴ ἀπαίτει, εἰ μὴ μετὰ χαρᾶς ὑπομείνω κατὰ τὸ ἀποστολικὸν λόγιον τὴν τῶν προσόντων μοι διαρπαγὴν πραγμάτων, ὁπότε οὐδὲ δικασάμενός τις καὶ ἀπολαβὼν ὅσαπερ ἠβουλήθη, τῆς ἁμαρτίας τὸν πλεονέκτην ἐλευθεροῖ; Ἐπειδὴ τὰ
5 φθαρτὰ δικαστήρια τὸ ἄφθαρτον τοῦ θεοῦ κριτήριον ὁρίζειν οὐ δύναται· τούτους γὰρ πάντως ὁ αἴτιος τοὺς νόμους πληροφορεῖ παρ' οἷς καὶ ὑπὲρ τῆς αἰτίας αὐτὸν ἀπολογεῖσθαι συμβαίνει. Ὥστε καλὸν τὸ τὴν τῶν θελόντων ἡμᾶς ἀδικεῖν φέρειν βίαν καὶ εὔχεσθαι ὑπὲρ αὐτῶν, ἵνα διὰ μετανοίας, οὐ μὴν διὰ τῆς ἀποδόσεως ὧν ἡμῶν ἥρπαξαν, ἀπολυθῶσι τοῦ
10 τῆς πλεονεξίας ἐγκλήματος. Τοῦτο γὰρ θέλει ἡ δικαιοσύνη τοῦ θεοῦ, ἵνα τὸν πλεονέκτην, οὐχὶ τὸ πλεονεκτηθέν, ἀπολάβωμέν ποτε τῆς ἁμαρτίας διὰ τῆς μετανοίας ἐλεύθερον.

ξε'.

15 Λίαν ἁρμόδιον καὶ διὰ πάντων ἐπωφελὲς τὸ ἐπιγνόντας ἡμᾶς τὴν ὁδὸν τῆς εὐσεβείας εὐθέως πάντα τὰ προσόντα ἡμῖν διαπωλεῖν καὶ τὰ ἀπὸ τούτων χρήματα διοικεῖν κατὰ τὴν ἐντολὴν τοῦ κυρίου καὶ μὴ προφάσει τοῦ διὰ παντὸς θέλειν ἐντολὰς ποιεῖν παρακούειν τοῦ σωτηρίου κελεύσματος. Ἔσται γὰρ ἡμῖν ἐκ τούτου πρῶτον μὲν ἡ καλὴ
20 ἀμεριμνία καὶ ἡ ἐντεῦθεν λοιπὸν ἀνεπιβούλευτος πενία, ἥτις πάσης ἀδικίας καὶ πάσης δίκης ἐπάνω φρονεῖ διὰ τὸ μὴ ἔχειν ἡμᾶς μηκέτι τὴν τὸ πῦρ τῶν πλεονεκτῶν ὕλην ἀνάπτουσαν. Περιθάλψει δὲ ἡμᾶς τότε πλέον τῶν ἄλλων ἡ ταπεινοφροσύνη τῶν ἀρετῶν καὶ εἰς τοὺς οἰκείους ὡς γυμνοὺς ὑπάρχοντας ἀναπαύσει κόλπους, οἷα μήτηρ τὸ ἑαυτῆς

---

1 καὶ om. N ‖ ἀπαίτει] κωλύσῃς a ‖ 2 κατὰ om. Nb ‖ τὸ . . . λόγιον] τὸν . . . λόγον a ‖ 3 διαρπαγὴν] ἁρπαγὴν N ‖ οὐδὲ NR: οὔτε BMSTa ‖ 4 ὅσαπερ] ἅπερ B εἰς ἅπερ RS ‖ ἠβουλήθη BM: ἐβουλήθη a ἐβιάσθη NRST ‖ 5 κριτήριον] δικαστήριον Sc ‖ δύναται MNR: δύνανται BSTa ‖ 8 ἡμᾶς om. Mac ‖ 9 ἀποδόσεως] ἀνταποδόσεως NTb ‖ ἡμῶν] ἡμῖν a ἀφ' ἡμῶν RS ‖ ἥπαρξαν MNR: ἥρπασαν BSTa ‖ 10 θεοῦ RSTa: κυρίου ceteri ‖ 11 τὸν] αὐτὸν τὸν RSTa ‖ οὐχὶ] οὐ a ‖ ἀπολάβωμέν] ἀπολαβόντες Mc ‖ ποτε BNT: ἀπὸ MRS om. ac ‖ 12 ἐλεύθερον] ἐλευθερώσωμεν Mc ‖ 15 τὸ om. MTc ‖ ἐπιγνόντας] ἐπεγνωκότας S ‖ 16 πάντα] ἅπαντα RS ‖ διαπωλεῖν] διαπωλῆσαι B ‖ 17 τούτων] αὐτῶν Mc ‖ ἐντολὴν] φωνὴν a ‖ 20 ἡ om. MSc ‖ 22 περιθάλψει BNa: περιθάλψοι M(R)ST ‖ 23 pr. τῶν BNR: om. MSTa ‖ 24 ἀναπαύσει] διαναπαύσει a ‖ κόλπους] κόλποις a.

orders me: 'Do not ask him who takes your things to return them,'[63] unless I am steadfast with joy (according to the apostolic statement) in the theft of my own things;[64] when, after one has gone to law and received back what was intended, it does not free the greedy one from sin? For mortal law-courts cannot determine the immortal standard of God, since the accused always satisfies those laws by which it happens that he pleads against the accusation. So it is good to bear the violence of those who want to do us injustice, and to pray for them, that through repentance–not through their returning what they took from us–they might be released from the charge of greed. This is what the justice of God wills, that we might receive back not the object of greed but the greedy one, whenever he becomes free from sin through repentance.

65. As soon as we recognise the path of piety, it is very proper and in every way useful to sell publicly all that we have, and to administer the proceeds from it according to the commandment of the Lord;[65] and not to disobey this salvific command, under the pretext of wanting to perform the commandments continually. For from this there will accrue to us first a beautiful freedom from care, and later (from that) an unscheming poverty, which has thoughts above all injustice and all judgement, due to our no longer having the material which kindles the fire of the greedy. Then humble-mindedness, more than the other virtues, will warm us, and give us rest in its own bosom, since we are naked; just like a mother who takes

---

[63] Luke 6:30.
[64] Hebrews 10:34.
[65] Matthew 19:21.

ΔΙΑΔΟΧΟΥ

παιδίον εἰς τὰς οἰκείας προσλαμβανομένη καταθάλπει ἀγκάλας, ὅταν διὰ τὴν νηπιώδη ἁπλότητα τὴν ἑαυτοῦ ἐκδυσάμενον πόρρω που ἀπορρίψῃ ἐσθῆτα τῇ γυμνότητι μᾶλλον διὰ πολλὴν ἀκακίαν ἢ τῇ ποικιλίᾳ τῆς ἐσθῆτος τερπόμενον. Φυλάσσων γάρ, φησίν, τὰ νήπια ὁ κύριος·
5 ἐταπεινώθην καὶ ἔσωσέ με.

ξς'.
Καθ' ὃ ἔχομεν πάντως ὁ κύριος ἡμᾶς ἀπαιτήσει τὸν λόγον τῆς ἐλεημοσύνης, οὐ καθ' ὃ οὐκ ἔχομεν. Ἐὰν οὖν, ὅπερ εἶχον δοῦναι εἰς
10 πολλοὺς χρόνους, ἐν ὀλίγῳ χρόνῳ διὰ τὸν φόβον τοῦ θεοῦ χρηστῶς διασπείρω κελεύσματι, περὶ τίνος ἔτι ὁ μηδὲν ἔχων ἐγκληθήσομαι; Ἀλλ' ἐρεῖ τις· Πόθεν οὖν ἐλεηθήσονται τοῦ λοιποῦ οἱ ἐκ τῶν ἡμετέρων μετρίων ἐθισθέντες κατ' ὀλίγον διοικεῖσθαι πένητες; Μανθανέτω δὲ ὁ τοιοῦτος μὴ προφάσει τῆς ἰδίας φιλοχρηματίας ὀνειδίζειν τῷ θεῷ· οὐχ
15 ὑστερήσει γὰρ ὁ θεὸς τὸ οἰκεῖον οἰκονομῶν ὡς ἀπ' ἀρχῆς κτίσμα· οὔτε γὰρ πρὶν οὗτος ἢ ἐκεῖνος εἰς τὴν ἐλεημοσύνην ἐξηγείροντο, ὑστεροῦντο τροφῆς ἢ σκεπασμάτων οἱ πτωχοί. Καλὸν οὖν τὸ παρ' αὐτὴν τὴν ἐπίγνωσιν μετὰ χρηστῆς διακονίας ἀπορρῖψαι τὸ ἐκ τοῦ πλούτου ἀλόγιστον καύχημα τὰς οἰκείας ἐπιθυμίας μισήσαντα, ὅπερ ἐστὶ μισῆσαι
20 τὴν ἑαυτοῦ ψυχήν, ἵνα μηκέτι χαίροντες ἐπὶ τῇ τῶν χρημάτων διασπορᾷ ἐξουδενώσωμεν ἡμῶν τὴν ψυχὴν σφόδρα ὡς μηδὲν τῶν καλῶν ἐργαζόμενοι. Ἕως μὲν γάρ που χρημάτων εὐποροῦμεν, χαίρομεν μεγάλως, εἴπερ ἐστὶν εἰς ἡμᾶς τοῦ ἀγαθοῦ ἐνέργεια, ἐπὶ τῷ τούτων διασκορπισμῷ, ὡς ἱλαρῶς ὑπηρετούμενοι τῷ θείῳ κελεύσματι· ἐπειδὰν δὲ

1 καταθάλπει BM(R)S: καταθάλποι Na κατακολποῖ T ‖ 1-2 διὰ τὴν νηπιώδη ἁπλότητα BNRST: νηπιώδει ἁπλότητι Ma ‖ 2 ἀπορρίψῃ (R)Sa.c.Ta: ἀπορρίψει N ἀπορρίπτει M ἀπορρίψοι BSp.c. ‖ 4 φησίν om. Ra ‖ 8 κύριος] χριστὸς N ‖ 10 διὰ - θεοῦ om. M ‖ θεοῦ] θείου κελεύσματος Nb ‖ χρηστῶς] χρηστῷ R ‖ 11 διασπείρω κελεύσματι RT: δαπανήσω a διασπείρω ceteri ‖ ὁ] ὃ Nb ‖ ἔχων] ἔχω Nb ‖ 12 ἐλεηθήσονται] ἐλεηθῶσιν a ‖ τοῦ λοιποῦ om. Mc ‖ 13 μετρίων om. Ra ‖ δὲ om. BRSa ‖ 14 τῷ om. a ‖ 15 ὁ om. Nb ‖ θεὸς] κύριος Nb ‖ ὡς ἀπ' ἀρχῆς om. a ‖ κτίσμα] πλάσμα a ‖ 16 οὗτος] οὓς ὄντως R ‖ εἰς BNT: πρὸς MRSa ‖ 17 πτωχοί] πένητες a ‖ 18 ἐπίγνωσιν] ἐπίγνωσιν τῆς ἀληθείας a ‖ 19 καύχημα] φρόνημά τε καὶ καύχημα TV ‖ τὰς] τῆς R ‖ 21 ἐξουδενώσωμεν] ἐχουθενήσωμεν N ἐχουδενίσωμεν b ‖ σφόδρα om. a ‖ τῶν καλῶν] καλὸν Nab ‖ 22 που BRST: οὖν N om. Ma ‖ 23 εἰς ἡμᾶς] ἐν ἡμῖν S ‖ ἐνέργεια] ἡ ἐνέργεια a ‖ 24 ὑπηρετούμενοι] ὑπηρετοῦμεν Nb ὑπηρετουμένοις c.

her child up into her arms and warms it, whenever it throws its clothing away due to childish simplicity, delighted more by nudity (because of great freedom from evil) than by the many colours of the garment. For it says, 'The Lord preserves the little children; I was brought low and he saved me.'[66]

66. It is only in terms of what we have that the Lord will ask us for a statement of charity, not in terms of what we do not have.[67] Therefore if ever by the command of God I dispensed properly from fear in a short time that which I had available to give for many years, about what would I who have nothing be blamed any longer? But someone will say, 'From what source will those poor who are accustomed to receive charity little by little from our means do so in future?' But let such a man learn not to reproach God on the pretext of his own affection for possessions, since God will not fail, managing his own creation as he has from the beginning; for it is not the case that before this man or that man was roused into charity, the poor lacked food or clothing. So recognising this it is good to throw away irrational boasting of riches, for a better sort of service: hating one's own desires–which is to hate one's own soul;[68] so that no longer rejoicing in the dispersal of possessions, we might set our own soul strictly at naught, as being people who do nothing of what is good. For so long as we abound in possessions, we rejoice greatly (if indeed there is an activity of good in us) in their dispersion, as we gladly comply with the divine command;

---

[66] Psalms 114:6.
[67] 2 Corinthians 8:18.
[68] Luke 14:26.

ΔΙΑΔΟΧΟΥ

πάντα ἐξαντλήσωμεν, λύπη ἡμῖν ἄπειρος καὶ ταπείνωσις ὑπεισέρχεται ὡς μηδὲν δικαιοσύνης ἄξιον διαπραττομένοις. Ὅθεν λοιπὸν ἐφ' ἑαυτὴν ἐπιστρέφει ἡ ψυχὴ ἐν πολλῇ ταπεινώσει, ἵνα, ὅπερ οὐκ ἔχει κτᾶσθαι καθ' ἡμέραν διὰ τῆς ἐλεημοσύνης, τοῦτο ἐκ τῆς ἐπιπόνου εὐχῆς καὶ τῆς
5 ὑπομονῆς καὶ τῆς ταπεινοφροσύνης ἑαυτῇ περιποιῇ. Πτωχὸς γάρ, φησίν, καὶ πένης αἰνέσουσι τὸ ὄνομά σου, κύριε. Οὔτε γὰρ τὸ τῆς θεολογίας χάρισμα ἑτοιμάζεταί τινι ὑπὸ τοῦ θεοῦ, εἰ μή τις ἑτοιμάσῃ ἑαυτόν, ὥστε πάντα τὰ προσόντα αὐτῷ ἀποκτήσασθαι αὐτὸν ἕνεκεν τῆς δόξης τοῦ εὐαγγελίου τοῦ θεοῦ, ἵνα ἐν θεοφιλεῖ πενίᾳ τὸν πλοῦτον
10 εὐαγγελίζηται τῆς βασιλείας τοῦ θεοῦ. Ὁ γὰρ εἰρηκώς· Ἡτοίμασας ἐν τῇ χρηστότητί σου τῷ πτωχῷ, ὁ θεός, καὶ ἐπαγαγών· Κύριος δώσει ῥῆμα τοῖς εὐαγγελιζομένοις δυνάμει πολλῇ, τοῦτο σαφῶς σημαίνει.

ξζ'.

15 Πάντα μὲν τὰ χαρίσματα τοῦ θεοῦ ἡμῶν καλὰ λίαν καὶ πάσης ἀγαθότητος παρεκτικά, οὐδὲν δὲ οὕτως ἡμῶν ἀναφλέγει καὶ κινεῖ τὴν καρδίαν εἰς τὴν ἀγάπην τῆς αὐτοῦ ἀγαθότητος ὡς ἡ θεολογία. Γέννημα γὰρ οὖσα αὕτη πρώϊμον τῆς τοῦ θεοῦ χάριτος πρῶτα πάντως καὶ δῶρα τῇ ψυχῇ χαρίζεται. Πρῶτον μὲν γὰρ παρασκευάζει ἡμᾶς πάσης τῆς τοῦ
20 βίου χαίροντας καταφρονεῖν φιλίας ὡς ἔχοντας ἀντὶ φθαρτῶν ἐπιθυμιῶν ἀνεκλάλητον πλοῦτον τὰ λόγια τοῦ θεοῦ. Ἔπειτα δὲ τῷ πυρὶ τὸν νοῦν ἡμῶν περιαυγάζει τῆς ἀλλαγῆς, ὅθεν αὐτὸν καὶ κοινωνικὸν τῶν λειτουργικῶν πνευμάτων ποιεῖ. Γνησίως οὖν ταύτην οἱ εἰς τοῦτο προετοιμασθέντες τὴν ἀρετὴν ποθοῦμεν, ἀγαπητοί, τὴν εὐπρεπῆ, τὴν
25 πανθέωρον, τὴν πάσης ἀμεριμνίας πρόξενον, τὴν ἐν αὐγῇ φωτὸς ἀρρήτου

---

1 λύπη] λύπη τις a ‖ ὑπεισέρχεται BMRS: ἐπεισέρχεται NTab ‖ 4 ἐκ] διὰ Mc ‖ ἐπιπόνου] ἐπιμόνου a ‖ 5 τῆς om. ac ‖ ἑαυτῇ περιποιῇ (R)S: ἑαυτῇ περιποιεῖ BN ἑξῆς ἑαυτῇ περιποιῇ c ἑχῇς ἑαυτῇ περιποιῆται Μ ἕξιν ἑαυτῇ περιποιεῖται a om. T ‖ 6 γὰρ BMS: δὲ NRTa ‖ 8 ἀποκτήσασθαι] ἀποκτᾶσθαι Mac ‖ αὐτὸν] αὐτοῦ c om. a ‖ 9 θεοῦ] χριστοῦ Mc ‖ 11 ἐπαγαγών] ἐπαγών R ‖ 12 σημαίνει] ἐπισημαίνεται a ‖ 15 μὲν om. Mac ‖ 18 χάριτος] ἀγαθότητος a ‖ 20 χαίροντας om. Ta ‖ ἀντὶ φθαρτῶν ἐπιθυμιῶν om. a ‖ 22 ἀλλαγῆς] ἀλλοιώσεως a ‖ 23 οἱ εἰς τοῦτο om. A ‖ 23-24 τοῦτο προετοιμασθέντες MNRST: αὐτὴν ἑτοιμασθέντες Ba ἑτοιμασθέντες T ‖ 24 ποθοῦμεν MNR: ποθῶμεν T πορευθῶμεν ABSa ‖ εὐπρεπῆ] εὐπρέπειαν A ‖ 25 αὐγῇ] αὐτῇ Nb.

DIADOCHOS

but whenever we dispense with everything, boundless grief and humility slip into us as there is nothing for us to effect which is worthy of justice. And so the soul then turns back in great humility, that through laborious prayer, and steadfastness, and humble-mindedness, it might save up for itself what it is not able to acquire daily through acts of charity; for 'the poor man,' it says, 'and the needy man shall praise your name, Lord'.[69] For the free gift of divine converse is not prepared for anyone by God unless that man prepare himself, losing all that he has for the sake of the glory of the gospel of God so that in godly penury he might preach the abundance of the kingdom of God. For he who said, 'You prepared something for the poor man in your exceeding goodness, O God' clearly indicated this by adding 'The Lord will give speech to those who preach good news, in great power.[70]

67. All the free gifts of our God are exceedingly beautiful, and causative of all goodness, but nothing so kindles and moves the heart into the love of his excellence as divine converse. Being an early product of the grace of God, it is this which gives the first gifts to the soul, freely and completely; for it first prepares us to despise all affection for this life with rejoicing, as having an inexpressible abundance in place of mortal desires: the utterances of God. Then it enflames our intellect in the fire of transformation, so that it also makes the intellect be one of the ministering spirits.[71] Therefore, beloved, we who are genuinely prepared in advance for this long for this virtue which is seemly and all-contemplating, which is an aid to all freedom from care, which feeds the intellect with the utterances of God in the sunshine of inexpressible light, which through the

---

[69] Psalms 73:21.
[70] Psalms 67:11f.
[71] See Hebrews 1:14.

ΔΙΑΔΟΧΟΥ

τὸν νοῦν τρέφουσαν τὰ λόγια τοῦ θεοῦ, τὴν τῷ θεῷ λόγῳ, ἵνα μὴ πολλὰ λέγω, τὴν λογικὴν ψυχὴν διὰ τῶν ἁγίων προφητῶν πρὸς κοινωνίαν ἁρμοσαμένην ἀχώριστον, ἵνα καὶ παρὰ ἀνθρώποις, ὢ τοῦ θαύματος, τοὺς θεῳδοὺς φθόγγους ἡ νυμφαγωγὸς ἐναρμόσῃ ἡ θεία τρανῶς ᾄδοντας τὰς
5 δυναστείας τοῦ θεοῦ.

ξη΄.

Ὁ νοῦς ἡμῶν τὰ πολλὰ περὶ μὲν τὴν προσευχὴν δυσανασχέτως ἔχει διὰ τὸ στενὸν ἄγαν καὶ περιεσταλμένον τῆς εὐκτικῆς ἀρετῆς, εἰς δὲ τὴν
10 θεολογίαν χαίρων ἑαυτὸν ἐπιδίδωσι διὰ τὸ πλατὺ καὶ ἀπολελυμένον τῶν θείων θεωρημάτων. Ἵνα οὖν μὴ ὁδὸν αὐτῷ δῶμεν τοῦ πολλὰ θέλειν λέγειν ἢ καὶ ὑπὲρ τὸ μέτρον αὐτὸν πτεροῦσθαι παραχωρῶμεν τῇ χαρᾷ, τῇ προσευχῇ τὰ πλεῖστα καὶ τῇ ψαλμῳδίᾳ καὶ τῇ τῶν ἁγίων γραφῶν ἀναγνώσει σχολάζωμεν μήτε τῶν φιλολόγων ἀνδρῶν παρορῶντες τὰ
15 θεωρήματα, ὧν ἡ πίστις διὰ τῶν λόγων γνωρίζεται. Οὔτε γὰρ ἴδια αὐτὸν τοῦτο ποιοῦντες παρασκευάσομεν ῥήματα ἐπιμιγνύναι τοῖς λόγοις τῆς χάριτος οὔτε μὴν ὑπὸ τῆς κενοδοξίας αὐτὸν ὑποσυρῆναι διαφορηθέντα διὰ τῆς πολλῆς χαρᾶς καὶ τῆς πολυλογίας παραχωρήσομεν· ἀλλὰ καὶ πάσης φαντασίας ἐκτὸς αὐτὸν ἐν τῷ καιρῷ τῆς θεωρίας φυλάξομεν καὶ
20 δακρυώδεις αὐτῷ σχεδὸν τὰς πάσας ἐκ τούτου ἐννοίας περιποιήσομεν. Ἀναπαυόμενος γὰρ ἐν τοῖς καιροῖς τῆς ἡσυχίας καὶ καθηδυνόμενος ὑπὸ

1 τὰ λόγια ABMNTa: τοῖς λόγοις RS ‖ τῷ θεῷ λόγῳ] τοῦ θεοῦ λόγου NSb ‖ 2 ἁγίων om. Aa ‖ 3 ἁρμοσαμένην] ὁρμωσαμένην b ‖ ἵνα NRT: εἶναι ABMSa ‖ 3 ὢ om. Nb ‖ τοὺς] τοῦ M ‖ 4 θεῳδοὺς NRTc: θεοειδεῖς BSa θεῷ ἡδεῖς A θεοειδοὺς M ‖ φθόγγους] φθόγγου M ‖ ἡ νυμφαγωγὸς ἐναρμόσῃ ἡ θεία t: ἡ νυμφαγωγὸς ἐναρμόσοι ἡ θεία BMNV ἡ νυμφαγωγὸς ἐναρμόσει ἡ θεία Tb ἡ νυμφαγωγὸς ἐν ἁρμοσύνῃ θεία Aa (θεία a) ἡ νυμφαγωγὸς ἐναρμόσασα ἡ θεία S ἐναρμόσασα ἡ θεία νυμφαγωγὸς R ‖ ᾄδοντας] ᾄδει RS ‖ 5 δυναστείας] θεολογίας Mc ‖ 8 μὲν om. a ‖ δυσανασχέτως ἔχει] δυσανασχετεῖ a ‖ 12 τὸ om. R ‖ παραχωρῶμεν ABRST: παραχωροῦμεν MN παράσχωμεν a ‖ 13 med. τῇ om. B ‖ ἁγίων om. Aa ‖ 14 σχολάζωμεν (R)Tac: σχολάσωμεν S σχολάζομεν ABMN ‖ φιλολόγων MNRSTa: θεολόγων A φιλονίκων B ‖ 15-16 ὧν - ῥήματα om. Nb ‖ 15 οὔτε ARSa: οὐδὲ BMT ‖ ἴδια] τι RS ‖ αὐτὸν M(R)Sa: αὐτῶν ABT ‖ 16 παρασκευάσομεν BM(R)Sa: παρασκευάσωμεν T παρασκευάσε μὲν A παρασκευάζομεν c ‖ 17 τῆς om. a ‖ 18 παραχωρήσομεν BN(R)a: παραχωρήσωμεν AMST et (ut vid.) ba.c. καταφρονήσωμεν (κατα ex παρα) bp.c. ‖ 19 φυλάξομεν ABN(R)Sa: φυλάξωμεν MTb ‖ 20 περιποιήσομεν AB(R)Sa: περιποιήσωμεν MNT.

holy prophets bound the rational soul inseparably into a fellowship with God the Logos (lest I say more), so that even among men–O the wonder!– the divine bridesmaid might tune the God-given voices which clearly hymn the powers of God.

68. It is with difficulty that our intellect holds the many things concerning prayer, because of the extreme constraint and hiddenness of this wished-for virtue; but our intellect gives itself up into divine converse rejoicing because of the breadth and release of divine contemplations. Therefore, so that we might not give the intellect scope for wanting to say many things, or allow it, in joy, to take flight immoderately, let us spend time for the most part in prayer and psalmody and the reading of holy Scripture–not overlooking the contemplations of learned men, whose faith is made known through words. For doing this we will neither accustom the intellect to mingle its own speech with the utterances of grace nor allow it to be undermined by vainglory, dispersed through great joy and garrulousness; rather we will keep it outside all fantasy in the time of contemplation and as a result make nearly all its intellectual conceptions tearful. For resting in times of stillness, and especially being gratified by

ΔΙΑΔΟΧΟΥ

τοῦ τῆς εὐχῆς μάλιστα γλυκάσματος οὐ μόνον τῶν προειρημένων αἰτιῶν ἐκτὸς γίνεται, ἀλλὰ πλέον καὶ πλέον ἀνανεοῦται εἰς τὸ ὀξέως καὶ δίχα πόνου τοῖς θείοις ἐπιβάλλειν θεωρήμασι μετὰ τοῦ καὶ εἰς τὴν θεωρίαν αὐτὸν τῆς διακρίσεως ἐν πολλῇ προκόπτειν ταπεινώσει. Πλὴν δεῖ
5 εἰδέναι ὅτι ἔστιν εὐχὴ παντὸς πλάτους ἐπάνω· αὕτη δὲ ἐκείνων μόνων ὑπάρχει τῶν ἐν πάσῃ αἰσθήσει καὶ πληροφορίᾳ ἐμπεπλησμένων τῆς ἁγίας χάριτος.

ξθ'.

10 Ἡ χάρις τὴν ἀρχὴν ἐν αἰσθήσει πολλῇ τὴν ψυχὴν τῷ οἰκείῳ εἴωθε περιαυγάζειν φωτί· προϊόντων δὲ τῶν ἀγώνων ἀγνώστως τὰ πολλὰ ἐνεργείᾳ τῇ θεολόγῳ τὰ ἑαυτῆς μυστήρια ἐνεργεῖ διανοίᾳ, ἵνα τότε μὲν ἡμᾶς χαίροντας εἰς τὸ ἴχνος ἐπιβάλλοι τῶν θείων θεωρημάτων ὡς ἐξ ἀγνοίας εἰς γνῶσιν καλουμένους, ἐν δὲ τῷ μέσῳ τῶν ἀγώνων ἀκενόδοξον
15 ἡμῶν τὴν γνῶσιν διαφυλάττοι. Δεῖ οὖν λυπεῖσθαι μὲν ἡμᾶς συμμέτρως ὡς ἐγκαταλειφθέντας, ἵνα πλέον ταπεινωθῶμεν καὶ ὑποταγῶμεν τῇ δόξῃ τοῦ κυρίου, χαίρειν δὲ εὐκαίρως τῇ ἀγαθῇ ἐλπίδι πτερουμένους. Ὡς γὰρ ἡ πολλὴ λύπη εἰς ἀπελπισμὸν καὶ ἀπιστίαν τὴν ψυχὴν περιΐστησιν, οὕτως καὶ ἡ πολλὴ χαρὰ εἰς οἴησιν αὐτὴν προκαλεῖται· ἐπὶ τῶν ἔτι δὲ
20 νηπιαζόντων λέγω· φωτισμοῦ μὲν γὰρ καὶ ἐγκαταλείψεως τὸ μέσον πεῖρα, λύπης δὲ καὶ χαρᾶς τὸ μέσον ἐλπίς. Ὑπομένων γάρ, φησίν, ὑπέμεινα τὸν κύριον καὶ προσέσχε μοι, καὶ πάλιν· Κατὰ τὸ πλῆθος τῶν ὀδυνῶν μου ἐν τῇ καρδίᾳ μου αἱ παρακλήσεις σου ηὔφραναν τὴν ψυχήν μου.

---

1 εὐχῆς] προσευχῆς N ‖ γλυκάσματος] γλυκασμοῦ MRSc ‖ προειρημένων] εἰρημένων a ‖ 2 γίνεται] εὑρίσκεται a ‖ ἀλλὰ πλέον] ἀλλὰ καὶ πλέον B ἀλλὰ Sa ‖ 3 θείοις] θείοις οἷς R ‖ θεωρήμασι] νοήμασι Aa ‖ τὴν om. R ‖ 5 εὐχὴ] προσευχὴ a ‖ πλάτους] πλούτου R ‖ 6 ὑπάρχει] ἐστὶ A ‖ 12 ἐνεργείᾳ τῇ θεολόγῳ τὰ ἑαυτῆς μυστήρια ἐνεργεῖ διανοίᾳ ARS: ἐνεργεῖ τῇ θεολόγῳ ψυχῇ τὰ ἑαυτῆς μυστήρια ceteri ‖ 13 ἐπιβάλλοι ABMRb: ἐπιβάλοι NSc ἐμβάλῃ a ἐπικαλεῖ T ‖ 14 ἀγνοίας] ἀγνωσίας B ‖ καλουμένους] καλουμένη T ‖ 15 μὲν om. R ‖ 17 πτερουμένους] πτερούμενος c κρατουμένους T a.c. κραταιουμένους Tp.c. ‖ 18 ἡ om. R ‖ 19 αὐτὴν om. Aa ‖ προκαλεῖται] προσκαλεῖται S ‖ δὲ om. A.

the sweetness of prayer, not only is the intellect clear of the charges previously stated, it is also increasingly renewed into the undertaking of divine contemplations quickly and effortlessly, advancing also into the contemplation of discernment, in great humility. But one must know that there is prayer beyond all expansiveness; this is characteristic only of those who are filled with holy grace with a whole Sense and complete assurance.

69. At first grace is wont to illumine the soul in its own light, with a great sensation; but as contests progress it activates its mysteries in the reason unperceived for the most part, by a divinely conversant activity; so that then as we rejoice it might set us on the track of divine contemplations, being called from lack of perception into perception; and in the midst of our contests it carefully keeps our perception free from vainglory. And so we must grieve moderately, as being forsaken, so that we might be humbled further and subordinated to the glory of the Lord; but we must also rejoice as is fitting, given wings by the good hope. Just as great grief brings the soul round into hopelessness and faithlessness, so great joy entices it into presumption (I speak in respect of those who are still like children[72]) since the middle degree between enlightenment and forsakenness is testing, and the middle degree between grief and joy is hope; for 'being steadfast', it says, 'I was steadfast in the Lord, and he gave heed to me;'[73] and again, 'according to the multitude of my distresses in my heart your consolations cheered my soul.'[74]

---

[72] See 1 Corinthians 13:11; Ephesians 4:14; 1 Thessalonians 2:7; Hebrews 5:12f.
[73] Psalms 39:2.
[74] Psalms 93:19.

ΔΙΑΔΟΧΟΥ

ο'.

Ὥσπερ αἱ τῶν λουτρῶν συνεχῶς ἐξανοιγόμεναι θύραι τὴν ἔνδον θᾶττον θέρμην ὠθοῦνται πρὸς τὰ ἔξω, οὕτως καὶ ἡ ψυχή, ὅταν πολλὰ θέλῃ διαλέγεσθαι, κἂν πάντα καλὰ λέγῃ, τὴν ἑαυτῆς μνήμην διὰ τῆς
5 φωνητικῆς πύλης διαφορεῖ. Ὅθεν λοιπὸν στερεῖται μὲν τῶν καιρίων ἐννοιῶν, αὐτὴν δὲ τὴν τῶν λογισμῶν συμπληγάδα ὀχληδόν πως τοῖς τυχοῦσι διαλέγεται, ἐπειδὴ οὔτε τὸ ἅγιον λοιπὸν ἔχει πνεῦμα εἰς ἀφάνταστον αὐτὴν συντηροῦν διάνοιαν· φεύγει γὰρ ἀεὶ τὸ ἀγαθὸν τὴν πολυλογίαν ὡς ταραχῆς ὂν πάσης καὶ φαντασίας ξένον. Καλὴ οὖν ἡ
10 εὔκαιρος σιωπή, οὐδὲν ἕτερον οὖσα ἢ μήτηρ ἐννοιῶν σοφωτάτων.

οα'.

Πολλὰ μὲν οὖν τῇ θεολόγῳ ψυχῇ τὴν ἀρχὴν διενοχλεῖν αὐτὸς ἡμᾶς ὁ λόγος τῆς γνώσεως διδάσκει πάθη, πλέον δὲ πάντων ὁ θυμὸς καὶ τὸ
15 μῖσος· τοῦτο δὲ πάσχει οὐ τοσοῦτον διὰ τοὺς ἐνεργοῦντας ταῦτα δαίμονας ὅσον διὰ τὴν οἰκείαν προκοπήν. Ἕως μὲν γὰρ τῷ τοῦ κόσμου ἡ ψυχὴ φρονήματι συναπάγεται, κἂν ὁπωσοῦν ἴδῃ τὸ δίκαιον παρά τινων καταπατούμενον, ἀκίνητος καὶ ἀτάραχος μένει· τῶν γὰρ ἰδίων ἐπιθυμιῶν φροντίζουσα εἰς τὸ δίκαιον οὐκ ἀφορᾷ τοῦ θεοῦ. Ὅτε δὲ τῶν
20 ἑαυτῆς ἐπάνω ἄρξηται γίνεσθαι παθῶν, διά τε τὴν τῶν παρόντων καταφρόνησιν καὶ τὴν ἀγάπην τοῦ θεοῦ οὐδὲ ἐν ὀνείρῳ τὸ δίκαιον ἀθετούμενον ἰδεῖν φέρει, ἀλλὰ χολᾷ κατὰ τῶν κακούργων καὶ ταράττεται, ἕως ὅτε τοὺς ὑβριστὰς ἴδοι τῆς δικαιοσύνης εὐσεβεῖ λογισμῷ τῷ ταύτης ἀπολογουμένους ἀξιώματι. Διὰ τοῦτο οὖν τοὺς μὲν
25 ἀδίκους μισεῖ, τοὺς δὲ δικαίους ὑπεραγαπᾷ· ἀσυνάρπακτον γὰρ πάντως

2 συνεχῶς] συχνῶς T ‖ ἐξανοιγόμεναι ABNRSa: ἀνοιγόμεναι MTb ‖ ἔνδον] ἔνδοθεν c ‖ 3 ὅταν] ὅτε RS ‖ 4 θέλῃ ABac: θέλει MN(R)S θελήσει T ‖ πάντα] πάντα ποτὲ A πάντοτε RS ‖ λέγῃ Ac: λέγει BMN(R)ST λίαν λαλῇ a ‖ 5 διαφορεῖ] διαφέρει B διαφθείρει Ra ‖ στερεῖται ABN: στερίσκεται MRTa ὁ νοῦς στερίσκεται S ‖ καιρίων] κυρίων M ‖ 8 συντηροῦν] συντηρεῖν Nb ‖ 9 ὂν MN(R)STa: ὢν b ὧν A οὖσαν B ‖ πάσης] ἁπάσης T ‖ ξένον AMNTa: ἐκτὸς RS πρόξενον Bb ‖ καλὴ] καλὸν N ‖ 10 σιωπῇ] σιωπὴ καὶ MRSc ‖ 13 διενοχλεῖν] διοχλεῖν RSa ‖ 14 ὁ θυμὸς] τῶν θυμῶν R ‖ 15 ταῦτα] τοῦτο Nb ‖ 17 ἡ ψυχὴ ABRSa: om. MNT ‖ συναπάγεται ABRST: συνυπάγεται MN συναπάγοιτο a ‖ ὁπωσοῦν Ta: ὁπωσὰν ABMNRS ‖ ἴδῃ] ἴδοι a ‖ 18 ἰδίων om. Nb ‖ 20 παθῶν] ἐπιθυμιῶν a ‖ 21 οὐδὲ Ra: οὔτε ceteri ‖ ὀνείρῳ ABMSa: ἑαυτῷ NRT ‖ 22 ἀθετούμενον] ἀδικούμενον Nb ‖ ἰδεῖν] εἰδέναι B om. Nb ‖ 22-23 καὶ ταράττεται om. Mc ‖ 23 ἴδοι] ἴδῃ T.

94

70. Just as the doors of the baths, in being opened continually, push the inner warmth quickly to the outside, so the soul also, whenever it wants to have many discussions (even if everything it says is good) disperses its recollection through the vocal gate. And so it is afterwards deprived of vital intellectual conceptions, and discusses the annoying jostling of imaginings with the first people who come along, since it doesn't have the holy Spirit any longer keeping it in a reasoning which is free from fantasy—because that which is good always flees garrulousness, since it is a stranger to all confusion and fantasy. So timely silence is good, being none other than the mother of the wisest intellectual conceptions.

71. The rationale of perception itself teaches us that in the beginning many passions disturb the divinely conversant soul, and most of all temper and hatred; the soul suffers this not so much because it is the demons which are activating them as because of its inherent progress. For as long as the soul is taken up in the mentality of the world it remains unmoved and untroubled, even if it sees what is just trampled down by someone in some way; because taking thought of its inherent desires, the soul does not look straight at that justness which is of God. But when it begins to be above its own passions (due to despising possessions, and to love of God) it cannot bear to see what is just slighted even in a dream, but is angry at the evil-doers, and upset until it sees those who insult justice speak in defence of its honour, in a pious imagining. So for this reason it hates the unjust, and loves the just exceedingly;[75] because the eye of the soul

---

[75] See Hebrews 1:9; Psalms 44:8.

ΔΙΑΔΟΧΟΥ

τὸ ὄμμα τῆς ψυχῆς γίνεται, ὅταν τὸ ἑαυτῆς παραπέτασμα, τὸ σῶμα λέγω, εἰς λεπτότητα πολλὴν διὰ τῆς ἐγκρατείας ἐξυφήνῃ. Πλὴν κρεῖττόν ἐστι πολὺ τοῦ μισεῖν τοὺς ἀδίκους τὸ κλαίειν τὴν αὐτῶν ἀναισθησίαν· εἰ γὰρ κἀκεῖνοι μίσους ὑπάρχουσιν ἄξιοι, ἀλλὰ τὴν
5 φιλόθεον ψυχὴν ὁ λόγος οὐ θέλει ὑπὸ μίσους ὀχλεῖσθαι, ἐπειδὴ μίσους ἐμπαρόντος τῇ ψυχῇ οὐκ ἐνεργεῖ ἡ γνῶσις.

οβ΄.

Ὁ θεολόγος νοῦς ὑπ᾽ αὐτῶν τῶν λογίων τοῦ θεοῦ καθηδυνόμενος τὴν
10 ψυχὴν καὶ διαπυρούμενος τοῖς τῆς ἀπαθείας προσβάλλει μέτροις ἐν εὐκαίροις πλάτεσιν. Τὰ λόγια γάρ, φησίν, κυρίου λόγια ἁγνά, ἀργύριον πεπυρωμένον, δοκίμιον τῇ γῇ. Ὁ δὲ γνωστικὸς ἐκ τῆς κατὰ τὴν ἐνέργειαν πείρας βεβαιούμενος ἐπάνω τῶν παθῶν γίνεται· γεύεται δὲ καὶ ὁ θεολόγος, εἴπερ ταπεινότερον ἑαυτὸν διαθοῖτο, τῆς πείρας τῆς
15 γνωστικῆς καὶ ὁ γνωστικός, εἴπερ ἄπταιστον τὸ διακριτικὸν τῆς ψυχῆς ἔχει μέρος, τῆς θεωρητικῆς πρὸς ὀλίγον ἀρετῆς. Τὰ γὰρ δύο οὐ συμβαίνει ἑκάστῳ ἐξ ὁλοκλήρου παραγίνεσθαι χαρίσματα, ἵνα τῶν ἀμφοτέρων θαυμαζόντων, εἰς ὃ ἕκαστος ἑκάστου περιττεύει, ἡ ταπεινοφροσύνη ἐν αὐτοῖς μετὰ ζήλου δικαιοσύνης πλεονάζῃ. Διὰ τοῦτο
20 ὁ ἀπόστολος λέγει· Ὧι μὲν γὰρ διὰ τοῦ πνεύματος δίδοται λόγος σοφίας, ἄλλῳ δὲ λόγος γνώσεως κατὰ τὸ αὐτὸ πνεῦμα.

ογ΄.

Ὅταν ἐν εὐθηνίᾳ ᾖ ἡ ψυχὴ τῶν φυσικῶν αὐτῆς καρπῶν,
25 μεγαλοφωνότερον καὶ τὴν ψαλμῳδίαν ποιεῖται καὶ φωνῇ μᾶλλον θέλει προσεύχεσθαι. Ὅτε δὲ ὑπὸ τοῦ ἁγίου πνεύματος ἐνεργεῖται, μετὰ πάσης ἀνέσεως καὶ ἡδύτητος ψάλλει καὶ εὔχεται ἐν μόνῃ τῇ καρδίᾳ.

2 τῆς] αὐτῆς τῆς BNb ǁ ἐξυφήνῃ AB(R)S: ἐξυφαίνηται a ἐξυφήνοι N ἐξυφαίνοι MT ǁ 3 ἐστι πολὺ om. a ǁ τοῦ om. B ǁ τὸ] καὶ τὸ Mc ǁ 4 ὑπάρχουσιν ἄξιοι] ἄχιοί εἰσιν a ǁ 5 φιλόθεον] θεοφιλῆ a ǁ θέλει] βούλεται a φέρει RS ǁ ὀχλεῖσθαι] διοχλεῖσθαι T ǁ 9 νοῦς ARSTa: om. BMN ǁ 10 διαπυρούμενος] συμπυρούμενος Aa ǁ προσβάλλει] προβάλλει b ǁ 10-11 μέτροις ἐν εὐκαίροις MRSTa: μετὰ καιροὺς ABN ǁ 13 γεύεται] τεύξεται Mac ǁ 14 διαθοῖτο B: διάθοιτο AMNSTa ǁ 16 πρὸς ὀλίγον om. A ǁ 17 παραγίνεσθαι] παραγενέσθαι A ǁ 18 ἀμφοτέρων] εὐσεβῶν A ǁ ἕκαστος om. M ǁ ἑκάστου] ἑκάστῳ A ǁ 19 αὐτοῖς] ἑαυτοῖς a ǁ δικαιοσύνης] τὸ δίκαιον A ǁ πλεονάζῃ Ma: πλεονάζει ABN(R)ST ǁ 21 λόγος om. A ǁ 24 ᾖ om. BMR ǁ 27 ψάλλει] καὶ ψάλλει a ǁ ἐν om. R.

becomes entirely undeluded whenever its lid (I speak of the body) unravels into a great thinness through self-control. However to lament the insensitivity of the unjust is very much better than to hate them; for even if they are worthy of hatred, the Logos does not want the godly soul to be disturbed by hatred, since perception is not active when hatred is in the soul.

72. When the soul is greatly gladdened and kindled by the very utterances of God, the divinely conversant intellect sends it out into the expanses of dispassion in fitting proportions. For 'the utterances of the Lord', it says, 'are pure utterances, silver refined by fire, tested for earth.'[76] But whoever is perceptive comes to be above passions, assured by the evidence which comes with activity. If indeed the divinely conversant man disposes himself to be humbler, he also tastes the evidence of perception together with him who is perceptive; and if that man holds the discerning part of the soul unfaltering, he tastes the contemplative virtue a little. For the two free gifts do not occur together in each completely, so that, both marvelling at what each excels the other in, humble-mindedness might abound in them both with the zeal of righteousness. Because of this the Apostle says, 'For to one the expression of wisdom is given, through the Spirit, but to another the expression of perception, according to the same Spirit.'[77]

73. Whenever the soul is in the abundance of its natural fruits, it makes its psalmody louder and wants to pray aloud more. But when it is activated by the holy Spirit, it sings and prays with all relaxation and gladness alone in a private place in the heart. A joy complete with fantasies follows

---

[76] Psalms 11:7.
[77] 1 Corinthians 12:8.

ΔΙΑΔΟΧΟΥ

Ἕπεται δὲ ἐκείνῃ μὲν τῇ διαθέσει χαρὰ πεφαντασμένη· ταύτῃ δὲ πνευματικὸν δάκρυον καὶ μετὰ ταῦτα θυμηδία τις φιλήσυχος· θερμὴ γὰρ ἡ μνήμη διὰ τὴν τῆς φωνῆς μένουσα συμμετρίαν δακρυώδεις τινὰς καὶ ἠπίους ἐννοίας τὴν καρδίαν πάντως παρασκευάζει φέρειν. Ὅθεν ὄντως
5 ἔστιν ἰδεῖν τὰ σπέρματα τῆς εὐχῆς μετὰ δακρύων ἐν τῇ γῇ τῆς καρδίας διὰ τὴν ἐλπίδα τῆς τοῦ θερισμοῦ ἐνσπειρόμενα χαρᾶς. Πλὴν ὅτε ὑπὸ πολλῆς δυσθυμίας βαρούμεθα, δεῖ ὀλίγον μείζονι τῇ φωνῇ ποιεῖσθαι ἡμᾶς τὴν ψαλμῳδίαν τῇ τῆς ἐλπίδος χαρᾷ τοὺς φθόγγους τῆς ψυχῆς ἀνακρούοντας, ἄχρις οὗ τὸ νέφος ἐκεῖνο τὸ βαρὺ ὑπὸ τῶν ἀνέμων τοῦ
10 μέλους διαλυθῇ.

οδ΄.

Ἡνίκα ἐν τῇ ἑαυτῆς ἐπιγνώσει ἡ ψυχὴ γένηται, φέρει καὶ ἐξ ἑαυτῆς θέρμην τινὰ θεοφιλῆ· μὴ συγχεομένη γὰρ ὑπὸ τῶν μεριμνῶν τοῦ βίου
15 ἔρωτά τινα ἀποτίκτει εἰρήνης συμμέτρως τὸν θεὸν ζητοῦντα τῆς εἰρήνης· ἀλλὰ ταύτης μὲν ταχέως διαφορεῖται ἢ ὑπὸ τῶν αἰσθήσεων προδιδομένης τῆς μνήμης ἢ καὶ ἀναλισκούσης τῆς φύσεως θᾶττον τὸ οἰκεῖον διὰ πενίαν καλόν· ὅθεν οἱ τῶν Ἑλλήνων σοφοί, οὕπερ διὰ τῆς ἐγκρατείας ἐπιτυγχάνειν ἐνόμιζον, τοῦτο οὐκ εἶχον ὡς ἔδει διὰ τὸ μὴ
20 ἐνεργεῖσθαι τὸν νοῦν αὐτῶν ὑπὸ τῆς ἀενάου καὶ πανταληθινῆς σοφίας. Ἡ δὲ ἐκ τοῦ ἁγίου πνεύματος φερομένη θέρμη τῇ καρδίᾳ πρῶτον μὲν εἰρηνική ἐστιν ὅλη καὶ ἀνένδοτος καὶ ὅλα τὰ μέρη τῆς ψυχῆς εἰς τὸν τοῦ θεοῦ προσκαλουμένη πόθον καὶ οὔτε ἔξω τῆς καρδίας ῥιπιζομένη, δι᾽ αὐτῆς δὲ μᾶλλον ὅλον τὸν ἄνθρωπον εἰς ἀγάπην τινὰ ἄπειρον
25 κατευφραίνουσα καὶ χαράν. Δεῖ μέντοι ἐπιγνόντας ἐκείνην εἰς ταύτην

---

3 ἡ om. A ‖ 4 ἠπίους MN(R)Sa: ἠπίους NT νηπίους B ‖ 7 δυσθυμίας] ἀθυμίας a ‖ δεῖ om. A ‖ 8 ἡμᾶς om. A ‖ ψαλμῳδίαν] ψαλμῳδίαν ἡμῶν A ‖ 9 βαρὺ] βαρύτατον B ‖ 10 μέλους διαλυθῇ] βάρους διαλυθεῖ Nb ‖ 13 alt. ἑαυτῆς ABSTa: αὐτῆς MNR ‖ 14 θέρμην] θερμήν A ‖ θεοφιλῆ MNR: καὶ θεοφιλῇ αἰδῶ ABSTa ‖ μὴ συγχεομένη γὰρ] ὅταν γὰρ μὴ συγχέηται A ὅταν γὰρ μὴ συγχῆται a ‖ 15 εἰρήνης] ἐν τῇ εἰρήνῃ RST ‖ 16 ταύτης μὲν] ταῦτα A ‖ διαφορεῖται] διαφορεῖται τῆς ἐνθυμήσεως ST ‖ 18 οὕπερ] ὅπερ A ‖ 19 τοῦτο] τοῦτον b ‖ 20 πανταληθινῆς ABRTa: πάντα ἀληθινῆς MN κατὰ πάντα ἀπηθινῆς S ‖ 21 φερομένη θέρμη] φαινομένη θερμῇ A ‖ 22 ἀνένδοτος] ἀνενδύαστος ST ‖ 24 αὐτῆς MNRT: ἑαυτῆς ABSa ‖ δὲ om. NT.

in the first disposition; but in the second there are spiritual tears, and after these a glad feeling–having affection for stillness; for when recollection remains ardent because of the moderation of the voice, it prepares the heart to bring forth its intellectual conceptions wholly with tears and gentleness. And from this it is truly seen that the seeds of prayer are sown with tears in the earth of the heart because of the hope of the joy of the harvest.[78] Except that when we are weighed down by great despair, we must perform the psalms with a slightly louder voice, with the joy of hope striking up the notes of the soul, to the point where that heavy cloud is dispersed by the winds of song.

74. When the soul comes to recognise itself, it bears from itself a godly ardour, since not being confounded by the cares of this life it produces a yearning for peace proportionately, seeking the God of peace; but it is quickly distracted from this, either by recollection being betrayed by the senses, or by nature expending its inherent good too quickly as a result of deficiency. And this is why the wise men of the Greeks did not have to the necessary extent that which they thought to find through self-control: because their intellect was not activated by ever-flowing and all-true wisdom. But that ardour which is borne into the heart first from the holy Spirit is entirely peaceful and unwavering, and invites all the parts of the soul into longing for God; it is not kindled outside the heart, but rather cheers the whole man into a boundless love and joy *through* the heart. Recognising the former sort of ardour, one must seize the latter. For

---

[78] See Psalms 125:5.

ΔΙΑΔΟΧΟΥ

καταφθάσαι· ὑγιαινούσης μὲν γάρ πως τῇ ἐγκρατείᾳ τῆς φύσεως ὑπάρχει γνώρισμα ἡ φυσικὴ ἀγάπη, ἀγαθῦναι δὲ τὸν νοῦν εἰς ἀπάθειαν ὡς ἡ πνευματικὴ ἀγάπη οὐδέποτε δύναται.

οε΄.

Ὥσπερ ὁ ἀὴρ οὗτος ὁ περὶ ἡμᾶς ἐμπνέοντος μὲν τοῦ βορρᾶ τῇ κτίσει καθαρὸς διαμένει διὰ τὴν τοῦ ἀνέμου λεπτήν τινα καὶ αἰθριοποιὸν φύσιν, τοῦ δὲ νότου πνέοντος ὅλος ὥσπερ δασύνεται τῆς τοῦ ἀνέμου τούτου ἀχλυοποιοῦ φύσεως λόγῳ τινὸς συγγενείας ἐκ τῶν ἑαυτοῦ μερῶν τὰς νεφέλας κατὰ πάσης ἐπιφέροντος τῆς οἰκουμένης· οὕτω καὶ ἡ ψυχή, ὅτε μὲν ὑπὸ τῆς τοῦ ἀληθινοῦ καὶ ἁγίου πνεύματος ἐμπνοίας ἐνεργεῖται, ἐκτὸς τῆς δαιμονικῆς ὅλη ἀχλύος εὑρίσκεται, ὅτε δὲ ὑπὸ τοῦ πνεύματος σφοδρῶς τῆς πλάνης ἐμπνέεται, ὑπὸ τῶν νεφῶν ὅλη τῆς ἁμαρτίας σκεπάζεται. Ἐχρῆν οὖν ἡμᾶς ἀεὶ τὴν πρόθεσιν ἐκ πάσης τῆς ἰσχύος πρὸς τὴν ζωοποιὸν καὶ καθαριστικὴν αὔραν ἐπιστρέφειν τοῦ ἁγίου πνεύματος, τοῦτ' ἔστιν πρὸς ὃ εἶδεν ἀπὸ βορρᾶ πνεῦμα ἐρχόμενον ἐν φωτὶ γνώσεως ὁ προφήτης Ἰεζεκιήλ, ἵνα αἴθριον ἡμῶν ἀεὶ τῆς ψυχῆς τὸ θεωρητικὸν μάλιστα διαμένοι μέρος πρὸς τὸ ἁπλανῶς ἡμᾶς τοῖς θείοις ἐπιβάλλειν θεωρήμασιν ἐν ἀέρι φωτὸς τὰ τοῦ φωτὸς ὁρῶντας· τοῦτο γάρ ἐστι φῶς ἀληθινῆς γνώσεως.

ος΄.

Τινὲς ὑπενόησαν τὴν χάριν ἅμα καὶ τὴν ἁμαρτίαν, τοῦτ' ἔστι τὸ πνεῦμα τῆς ἀληθείας καὶ τὸ πνεῦμα τῆς πλάνης, ἐπὶ τῶν βαπτιζομένων ἐγκρύπτεσθαι εἰς τὸν νοῦν. Ὅθεν, φησίν, τὸ μὲν ἓν πρόσωπον εἰς τὰ καλὰ παρακαλεῖ τὸν νοῦν, τὸ δὲ ἕτερον εὐθὺς πρὸς τὰ ἐναντία. Ἐγὼ δὲ ἐκ τῶν θείων γραφῶν καὶ ἐξ αὐτῆς δὲ τῆς τοῦ νοῦ αἰσθήσεως κατείληφα

---

1 μὲν om. Nb ‖ τῇ ἐγκρατείᾳ MNRTa: τῆς ἐγκρατείας ABS ‖ 2 ἀγαθῦναι] παραχθῆναι S ‖ 3 οὐδέποτε] οὐ T ‖ 6 οὗτος om. R ‖ 7 ἀνέμου] ἀνέμου τούτου a ‖ 9 φύσεως] αὔρας a om. c ‖ 10 ἐπιφέροντος] ἐπάγοντος a ‖ οἰκουμένης] κτίσεως a ‖ 11 ἐμπνοίας] ἐπιπνοίας Ta ‖ 12 ὅλη om. Aa ‖ 13 νεφῶν BMRS: νεφελῶν ANTa ‖ 14 ἀεὶ om. R ‖ τῆς om. N ‖ 15 ζωοποιὸν] ζωοποιὸν ἐκείνην a ‖ καθαριστικὴν] καθαρτικὴν a ‖ 18 μάλιστα διαμένοι] διαμένῃ a ‖ 19 τὰ τοῦ φωτὸς om. R ‖ 25 φησίν] φάσι S ‖ alt. εἰς MNT: πρὸς ABRSa ‖ 26 παρακαλεῖ] παρακαλεῖν BT ‖ εὐθὺς] εὐθέως B.

though natural love is the mark of a nature which is healthy by means of self-control, it can never exalt the intellect into dispassion as can spiritual love.

75. The air which is around us remains clean when the north wind is blowing on creation, because of the fine and clear nature of the wind, whereas when the south wind is blowing, the whole air becomes hazy (as it were) because of the misty nature of that wind, and it carries clouds from its own regions all over the inhabited world (by reason of a relationship with them). In the same way the soul also is found to be wholly clear of the demonic mist when it is activated by the blowing of the true and holy Spirit, whereas when it is blown violently by the spirit of error, it is entirely covered by the clouds of sin. So we must always turn round our purpose with all strength towards the life-giving and cleansing breeze of the holy Spirit (that is, towards that Spirit which the prophet Ezekiel, in the light of perception, saw coming from the north[79]) so that the contemplative part of our soul might above all remain always clear for our unerring assault on divine contemplations, seeing the things of light in an air of light;[80] for this is the light of true perception.

76. There are some who supposed grace to be hidden in the intellect of the baptised together with sin (that is, the spirit of truth and the spirit of error[81]). As a result, one says, the former persona summons the intellect into good things, while the latter immediately does so towards the opposite. But I have apprehended from divine Scripture and from the very

---

[79] Ezekiel 1:4.
[80] Psalms 36:9.
[81] See 1 Jn. 4:6.

ΔΙΑΔΟΧΟΥ

ὅτι πρὸ μὲν τοῦ ἁγίου βαπτίσματος ἔξωθεν ἡ χάρις πρὸς τὰ καλὰ προτρέπεται τὴν ψυχήν, ὁ δὲ Σατανᾶς ἐν τοῖς αὐτῆς ἐμφωλεύει βάθεσιν ὅλας τὰς τοῦ νοῦ ἀποφράττειν δεξιὰς πειρώμενος διεξόδους· ἀπὸ δὲ αὐτῆς τῆς ὥρας ἐν ᾗπερ ἀναγεννώμεθα, ἔξωθεν μὲν ὁ δαίμων γίνεται,
5   ἔσωθεν δὲ ἡ χάρις. Ὅθεν εὑρίσκομεν ὅτι, ὡς πάλαι ἐκυρίευεν ἡ πλάνη τῆς ψυχῆς, οὕτως μετὰ τὸ βάπτισμα αὐτῆς κυριεύει ἡ ἀλήθεια. Ἐνεργεῖ μέντοι καὶ ὁ Σατανᾶς μετὰ τοῦτο τῇ ψυχῇ καθάπερ τὸ πρὶν καὶ χείρω δὲ τὰ πολλά, οὐχ ὡς συμπαρὼν δὲ τῇ χάριτι, μὴ γένοιτο, ἀλλὰ καπνίζων ὥσπερ τὸν νοῦν διὰ τῆς ὑγρότητος τοῦ σώματος τὴν ἡδύτητα
10 τῶν ἀλόγων ἡδονῶν· παραχωρήσει δὲ τοῦ θεοῦ τοῦτο γίνεται, ἵνα διὰ τῆς ζάλης καὶ τοῦ πυρὸς τῆς δοκιμασίας διερχόμενος ὁ ἄνθρωπος οὕτως ἐν ἀπολαύσει, εἰ θέλει, γένηται τοῦ ἀγαθοῦ. Διήλθομεν γάρ, φησίν, διὰ πυρὸς καὶ ὕδατος καὶ ἐξήγαγες ἡμᾶς εἰς ἀναψυχήν.

15   οζ΄.

Ἡ χάρις, ὡς ἔφην, ἀπ' αὐτῆς τῆς ῥοπῆς ἐν ᾗ βαπτιζόμεθα, ἐν αὐτῷ τῷ βάθει τοῦ νοῦ ἐγκρύπτεται, αὐτὴν τὴν αἴσθησιν αὐτοῦ κρύπτουσα τὴν ἑαυτῆς παρουσίαν· ἐπειδὰν δὲ ἄρξηταί τις ἐκ πάσης προθέσεως ἐρᾶν τοῦ θεοῦ, τότε ἀρρήτῳ τινὶ λόγῳ διὰ τῆς τοῦ νοῦ αἰσθήσεως
20 προσομιλεῖ τῇ ψυχῇ μέρος τι τῶν ἑαυτῆς ἀγαθῶν. Ὅθεν εἰς ἐπιθυμίαν λοιπὸν ὁ τοῦτο ὅλως θέλων ἀσφαλῶς τὸ εὕρημα κρατεῖν ἔρχεται τοῦ πάντα τὰ παρόντα μετὰ πολλῆς χαρᾶς ἀποκτήσασθαι ἀγαθά, ἵνα τὸν ἀγρὸν ὄντως κτήσηται ἐν ᾧπερ εὗρε τὸν θησαυρὸν κεκρυμμένον τῆς ζωῆς. Ὅταν γὰρ πάντα τις ἀποκτήσηται τὸν βιωτικὸν πλοῦτον, τότε

---

2 τοῖς αὐτῆς Bp.c.MN(R)Sa: τοῖς αὐτοῖς Ba.c.Tbc αὐτοῖς τοῖς A ‖ 3 ἀποφράττειν] ἀναφράττειν Aa ‖ πειρώμενος] πειρώμενον R ‖ 5 ἔσωθεν] ἔνδοθεν R ‖ χάρις] χάρις εὑρίσκεται a ‖ εὑρίσκομεν] γινώσκομεν a ‖ ἐκυρίευεν ABNRS: ἐκυρίευσεν MTa ‖ 6 τὸ] τὸ ἅγιον a ‖ 7 καθάπερ AMNRS: καθάπερ καὶ BTa ‖ 8 συμπαρὼν BNRSTa: παρὼν M σὺν ἡμῖν παρὼν A ‖ alt. δὲ om. A ‖ 10 ἡδονῶν] ἡδυνὴν R ‖ τοῦτο om. Nb ‖ 11 πυρὸς] πυρὸς καὶ Mc ‖ δοκιμασίας] δοκιμῆς a ‖ 12 θέλει MN: θέλοι A(R)STa θέλοιτο B ‖ γένηται NRT: γένοιτο Ba γίνοιτο AS γίνεται M ‖ 16 αὐτῷ om. Aa ‖ 17 ἐγκρύπτεται] ἐγκεκρύπται Aa ‖ αὐτὴν τὴν αἴσθησιν BMNRa: αὐτῇ τῇ αἰσθήσει AST ‖ 18 τὴν ἑαυτῆς παρουσίαν] τῇ ἑαυτῆς παρουσίᾳ a ‖ τις om. a ‖ προθέσεως] προαιρέσεως R ‖ 19 ἐρᾶν τοῦ θεοῦ] ἀγαπᾶν τὸν θεὸν a ἀγαπᾶν A ‖ 20 ἑαυτῆς om. NRSb ‖ 21 ἔρχεται] ἄρχεται AS ‖ τοῦ] πρὸς τὸ R ‖ 22 πολλῆς om. a ‖ ἀποκτήσασθαι] ἀποκτᾶσθαι A ‖ 24 ὅταν] ὅτε BNb ‖ ἀποκτήσηται] ἀποκτίσεται A ἀποκτίσηται S.

DIADOCHOS

Sense of the intellect that before holy baptism grace urges the soul forward to what is good *from outside*, while Satan lurks in its depths trying to block up all the exits that are right; but from the time that we are born again, the devil come to be outside and grace inside. And so we find that as error ruled the soul before, so after baptism truth rules it. After this Satan acts on the soul just as before, and in many cases worse; not as co-existing with grace–heaven forbid!–rather obscuring the intellect with the pleasantness of irrational pleasures through the malleability of the body. But this comes about with the consent of God, so that man, going through the testing of the storm and the fire comes, if he decides, into the enjoyment of good; for it says, 'We went through fire and water, and you led us into the soul's renewal.'[82]

77. Grace (as I said) is hidden away in the very depths of the intellect from the very point at which we are baptised, hiding its own presence from the intellect's very Sense; but whenever one begins to yearn for God with a complete purpose, then by an inexpressible utterance grace communicates to the soul some part of its own goods through the Sense of the intellect. And then he who completely intends to secure this discovery safely begins to desire to lose possession of all his goods with great joy, in order truly to gain the field in which he found the hidden treasure of life;[83] for whenever anyone gives up possession of all the wealth of this life, he then finds the place in which the grace of God has been hidden away.

---

[82] Psalms 65:12.
[83] Matthew 13:44.

ΔΙΑΔΟΧΟΥ

εὑρίσκει τὸν τόπον ἐν ᾧ ἡ χάρις κατεκέκρυπται τοῦ θεοῦ. Κατὰ γὰρ τὴν προκοπὴν τῆς ψυχῆς καὶ τὸ θεῖον δῶρον τὴν ἑαυτοῦ τῷ νοΐ ἐμφανίζει χρηστότητα· πλέον μέντοι τότε ὑπὸ τῶν δαιμόνων τὴν ψυχὴν ὀχλεῖσθαι παραχωρεῖ ὁ κύριος, ἵνα καὶ τὴν διάκρισιν αὐτὴν δεόντως ἐκδιδάσκῃ
5 καλοῦ τε καὶ κακοῦ καὶ ταπεινοτέραν αὐτὴν ἀπεργάζηται διὰ τὸ πολλὴν αὐτῇ, ὅτε καθαίρεται, αἰσχύνην ἐκ τῆς τῶν δαιμονικῶν λογισμῶν ἐγγίνεσθαι αἰσχρότητος.

οη′.
10 Κατ᾽ εἰκόνα ἐσμὲν τοῦ θεοῦ τῷ νοερῷ τῆς ψυχῆς κινήματι· τὸ γὰρ σῶμα ὥσπερ οἶκος αὐτῆς ἐστιν. Ἐπειδὴ οὖν διὰ τῆς παραβάσεως τοῦ Ἀδὰμ οὐ μόνον αἱ γραμμαὶ τοῦ χαρακτῆρος τῆς ψυχῆς ἐρρυπώθησαν, ἀλλὰ καὶ τὸ σῶμα ἡμῶν τῇ φθορᾷ ὑπέπεσεν, διὰ τοῦτο ὁ ἅγιος τοῦ θεοῦ λόγος ἐσαρκώθη, ὕδωρ ἡμῖν σωτηρίου διὰ τοῦ οἰκείου ὡς θεὸς
15 βαπτίσματος εἰς ἀναγέννησιν χαρισάμενος. Ἀναγεννώμεθα δὲ διὰ τοῦ ὕδατος τῇ ἐνεργείᾳ τοῦ ἁγίου καὶ ζωοποιοῦ πνεύματος, ὅθεν εὐθέως καὶ τὴν ψυχὴν καὶ τὸ σῶμα, εἴπερ ἐξ ὁλοκλήρου διαθέσεως προσέρχεταί τις τῷ θεῷ, καθαριζόμεθα τοῦ μὲν ἁγίου πνεύματος εἰς ἡμᾶς κατασκηνοῦντος, τῆς δὲ ἁμαρτίας ὑπ᾽ αὐτοῦ φυγαδευομένης. Οὐ γάρ
20 ἐστι δυνατὸν ἑνὸς ὄντος καὶ ἁπλοῦ τοῦ χαρακτῆρος τῆς ψυχῆς δύο πρόσωπα εἰς αὐτήν, ὡς ἐνόμισάν τινες, ἐμπαρεῖναι. Τῆς γὰρ θείας χάριτος προσαρμοζούσης ἑαυτὴν διὰ τοῦ ἁγίου βαπτίσματος ἐν στοργῇ τινι ἀπείρῳ ταῖς γραμμαῖς τοῦ κατ᾽ εἰκόνα ἐπὶ ἀρραβῶνι τῆς ὁμοιώσεως, ποῦ δύναται χωρηθῆναι τὸ τοῦ πονηροῦ πρόσωπον μηδεμιᾶς μάλιστα
25 οὔσης κοινωνίας τῷ φωτὶ πρὸς τὸ σκότος; Ἐκβάλλεσθαι οὖν πιστεύομεν

---

1 κατακέκρυπται] κατακρύπτεται Ba ἀποκέκρυπται T || 2-3 δῶρον - χρηστότητα] ἀποκαλύπτεται δῶρον a || 2 τῷ MNR: ἐν τῷ ABST || 4 αὐτὴν om. Aa || ἐκδιδάσκῃ a: ἐκδιδάσκει N ἐκδιδάσκοι AB(R)STc διδάσκοι M || 5 ἀπεργάζηται BTa: ἀπεργάζεται MN ἀπεργάζοιτο ARS || 6 δαιμονικῶν om. a || 7 ἐγγίνεσθαι] γίνεσθαι a || 11 διὰ] ἐκ ATa || 12 γραμμαὶ] γραφαὶ B || ἐρρυπώθησαν] ἐμαυρώθησαν R || 13 ὑπέπεσεν] ἐπέπεσεν M || 14 σωτηρίου] σωτήριον M || ὡς θεὸς BNRSTc: ὁ θεὸς AMb om. a || 15 δὲ] γὰρ a || 16 τῇ ABNa: ἐν τῇ MRST || ἐνεργείᾳ] συνεργείᾳ Nb || καὶ ζωοποιοῦ om. a || alt. καὶ om. M || 17 προσέρχεταί τις] προσερχόμεθα a προσέλθωμεν S || 20 ὄντος] ὄντως Mb || τοῦ om. R || 21 εἰς αὐτήν om. MRSc || ἐμπαρεῖναι] παρεῖναι R || 22 προσαρμοζούσης] ἐναρμοζούσης A || ἁγίου om. Mc || 23 ἀρραβῶνι] ἀρραβῶνα MTc || 25 τῷ φωτὶ BMNRS: φωτὶ Aa τοῦ φωτὸς T || τὸ om. ABa.

DIADOCHOS

For the divine gift makes its own excellence clear to the intellect according to the progress of the soul; then the Lord allows the soul to be troubled more by the demons, so that he might thoroughly teach the very discernment of good and evil as is necessary, and render the soul more humble because of the great shame which is engendered in it (when it is cleansed) from the shamefulness of demonic imaginings.

78. We are in the image of God in the intelligent movement of the soul; for the body is as its house. Because through the disobedience of Adam not only were the outlines of the figure of the soul smudged, but our body also fell into mortality; and so it was for this reason that the holy Logos of God was made flesh, freely giving us water of salvation into regeneration through his own baptism, as God. So we are regenerated through water by the activity of the holy and life-giving Spirit, through which we are immediately cleansed, both soul and body (if indeed one comes to God from a complete disposition) when the holy Spirit encamps in us, and sin is put to flight by it. For it is not possible since the soul is one and of one simple character, that two personas should co-exist in it, as some supposed. For when through holy baptism divine grace with boundless affection fits itself closely to the outlines of what is in the image (on a pledge of likeness) where can the persona of the evil one find room, especially when 'there is nothing in common between the light and the darkness'?[84] So we who run in sacred contests believe that the many-

---

[84] 2 Corinthians 6:14.

ΔΙΑΔΟΧΟΥ

ἐκ τῶν ταμιείων τοῦ νοῦ διὰ τοῦ λουτροῦ τῆς ἀφθαρσίας οἱ τῶν ἱερῶν ἀγώνων δρομεῖς τὸν πολύμορφον ὄφιν, καὶ μὴ θαυμάζωμεν τίνος ἕνεκεν μετὰ τὸ βάπτισμα πάλιν φαῦλα μετὰ τῶν καλῶν λογιζόμεθα. Τὸ γὰρ λουτρὸν τῆς ἁγιότητος τὸν μὲν ἐκ τῆς ἁμαρτίας περιαίρει ἐξ ἡμῶν
5 ῥύπον, τὸ δὲ διπλοῦν τῆς θελήσεως ἡμῶν οὐκ ἀλλάσσει νῦν οὔτε μὴν τοὺς δαίμονας τοῦ πολεμεῖν ἡμῖν ἢ ἀπάτης προσλαλεῖν ῥήματα κωλύει, ἵνα, ἅπερ οὐκ ἐφυλαξάμεθα ψυχικοὶ ὑπάρχοντες, τὰ ὅπλα τῆς δικαιοσύνης λαβόντες ἐν τῇ δυνάμει τηρήσωμεν τοῦ θεοῦ.

10 οθ'.

Ὁ Σατανᾶς, ὡς εἶπον, διὰ μὲν τοῦ ἁγίου βαπτίσματος ἐκβάλλεται ἀπὸ τῆς ψυχῆς, συγχωρεῖται δὲ αὐτῷ ἕνεκεν τῶν προειρημένων αἰτιῶν ἐνεργεῖν αὐτῇ διὰ τοῦ σώματος· ἡ μὲν γὰρ χάρις τοῦ θεοῦ εἰς αὐτὸ τὸ βάθος τῆς ψυχῆς, τοῦτ' ἔστιν εἰς τὸν νοῦν, κατασκηνοῖ. Πᾶσα γάρ,
15 φησίν, ἡ δόξα τῆς θυγατρὸς τοῦ βασιλέως ἔσωθεν, οὐ φαινομένη τοῖς δαίμοσιν. Διόπερ ἐξ αὐτοῦ τοῦ βάθους τῆς καρδίας ἡμῶν αἰσθανόμεθα τοῦ θείου ὥσπερ ἀναβλύζοντος πόθου, ὅτε θερμῶς τοῦ θεοῦ μεμνήμεθα· τὰ δὲ πονηρὰ πνεύματα λοιπὸν ταῖς αἰσθήσεσι τοῦ σώματος ἐνάλλεταί τε καὶ ἐμφωλεύει διὰ τῆς εὐχερείας τῆς σαρκὸς ἐνεργοῦντα ἐπὶ τῶν ἔτι
20 νηπιαζόντων τῇ ψυχῇ. Οὕτως οὖν ὁ μὲν νοῦς ἡμῶν ἀεὶ κατὰ τὸν ἀπόστολον συνήδεται τοῖς νόμοις τοῦ πνεύματος, τὰ δὲ αἰσθητήρια τῆς σαρκὸς τῷ λείῳ τῶν ἡδονῶν συναπάγεσθαι θέλει. Ὅθεν ἡ μὲν χάρις διὰ τῆς τοῦ νοῦ αἰσθήσεως τὸ σῶμα εἰς ἀγαλλίασιν ἄρρητον ἐπὶ τῶν προκοπτόντων τῇ γνώσει κατευφραίνει. Οἱ δὲ δαίμονες διὰ τῶν
25 αἰσθήσεων τοῦ σώματος, ὅταν ἡμᾶς εὕρωσι μάλιστα ὀλιγώρως τὸν δρόμον

1 τῆς om. R ǁ οἱ] ἡμεῖς οἱ R ǁ 2 θαυμάζωμεν BTac: θαυμάζομεν AMN(R)S ǁ ἕνεκεν] ἕνεκα A ǁ 4 ἐκ om. RSa ǁ 5 ῥύπον BMNT: σπῖλον ASa et (post ἁμαρτίας) R ǁ τὸ] τὸν Nb ǁ νῦν] νοῦν Nb ǁ 6 ἡμῖν] ἡμᾶς A ǁ προσλαλεῖν] προσομιλεῖν A ǁ 7 ἅπερ] ὅπερ ASa ǁ ἐφυλαξάμεθα] ἐφυλάξαμεν a ǁ ψυχικοὶ ANRSa: φυσικοὶ BMT ǁ 8 λαβόντες] λαμβάνοντες a ǁ 11 εἶπον] προεῖπον A εἴπομεν R ǁ μὲν om. a ǁ 12 ἀπὸ om. Aa ǁ ἕνεκεν] ἕνεκα Aa ǁ 13 αὐτῇ] αὐτὴν R ǁ 15 φησίν om. A ǁ 16 αἰσθανόμεθα] αἰσθόμεθα AR ǁ 17 πόθου] ἔρωτος a ǁ ὅτε] ὅτε μάλιστα a ǁ 18 σώματος] σώματος ἡμῶν B ǁ ἐνάλλεταί MNRSa: ἐνάλλονταί ABT ǁ 19 τε om. RSp.c.Ta ǁ ἐμφωλεύει MNRS: ἐμφωλεύουσι ABTa ǁ εὐχερείας] εὐχαριστίας A ǁ τῆς σαρκὸς] τοῦ σώματος a ǁ ἐνεργοῦντα] ἐνεργοῦντες A ἐνεργοῦντες τὰ ἑαυτῶν a ǁ ἔτι om. A ǁ 20 τῇ ψυχῇ ANRT: τὴν ψυχὴν MS τὴν διάνοιαν a ψυχῶν B ǁ οὖν] γοῦν Nb om. R ǁ ἀεὶ ABRSb: om. MNTa ǁ 22 συναπάγεσθαι] συνυπάγεσθαι N ǁ μὲν om. Nb ǁ 25 ὅταν a: ὅτε ceteri ǁ μάλιστα] ἀμελῶς R ἀμελῶς καὶ S om. Aa.

106

shaped serpent is cast out of the treasuries of the intellect through the cleansing bath of immortality; then let us not be amazed why it is that after baptism we still reckon foul things together with good. For the bath of sanctity removes from us the smudge which comes from sin, but it does not transform the duality of our will yet, nor stop the demons making war on us or telling tales of beguilement; this is so that in taking up the weapons of justice, we might keep, in the power of God, that which we have not preserved through having souls.

79. Satan, as I said, is cast out from the soul through holy baptism, but it is granted to him (for the aforementioned reasons) to be active in the soul through the body; for the grace of God is encamped in the very depth of the soul, that is in the intellect. Thus it says, 'All the glory of the daughter of the king is within,'[85] not apparent to the demons. And so we sense the divine as an overflowing of longing, as it were, from the very depth of our heart when we recollect him ardently; then the evil spirits leap into the senses of the body and lurk there through the pliancy of the flesh,[86] being active in those who are still like children in the soul. So our intellect always rejoices (according to the Apostle) in the laws of the Spirit, while the sense faculties of the flesh want to be led away by the smoothness of pleasures.[87] As a result of this, grace cheers the body exceedingly into unutterable exultation through the Sense of the intellect, in those who are progressing in perception. But the demons take the soul prisoner by force through the senses of the body, especially whenever

---

[85] Psalms 44:14.
[86] See Matthew 26:41.
[87] Romans 7:21ff.

ΔΙΑΔΟΧΟΥ

τῆς εὐσεβείας τρέχοντας, τὴν ψυχὴν αἰχμαλωτίζουσι βιαίως, αὐτὴν εἰς ἃ μὴ θέλει παρακαλοῦντες οἱ φόνιοι.

π'.

5 Οἱ λέγοντες ὁμοῦ τὰ δύο πρόσωπα τῆς τε χάριτος καὶ τῆς ἁμαρτίας ταῖς τῶν πιστῶν ἐμπαρεῖναι καρδίαις ἐκ τοῦ εἰρηκέναι τὸν εὐαγγελιστήν· Καὶ τὸ φῶς ἐν τῇ σκοτίᾳ φαίνει καὶ ἡ σκοτία αὐτὸ οὐ κατέλαβεν, συνίστασθαι τὴν ἑαυτῶν θέλουσιν ὑπόνοιαν λέγοντες μηδαμῶς τὴν θείαν λαμπρότητα ὑπὸ τῆς τοῦ πονηροῦ συνδιατριβῆς
10 μολύνεσθαι, κἂν ὁπωσοῦν πλησιάζοι, φησίν, ἐν τῇ ψυχῇ τὸ φῶς τὸ θεῖον τῇ σκοτίᾳ τοῦ δαίμονος. Ὑπὸ δὲ αὐτοῦ τοῦ εὐαγγελικοῦ ῥητοῦ ἔξω τῶν ἁγίων γραφῶν φρονοῦντες ἐλέγχονται. Ἐπειδὴ γὰρ ὁ λόγος τοῦ θεοῦ τὸ φῶς τὸ ἀληθινὸν τῇ ἑαυτοῦ ἐν σαρκὶ ἐπιφανῆναι κατηξίωσε κτίσει, ἀμέτρῳ φιλανθρωπίᾳ τὸ φῶς αὐτοῦ παρ' ἡμῖν ἀνάψας τῆς ἁγίας
15 γνώσεως, τὸ δὲ φρόνημα τοῦ κόσμου τὴν βουλὴν οὐ κατέλαβε τοῦ θεοῦ, τοῦτ' ἔστιν οὐκ ἔγνω, ἐπειδὴ τὸ φρόνημα τῆς σαρκὸς ἔχθρα εἰς θεόν· τούτου χάριν τοιούτῳ ὁ θεολόγος ἐχρήσατο ῥήματι· ἀμέλει ὀλίγα εἰρηκὼς μέσα ὁ θεσπέσιος ἐπάγει· Ἦν τὸ φῶς τὸ ἀληθινόν, ὃ φωτίζει πάντα ἄνθρωπον ἐρχόμενον εἰς τὸν κόσμον, ἀντὶ τοῦ ὁδηγεῖ καὶ
20 ζωοποιεῖ· ἐν τῷ κόσμῳ ἦν καὶ ὁ κόσμος δι' αὐτοῦ ἐγένετο καὶ ὁ κόσμος αὐτὸν οὐκ ἔγνω· εἰς τὰ ἴδια ἦλθε καὶ οἱ ἴδιοι αὐτὸν οὐ παρέλαβον· ὅσοι δὲ ἔλαβον αὐτόν, ἔδωκεν αὐτοῖς ἐξουσίαν τέκνα θεοῦ γενέσθαι τοῖς πιστεύουσιν εἰς τὸ ὄνομα αὐτοῦ. Λέγει δὲ καὶ ὁ σοφώτατος Παῦλος ἑρμηνεύων τὸ οὐ κατέλαβεν· Οὐχ ὅτι ἤδη ἔλαβον ἢ ἤδη τετελείωμαι,
25 διώκω δέ, εἰ καὶ καταλάβω, ἐφ' ᾧ καὶ κατελήφθην ὑπὸ Χριστοῦ Ἰησοῦ. Ὥστε οὐ τὸν Σατανᾶν λέγει ὁ εὐαγγελιστὴς μὴ κατειληφέναι τὸ φῶς τὸ ἀληθινόν· ἀπ' ἀρχῆς γὰρ ἀλλότριος αὐτοῦ ἐστιν, ἐπειδὴ οὐδὲ ἐν

2 θέλει] θέλῃ AB(R)S || 5 τε om. R || χάριτος] χάριτος τοῦ θεοῦ Aa || 8 τὴν MRTa: τῇ ABNS || ὑπόνοιαν MRTa: ὑπονοίᾳ ABNS || 10 ὁπωσοῦν BRST: ὅπως ἂν AMNa || φησίν, ἐν om. A || 12 γὰρ om. c || 13 ἑαυτοῦ] αὐτοῦ Mc || ἐν MNRST: om. ABac || κτίσει MNRST: τῇ κτίσει ABa || 14 ἀμέτρῳ] ἀμετρήτῳ AS || φιλανθρωπίᾳ BMT: φιλοτιμίᾳ ANRSa || παρ'] ἐν R || 15 φρόνημα] φρόνημα τῆς σαρκὸς A || βουλὴν] βουλὴν αὐτοῦ A || κατέλαβε] ἐκατελάμβανε c || 15-16 τοῦ - ἔγνω om. M || 16 τοῦτ' - ἔγνω om. c || θεόν] θεόν ἐστιν Aa || 17 ῥήματι] σχήματι BNRb || 18 ἐπάγει] ἐπάγει λέγων a || 24 οὐ κατέλαβεν] οὐκ ἔλαβεν R || 25 Ἰησοῦ om. a || 26 κατειληφέναι] καταληφθῆναι Mc || 27 οὐδὲ MRa: οὔτε ABNST.

108

they find us running the race of piety carelessly: murderers inviting the soul into those things it does not intend.

80. Those who say the two personas of grace and of sin co-exist in the hearts of the faithful, from what the Evangelist has said ('And the light shines in the darkness and the darkness did not apprehend it'[88]) are wanting to support a supposition of their own–saying that the divine splendour is in no way sullied by association with evil, no matter how close the divine light might come in the soul to the darkness of the devil (as it says). They are refuted by the evangelical statement itself as departing from holy Scripture in their thinking. For it was because the Logos of God deemed it fit that the true light be manifest to his own creation in flesh (when by immeasurable benevolence he struck up his light of holy perception in us) and the mentality of the world did not apprehend the purpose of God (that is did not perceive it, since 'the mentality of the flesh is inimical to God'[89]), that thanks to this the Divinely Conversant one used such a statement; the Inspired one added (saying a few things between of course), 'He was the true light, which, coming into the world, illuminates all mankind' (that is, guides and gives life) 'he was in the world and the world came into being through him and the world did not perceive him; he came to his own and his own did not receive him; but to those who received him, who believed in his name, he gave authority to become children of God.'[90] And the most wise Paul (interpreting 'did not apprehend'): 'Not that I have already received or am already made perfect, but I pursue this that I might apprehend it, because I have myself been apprehended by Jesus Christ.'[91] In the same way the Evangelist does not say it is Satan who was not apprehending the true light (for from the

---

[88] John 1:5.
[89] Romans 8:7.
[90] John 1:9-12.
[91] Philippians 3:12.

ΔΙΑΔΟΧΟΥ

αὐτῷ φαίνει· ἀλλὰ τοὺς ἀκούοντας μὲν ἀνθρώπους τὰς δυναστείας καὶ τὰ θαυμάσια τοῦ υἱοῦ τοῦ θεοῦ, μὴ θέλοντας δὲ προσεγγίσαι διὰ τὴν ἐσκοτισμένην αὐτῶν καρδίαν τῷ φωτὶ τῆς γνώσεως αὐτοῦ, διὰ τοῦ λόγου ἀξίως ἀτιμάζει.

πα΄.

Δύο ὥσπερ γένη εἶναι ὁ λόγος ἡμᾶς διδάσκει τῆς γνώσεως τῶν πονηρῶν πνευμάτων. Τὰ μὲν γὰρ αὐτῶν εἰσιν ὥσπερ λεπτότερα, τὰ δὲ ὑλωδέστερα. Τὰ οὖν λεπτότερα τῇ ψυχῇ πολεμεῖ, τὰ δὲ ἄλλα τὴν σάρκα διὰ λιπαρῶν τινων παρακλήσεων αἰχμαλωτίζειν εἴωθεν. Διόπερ ἐναντίως ἔχουσιν ἀεὶ πρὸς ἑαυτοὺς οἵ τε τῇ ψυχῇ προσπαλαίοντες δαίμονες καὶ οἱ τῷ σώματι κἂν εἰς τὸ βλάπτειν τοὺς ἀνθρώπους τὴν ἴσην ἔχωσι πρόθεσιν. Ὅτε οὖν ἡ χάρις οὐ κατοικεῖ εἰς τὸν ἄνθρωπον, εἰς τὰ βάθη τῆς καρδίας δίκην ὄντως ὄφεων ἐμφωλεύουσι, μὴ συγχωροῦντες ὅλως διαβλέψαι τὴν ψυχὴν πρὸς τὴν ἐπιθυμίαν τοῦ καλοῦ. Ὅτε δὲ εἰς τὸν νοῦν ἡ χάρις ἐγκέκρυπται, ὡσανεὶ νεφέλαι τινὲς ζοφώδεις λοιπὸν διὰ τῶν μερῶν τῆς καρδίας διατρέχουσιν εἰς τὰ πάθη τῆς ἁμαρτίας καὶ εἰς μετεωρισμοὺς ποικίλους σχηματιζόμενοι, ἵνα τὴν μνήμην μετεωρίζοντες τοῦ νοῦ τῆς πρὸς τὴν χάριν αὐτὸν ὁμιλίας ἀποσπῶσιν. Ὅτε τοίνυν ὑπὸ τῶν τῇ ψυχῇ διοχλούντων δαιμόνων εἰς τὰ ψυχικὰ ἐκπυρούμεθα πάθη καὶ μάλιστα εἰς τὴν οἴησιν, ἥτις ἐστὶ μήτηρ πάντων τῶν κακῶν, τὴν ἀνάλυσιν τοῦ σώματος ἡμῶν λογιζόμενοι τὸν ὄγκον μάλιστα τῆς φιλοδοξίας καταισχύνομεν. Τὸ αὐτὸ δὲ δεῖ ποιεῖν καὶ ὅταν οἱ τῷ σώματι προσπαλαίοντες δαίμονες εἰς αἰσχρὰς ἐπιθυμίας τὴν καρδίαν ἡμῶν ἀναζέειν παρασκευάζωσιν· αὕτη γὰρ μόνη ἡ ἐνθύμησις πάσας τὰς

1 φαίνει] φαίνεται Β ‖ μὲν om. Ra ‖ 2 τοῦ υἱοῦ om. AT ‖ 3 αὐτῶν om. R ‖ 8 εἰσιν] ἔστιν a ‖ 9 τὰ μὲν οὖν] τὰ μὲν οὖν, a ‖ τῇ ψυχῇ] τὴν ψυχὴν Tc ‖ πολεμεῖ] παρενοχλεῖ a ‖ 11 ἑαυτοὺς] αὐτοὺς a ‖ 12 τὸ om. A ‖ ἔχωσι ΒΤ: ἔχουσι AMNRSa ‖ 13 ὅτε] ὅταν R ‖ τὰ om. A ‖ 14 ὄντως om. Nb ‖ 16 ἐγκέκρυπται MNRST: ἐγκρύπτεται ABa ‖ ὡσανεὶ BNSp.c.a: ὡσὰν AMRSa.c.T ‖ λοιπὸν om. a ‖ διὰ om. Aa ‖ 17 πάθη] βάθη MTc ‖ καὶ] εἰ καὶ A(R) ἢ καὶ a ‖ 18-19 τὴν μνήμην . . . τοῦ νοῦ] τῇ μνήμῃ . . . τὸν νοῦν T ‖ 18 μετεωρίζοντες] μεγαλύνοντες A ‖ 19 τῆς πρὸς τὴν χάριν αὐτὸν] χάριν τῆς πρὸς αὐτοὺς R ‖ ὁμιλίας] ἀφήξεως Nb ‖ ὅτε] ὥστε MSa.c.c ‖ 20 διοχλούντων] διενοχλούντων Ba ‖ ψυχικὰ] φυσικὰ R ‖ ἐκπυρούμεθα] ἐκφερόμεθα B ‖ 22 ἡμῶν om. R ‖ μάλιστα] μᾶλλον B ‖ 23 φιλοδοξίας] κενοδοξίας ἡμῶν a ‖ 25 ἀναζέειν] ἀναζῆν a ‖ παρασκευάζωσιν BTa: παρασκευάζουσιν ANRS παρασκευάσωσιν c παρασκευάσουσιν M ‖ αὕτη] αὐτὴ B ‖ μόνη] μόνον A.

beginning he is alien to it, since it does not shine in him), but rather on this rationale he rightly disdains those who hear of the dominions and wonders of the Son of God, but do not want to draw near because their heart has been darkened to the light of his perception.

81. The rationale of perception teaches us that there are two kinds of evil spirits; for some of them are (as it were) more rarefied, but others are more material. Thus the more rarefied make war on the soul, while the others are wont to take the flesh captive through certain heady consolations. As a result those demons which wrestle with the soul and those which do so with the body always conduct themselves in opposite ways, even though they hold to the same purpose: that is, to thwart men. So when grace does not dwell in a person, the demons lurk in the depths of the heart, truly after the manner of serpents, not allowing the soul to look completely straight towards the desire for good. But when grace has hidden itself in the intellect, then the demons run through the parts of the heart like dark clouds, forming themselves into the passions of sin and various elations, so that elating the recollection of the intellect they might tear it away from relationship with grace. Accordingly when we are inflamed into the soul-type passions (and particularly into presumption, which is the mother of all ills) by the demons which crowd in on the soul, it is especially in considering the destruction of our body that we shame the pretension of affection for glory. One must do the same thing also whenever the demons wrestling with the body prepare to bring our heart to a boil in base desires; for this consideration by itself can make all the

ΔΙΑΔΟΧΟΥ

διαφορὰς τῶν πονηρῶν πνευμάτων καταργεῖν δύναται ἐν τῇ μνήμῃ τοῦ θεοῦ. Εἰ δὲ ἀπὸ ταύτης τῆς ἐνθυμήσεως ἐξουδένωσιν ἡμῖν ἄπειρον τῆς ἀνθρωπείας φύσεως οἱ ψυχικοὶ ὑποβάλλουσι δαίμονες ὡς οὐδενὸς οὔσης αὐτῆς ἀξίας διὰ τὴν σάρκα λόγου (τοῦτο γὰρ φιλοῦσι ποιεῖν ὅταν
5 αὐτούς τις βασανίσαι θέλῃ τῇ τοιαύτῃ ἐννοίᾳ), τὴν τῆς ἐπουρανίου λοιπὸν βασιλείας τιμήν τε καὶ δόξαν ἐνθυμώμεθα μήτε τὸ πικρὸν καὶ ζοφῶδες παρορῶντες τῆς κρίσεως, ἵνα τῷ μὲν τὴν ἀθυμίαν ἡμῶν παραμυθώμεθα, τῷ δὲ τὸ εὔκολον τῆς καρδίας ἡμῶν ἐπιστύφωμεν.

10 πβ'.

Ὁ κύριος ἐν τοῖς εὐαγγελίοις ἡμᾶς διδάσκει ὅτι, ὅταν ὑποστρέψας εὕρῃ σεσαρωμένον καὶ σχολάζοντα τὸν ἑαυτοῦ οἶκον, τοῦτ' ἔστιν τὴν ἄκαρπον καρδίαν, ὁ Σατανᾶς, τότε παραλαμβάνει ἕτερα ἑπτὰ πνεύματα καὶ εἰσέρχεται εἰς αὐτὴν καὶ ἐμφωλεύει χείρονα τῶν πρώτων τὰ τοῦ
15 ἀνθρώπου ἔσχατα ποιῶν. Ὅθεν δεῖ νοεῖν ὅτι, ἐφ' ὅσον ἐστὶ τὸ ἅγιον πνεῦμα ἐν ἡμῖν, οὐ δύναται εἰσελθὼν ὁ Σατανᾶς ἐν τῷ βάθει τῆς ψυχῆς καταμεῖναι, ἀλλὰ καὶ ὁ θεσπέσιος Παῦλος φανερῶς ταύτης ἡμᾶς διδάσκει τὸν νοῦν τῆς θεωρίας· ἐκ μὲν γὰρ τῆς ἀγωνιστικῆς γνώσεως θεωρήσας τὸ σχῆμα τῆς ὑποθέσεως, οὕτως λέγει· Συνήδομαι γὰρ τῷ
20 νόμῳ τοῦ θεοῦ κατὰ τὸν ἔσω ἄνθρωπον. Βλέπω δὲ ἕτερον νόμον ἐν τοῖς μέλεσί μου ἀντιστρατευόμενον τῷ νόμῳ τοῦ νοός μου καὶ αἰχμαλωτίζοντά με τῷ νόμῳ τῆς ἁμαρτίας τῷ ὄντι ἐν τοῖς μέλεσί μου· ἐκ δὲ τῆς τελειότητος· Οὐδὲν ἄρα νῦν, φησίν, κατάκριμα τοῖς ἐν Χριστῷ Ἰησοῦ· ὁ γὰρ νόμος τοῦ πνεύματος τῆς ζωῆς ἠλευθέρωσέ με

2 ἐνθυμήσεως MNa: ἐνθυμήσεως πάλιν ABST ἐπιθυμήσεως πάλιν R ‖ 3 ὡς om. R ‖ 5 βασανίσαι] βασανίσῃ S βαστάσαι A ‖ θέλῃ A: θέλει b θέλοι BMNTa om. RS ‖ τῇ] ἐν τῇ R om. B ‖ 6 λοιπὸν om. Sa ‖ ἐνθυμώμεθα BNTac: ἐνθυμούμεθα AM ἐνθυμεῖσθαι R ἐνθυμεῖσθαι δεῖ S ‖ πικρὸν] φρικτὸν R ‖ 7 ζοφῶδες] γνοφῶδες Aa ‖ 8 παραμυθώμεθα BRSTac: παραμυθούμεθα AMN ‖ εὔκολον] εὐήκοον Nb ‖ ἐπιστύφωμεν] ἐπιστρέφωμεν ARa ‖ 11 διδάσκει] διδάσκει λέγων a ‖ ὅτι om. a ‖ 12 εὕρῃ Aa: εὕροι BMN(R)ST ‖ σεσαρωμένον] σεσαρωμένον καὶ κεκοσμημένον a ‖ 13 ἕτερα om. c ‖ πνεύματα] πνεύματα πονηρότερα ἑαυτοῦ a ‖ 14 εἰσέρχεται ABT: εἰσέρχονται M ἔρχεται RS ἔρχονται N εἰσέλθοντα a ‖ εἰς αὐτὴν MNRST: εἰς αὐτὸν AB om. a ‖ καὶ ἐμφωλεύει] κατοικεῖ ἐκεῖ a ‖ 16 εἰσελθὼν] εἰσελθεῖν S ‖ 17 καταμεῖναι] καὶ καταμεῖναι S ‖ 17-18 ἡμᾶς διδάσκει] ἐκδιδάσκει a ‖ 19 οὕτως λέγει om. a ‖ γὰρ] φησὶ a ‖ 23 τελειότητος] τελειωτικῆς a ‖ νῦν om. a ‖ 24 Ἰησοῦ] Ἰησοῦ μὴ κατὰ σάρκα περιπατοῦσιν a.

categories of evil spirits ineffectual in the recollection of God. But if from this consideration the soul-type demons suggest to us a boundless contempt for human nature, as being of no value because of the flesh (for they like to do this whenever one decides to torture them with such thinking), let us then consider the value and glory of the heavenly kingdom, not overlooking the sharp and dark quality of the judgement: so that by the former we might relieve our dispiritedness, and by the latter we might reprove the contentedness of our heart.

82. The Lord teaches us in the gospels that whenever Satan in returning to his own house (that is the unfruitful heart) finds it swept and vacant, he takes seven other spirits and goes into it and lurks in it, making the last state of the man worse than the first.[92] And so one must observe that insofar as the holy Spirit is in us, Satan, entering into the depth of the soul, cannot remain. And the inspired Paul also clearly teaches us the meaning of this contemplation: contemplating the form of the hypothesis from contending perception he speaks thus: 'For I rejoice in the law of God according to the inner man. But I see another law in my members, fighting against the law of my intellect and taking me prisoner to the law of sin which is in my members';[93] but from perfection he says: 'But there is now no condemnation for those in Christ Jesus; for the law of the Spirit of life freed me from the law of sin and death.'[94] And he also says elsewhere

---

[92] Matthew 12:44ff.
[93] Romans 7:22f.
[94] Romans 8:1f.

ΔΙΑΔΟΧΟΥ

ἀπὸ τοῦ νόμου τῆς ἁμαρτίας καὶ τοῦ θανάτου. Λέγει δὲ καὶ ἀλλαχοῦ, ἵνα πάλιν διδάξῃ ἡμᾶς, ὅτι ἐκ τοῦ σώματος πολεμεῖ ὁ Σατανᾶς τὴν ψυχὴν τὴν μετέχουσαν τοῦ ἁγίου πνεύματος· Στῆτε οὖν περιζωσάμενοι τὴν ὀσφὺν ὑμῶν ἐν ἀληθείᾳ καὶ ἐνδυσάμενοι τὸν θώρακα τῆς
5 δικαιοσύνης καὶ ὑποδησάμενοι τοὺς πόδας ἐν ἑτοιμασίᾳ τοῦ εὐαγγελίου τῆς εἰρήνης, ἐπὶ πᾶσιν ἀναλαβόντες τὸν θυρεὸν τῆς πίστεως, ἐν ᾧ δυνήσεσθε πάντα τὰ βέλη τοῦ πονηροῦ τὰ πεπυρωμένα σβέσαι καὶ τὴν περικεφαλαίαν τοῦ σωτηρίου δέξασθαι καὶ τὴν μάχαιραν τοῦ πνεύματος, ὅ ἐστι ῥῆμα θεοῦ. Ἄλλο δέ τι αἰχμαλωτισμὸς καὶ ἄλλο πάλη· ἐπειδὴ
10 τὸ μὲν βιαίας ἀπαγωγῆς ἐστι σημαντικόν, τὸ δὲ ἰσοσθενοῦς τινος ἀγῶνος δηλωτικόν. Διόπερ ὅλως καὶ βέλεσι πεπυρωμένοις ταῖς χριστοφόροις ψυχαῖς ἐπέρχεσθαι λέγει ὁ ἀπόστολος τὸν διάβολον. Ὁ γὰρ μὴ ὢν ἐγκρατὴς τοῦ ἑαυτοῦ ἀνταγωνιστοῦ βέλεσι πάντως κατ' αὐτοῦ κέχρηται, ἵνα τὸν ἐκ μήκους αὐτῷ μαχόμενον τῷ πτερῷ δυνηθῇ
15 θηράσαι τῶν βελῶν· οὕτως καὶ ὁ Σατανᾶς, ἐπειδὴ οὐ δύναται διὰ τὴν παρουσίαν τῆς χάριτος ἐμφωλεῦσαι ὡς τὸ πρὶν τῷ τῶν ἀγωνιζομένων νοΐ, τῇ ὑγρότητι λοιπὸν ἐφίπταται καὶ ἐμφωλεύει τῷ σώματι, ἵνα διὰ τῆς αὐτοῦ εὐχερείας τὴν ψυχὴν δελεάζῃ· διόπερ δεῖ ἐκτήκειν αὐτὸ συμμέτρως, ἵνα μὴ διὰ τῆς αὐτοῦ ὑγρότητος ὀλισθαίνῃ ὁ νοῦς εἰς τὸ
20 λεῖον τῶν ἡδονῶν. Ὑπ' αὐτοῦ γὰρ τοῦ ἀποστολικοῦ ῥητοῦ προσήκει πείθεσθαι ὅτι ὁ μὲν νοῦς τῶν ἀγωνιζομένων ὑπὸ τοῦ θείου φωτὸς ἐνεργεῖται· διόπερ καὶ τῷ θείῳ νόμῳ δουλεύει καὶ συνήδεται. Ἡ δὲ σὰρξ τὰ πονηρὰ ἥδιον διὰ τὴν ἑαυτῆς εὐχέρειαν προσίεται πνεύματα· διόπερ τῇ αὐτῶν ποτε ἐξέλκεται δουλεύειν πονηρίᾳ. Ὅθεν μάλιστα
25 φαίνεται μὴ εἶναι κοινόν τι κατοικητήριον τὸν νοῦν θεοῦ τε καὶ

2 διδάξῃ] διδάξει NTb ‖ 4 ὑμῶν] ἡμῶν Nb ‖ 5 ὑποδησάμενοι] ὑποδυσάμενοι a ‖ 7 δυνήσεσθε] δύνασθαι A ‖ 9 τι] ἐστιν BST ‖ 10 ἀπαγωγῆς] τινος ἀπαγωγῆς a ‖ σημαντικόν om. a ‖ τινος om. ac ‖ 11 ἀγῶνος om. R ‖ ὅλως om. a ‖ 12 ἐπέρχεσθαι om. a ‖ 13 ἑαυτοῦ AMRSa: αὐτοῦ BNT ‖ 14 αὐτῷ] αὐτὸν R ‖ πτερῷ] πτερῷ καταβαλεῖν B ‖ 15 καὶ] οὖν καὶ BRS ‖ 16 παρουσίαν τῆς χάριτος] παροῦσαν τῆς χάριτος δύναμιν Aa ‖ ὡς τὸ] ὡς τῷ c ὡς S ‖ τῷ] ἐν τῷ R ‖ 18 δελεάζῃ a: δελεάζει A δελεάζοι BMN(R)ST ‖ ἐκτήκειν] ἐκτήκειν μὲν a ‖ αὐτὸ BM(R)STa: αυτῷ ANc ‖ 20 ὑπ'] ἀπ' ARST ‖ 21 πείθεσθαι] νοεῖν καὶ πείθεσθαι a ‖ 23 ἥδιον N: ἡδέως RST ἥδεται AB ἥδεται καὶ Μa ‖ ἑαυτῆς AMNS: αὐτῆς BTa ‖ εὐχέρειαν] εὐχέρειαν καὶ AB ‖ 24 διόπερ] διόπερ καὶ a ‖ ποτε om. A ‖ ἐξέλκεται] ἐφέλκεται A ‖ δουλεύειν πονηρίᾳ] δουλεία A ‖ 25 τι om. ASa ‖ τε καὶ] καὶ τοῦ Aa φημι καὶ RS.

(in order to teach us again that Satan wages war from the body against the soul which participates in the holy Spirit): 'Stand therefore, girded at the waist with truth and clothed with the breastplate of righteousness and feet shod in preparation of the good news of peace; as well as all these, taking up the shield of faith, by which you will be able to extinguish all the flaming arrows of the evil one; and receive the helmet of salvation and the sword of the Spirit, which is the utterance of God.'[95] Captivity is one thing and fighting is another; for the one signifies being led away by force whereas the other indicates a contest of equal strength. It is for just this reason that the Apostle says that the devil attacks Christ-bearing souls with fiery arrows. For whoever does not have control of his adversary always uses arrows against him, in order to be able to catch the one who fights against him from a distance by the flight of arrows. This is what Satan also does, since he cannot lurk as before in the intellect of those who contend, because of the presence of grace; he then flies at the body and lurks in it by means of its malleability, in order to bait the soul through the body's pliancy. This is why one must thin the body down in moderation, lest through its malleability the intellect should slip into the smoothness of pleasures. It is proper to be persuaded by this apostolic statement that the intellect of those who contend is activated by divine light; for this reason one both serves the divine law and rejoices.[96] But the flesh gladly admits evil spirits through its own pliancy, and so it is sometimes dragged away to serve their evil. For this reason especially it is evident that the intellect is not the common dwelling-place of God and of the devil, for how is it that

---

[95] Ephesians 6:14-17.
[96] Romans 7:22.

ΔΙΑΔΟΧΟΥ

διαβόλου· ἐπεὶ πῶς τῷ μὲν νοΐ μου δουλεύω νόμῳ θεοῦ, τῇ δὲ σαρκὶ νόμῳ ἁμαρτίας, εἰ μὴ ὁ μὲν νοῦς μου ἐν πάσῃ ἐλευθερίᾳ πρὸς μάχην ἵστατο τῶν δαιμόνων τῇ χρηστότητι τῆς χάριτος ἡδέως δουλούμενος, τὸ δὲ σῶμα ἥδιον τὴν ὀσμὴν προσίεται τῶν ἀλόγων ἡδονῶν; διὰ τὸ ἐν
5 αὐτῷ, ὡς ἔφην, παραχωρεῖσθαι ἐμφωλεύειν ἐπὶ τῶν ἀγωνιζομένων τὰ πονηρὰ τῆς ἀπάτης πνεύματα· Οἶδα γάρ, φησίν, ὅτι οὐκ οἰκεῖ ἐν ἐμοί, τοῦτ᾿ ἔστιν ἐν τῇ σαρκί μου, ἀγαθόν· ὥστε ἐπὶ τῶν κατὰ μέσον τινὰ ἀγῶνα ἀνθισταμένων τῇ ἁμαρτίᾳ. Οὐ γὰρ ἐξ ἑαυτοῦ τοῦτο ὁ ἀπόστολος λέγει· τῷ μὲν νοΐ μάχονται οἱ δαίμονες, τὴν δὲ σάρκα λιπαραῖς
10 ὑπεκλύειν πρὸς τὸ λεῖον τῶν ἡδονῶν ἐπιχειροῦσι παρακλήσεσιν. Παραχωροῦνται γὰρ ἅπαξ κατὰ δίκαιον κρίμα ἐνδιατρίβειν περὶ τὰ βάθη τοῦ σώματος καὶ ἐπὶ τῶν συντόνως ἀγωνιζομένων κατὰ τῆς ἁμαρτίας διὰ τὸ ὑπὸ δοκιμὴν εἶναι ἀεὶ τὸ αὐτεξούσιον τοῦ ἀνθρωπίνου φρονήματος. Εἰ δέ τις δυνηθείη ζῶν ἔτι διὰ τῶν πόνων ἀποθανεῖν, ὅλος λοιπὸν
15 γίνεται οἶκος τοῦ ἁγίου πνεύματος· πρὶν γὰρ ἀποθάνῃ ὁ τοιοῦτος, ἀνέστη, ὥσπερ ἦν αὐτὸς ὁ μακάριος Παῦλος καὶ ὅσοι τελείως ἠγωνίσαντο καὶ ἀγωνίζονται κατὰ τῆς ἁμαρτίας.

πγ'.

20 Φέρει μὲν ἡ καρδία καὶ ἐξ ἑαυτῆς λογισμοὺς καλούς τε καὶ οὐ καλούς, οὐ φύσει δὲ καρποφοροῦσα τὰς μὴ καλὰς ἐννοίας, ἀλλ᾿ ὥσπερ εἰς ἕξιν ἔχουσα διὰ τὴν πρώτην ἅπαξ ἀπάτην τὴν μνήμην τοῦ μὴ καλοῦ· τοὺς δὲ πλείστους καὶ πονηροὺς ἐκ τῆς τῶν δαιμόνων συλλαμβάνει πικρίας. Πάντων δὲ ἡμεῖς ὡς ἐκ τῆς καρδίας προϊόντων

---

1 μου om. MTc || 2 μου om. M || 3 δουλούμενος] δεδουλωμένος c || 4 ἥδιον BNRSTa: ἴδιον Mb ἡδεῖαν Ac || προσίεται] προσίετο A προΐεται M || 5 αὐτῷ] αὐτὴ a || 6 ἐμοί] ἐμοὶ ἀγαθόν A ἐμοὶ τὸ ἀγαθόν a || 7 ἀγαθόν om. Aa || τῶν] τὸν B || κατὰ] κατὰ τὸ a om. B || 7-8 μέσον τινὰ ἀγῶνα BMNR: μέσον τὸν ἀγῶνα A μέσον τῶν ἀγώνων a μέσον τινὰ τὸν ἀγῶνα T μέσον ἀγώνων S || 8 ἀνθισταμένων] τῶν ἀνθισταμένων B || ἑαυτοῦ ABMRa: αὐτοῦ NST || 9 μὲν om. A || λιπαραῖς] λιπαραῖς τισι a om. B || 10 ὑπεκλύειν] ὑπεκλύουσιν R || ἐπιχειροῦσι] σπουδάζουσι a || 11 κατὰ BNRST: κατὰ τὸ AMa || περὶ] κατὰ RS παρὰ T || βάθη] πάθη c || 13 δοκιμὴν] δίκην N || ἀεὶ om. a || ἀνθρωπίνου] ἀνθρωπείου A || 14 δυνηθείη BRa: δυνηθῇ ANTc δυνηθεῖ MSb || ἀποθανεῖν] ἀποθνήσκειν A || 15 οἶκος] ὁ τοιοῦτος οἰκητήριον a || ἀποθάνῃ AB(R)STa: ἀποθάνει MN || 16 ἀνέστη] εἰ δὲ ἀνέστη R || ὥσπερ ABNR: ὅπερ MSTa || 17 καὶ BMNR: ἢ καὶ AT ἢ S om. a || ἀγωνίζονται om. a || 20-21 οὐ καλούς] κακούς B || 21 καλὰς] ἀγαθὰς Aa || 22 ἔχουσα MNRS: ἐλθοῦσα ABTa || τὴν μνήμην MNRS: τῆς μνήμης ABTa.

'in my intellect I serve the law of God, but in flesh the law of sin,'[97] unless my intellect stands in complete freedom for the fight of the demons, gladly serving the excellence of grace, while the body gladly accepts the odour of irrational pleasures? Because as I said, it is granted to the evil spirits of deception to lurk in the body of those who contend: 'for I know,' it says, 'that what is good does not dwell in me, that is in my flesh'[98] (this is with respect to those who resist sin in the midst of combat). And the apostle does not say this from himself: the demons fight in the intellect, but they attempt to weaken the flesh gradually towards the smoothness of the pleasures by louche consolations. They are simply granted (according to a just judgement) to loiter around the depths of the body, even in those who contend earnestly against sin, because the independence of the human mentality is always under test. But if someone were able, still living, to die through labours, he would then become a complete home of the holy Spirit; for before such a one dies, he has risen, just as the blessed Paul himself, and as many as perfectly contended and do contend against sin.

83. The heart carries out of itself both good imaginings and those which are not good–not producing by nature intellectual conceptions which are not good, but having as a habit the recollection of what is not good, once and for all, because of the primal deception. It is rather from the bitterness of the demons that the heart conceives most (and evil) imaginings; but we sense all the things which are produced as being from the heart, and

---

[97] Romans 7:25.
[98] Romans 7:18.

ΔΙΑΔΟΧΟΥ

αἰσθανόμεθα· καὶ διὰ τοῦτό τινες ὑπενόησαν εἰς τὸν νοῦν εἶναι σὺν τῇ χάριτι καὶ τὴν ἁμαρτίαν. Διόπερ λέγουσι καὶ τὸν κύριον εἰρηκέναι· Τὰ δὲ ἐξερχόμενα ἐκ τοῦ στόματος ἐκ τῆς καρδίας ἐξέρχεται κἀκεῖνα κοινοῖ τὸν ἄνθρωπον· ἐκ γὰρ τῆς καρδίας ἐξέρχονται διαλογισμοὶ πονηροί,
5 μοιχεῖαι καὶ τὰ ἑξῆς. Οὐκ ἴσασι δὲ ὅτι ὁ νοῦς ἡμῶν λεπτοτάτης τινὸς αἰσθήσεως ἔχων ἐνέργειαν αὐτῶν τῶν ὑπὸ τῶν πονηρῶν πνευμάτων ὑποβαλλομένων αὐτῷ λογισμῶν οἰκειοῦται ὥσπερ διὰ τῆς σαρκὸς τὴν ἐνέργειαν, τῆς εὐχερείας τοῦ σώματος πλέον εἰς τοῦτο φερούσης διὰ τῆς συγκράσεως τὴν ψυχήν, ὡς οὐκ οἴδαμεν. Ἐπειδὴ ἀμέτρως φιλεῖ ἀεὶ ἡ
10 σὰρξ τὸ ὑπὸ τῆς ἀπάτης κολακεύεσθαι, καὶ διὰ τοῦτο ἐκ τῆς καρδίας καὶ οἱ ἐκ τῶν δαιμόνων ἐνσπειρόμενοι τῇ ψυχῇ λογισμοὶ ἐξερχόμενοι φαίνονται· ἰδιοποιούμεθα δὲ αὐτοὺς ὄντως, ὅταν αὐτοῖς συνήδεσθαι θέλωμεν. Ὅπερ ὁ κύριος μεμφόμενος, ὡς αὐτὸ τὸ θεῖον δηλοῖ λόγιον, τῷ προειρημένῳ ῥητῷ ἐχρήσατο. Ὁ γὰρ συνηδόμενος τοῖς ἐκ τῆς
15 πονηρίας τοῦ Σατανᾶ αὐτῷ ὑποβαλλομένοις λογισμοῖς καὶ τὴν μνήμην αὐτῶν ὥσπερ ἐγγράφων τῇ ἑαυτοῦ καρδίᾳ, οὐκ ἄδηλον ὅτι ἐκ τῆς ἑαυτοῦ αὐτοὺς λοιπὸν καρποφορεῖ ἐννοίας.

πδ´.

20 Λέγει ἐν τοῖς εὐαγγελίοις ὁ κύριος μὴ δύνασθαι ἐκβληθῆναι τὸν ἰσχυρὸν ἐκ τοῦ οἴκου αὐτοῦ, ἐὰν μὴ ὁ ἰσχυρότερος αὐτοῦ δήσας αὐτὸν καὶ σκυλεύσας ἐκβάλῃ. Πῶς οὖν δύναται ὁ μετὰ τοσαύτης αἰσχύνης ἐκβαλλόμενος πάλιν εἰσιέναι καὶ τῷ ἀληθινῷ συνδιατρίβειν οἰκοδεσπότῃ ἐν τῷ ἑαυτοῦ, ὡς ἐὰν καὶ θέλοι, ἀναπαυομένῳ οἴκῳ; Οὔτε γὰρ βασιλεὺς
25 τὸν ἀντιστάντα αὐτῷ ποτε καταγωνισάμενος τύραννον συμπαρεῖναι αὐτῷ τοῦτον ἐν ταῖς βασιλικαῖς αὐλαῖς ἐνθυμηθήσεται· ἀποσφάξει δὲ μᾶλλον εὐθέως ἢ δήσας πρὸς μακρὰν τιμωρίαν καὶ θάνατον οἴκτιστον παραδώσει τοῖς ἰδίοις στρατεύμασιν.

1 αἰσθανόμεθα] αἰσθανώμεθα M αἰσθόμεθα ARb ‖ εἶναι σὺν] συνεῖναι a ‖ 3-4 ἐξέρχεται - καρδίας om. R ‖ 3 ἐξέρχεται BN: ἐξέρχονται AMST ἐκπορεύονται a ‖ 5 μοιχεῖαι] μοιχεῖαι πλεονεξίαι Nb μοιχεῖαι πορνεῖαι T ‖ 9 ἀεὶ om. AS ‖ 10 τὸ om. R ‖ pr. καὶ om. a ‖ 16 τῇ] ἐν τῇ AT ‖ οὐκ ἄδηλον] δῆλον Nb ‖ 17 λοιπὸν om. M ‖ καρποφορεῖ] κρατεῖ A ‖ ἐννοίας] διανοίας RSa ‖ 20 ὁ κύριος om. M ‖ 21 ἰσχυρότερος αὐτοῦ] ἰσχυρὸς Nb ‖ 24 ἑαυτοῦ] αὐτοῦ BTa ‖ ὡς - ἀναπαυομένῳ om. a ‖ ἐὰν] ἂν BS ‖ ἀναπαυομένῳ] ἀναπαυόμενος NT ‖ 25 ἀντιστάντα] ἀνθιστάμενον Mc ‖ 26 αὐλαις R: om. ceteri ‖ 27 μακρὰν] μακρὰν τὴν M μακράν τινα T ‖ 28 στρατεύμασιν om. B.

because of this some supposed sin to be in the intellect together with grace. They say it was for this reason that the Lord also said: 'the things which come out of the mouth come out of the heart, these things defile man; for evil considerations come out of the heart, adulteries' etc.[99] But they don't know that our intellect (having the activity of a most refined Sense) appropriates, as it were through the flesh, the activity of the very imaginings which are insinuated into it by the evil spirits–the pliancy of the body rather carrying the soul into this (because of their blending), in a way we do not know. For the flesh always likes to be flattered immoderately by deception, and because of this even those imaginings sown in the soul by demons appear to come out of the heart; but we make them truly our own, whenever we decide to be gratified by them. It was this very thing the Lord censured (as the divine saying itself indicates) when he used the aforementioned statement. For whoever is gratified by the imaginings which are insinuated into him from the evil of Satan and as it were engraves the recollection of them on his own heart, clearly then bears their fruit from his own intellectual conception.

84. The Lord says in the Gospels[100] that the strong man is not able to be thrown out of his house, unless someone who is stronger than he is casts him out, binding and stripping him. And then how can he who has been thrown out with such a disgrace, even if he wanted to, enter in again and live constantly with the true ruler of the house, who resides in his own house? For when a king has contended against a tyrant who has rebelled against him, he will not consider living with him in the royal halls; he will rather immediately cut his throat, or binding him deliver him to his own soldiers for a long retribution and a most lamentable death.

---

[99] Matthew 15:18f.
[100] Matthew 12:29.

ΔΙΑΔΟΧΟΥ

πε'.

Εἴ τις διὰ τὸ καλὰ ἡμᾶς ὁμοῦ καὶ φαῦλα λογίζεσθαι ὁμοῦ τό τε ἅγιον πνεῦμα καὶ τὸν διάβολον ἐνοικεῖν ἐν τῷ νοῒ ὑπολαμβάνει, μανθανέτω ὅτι τοῦτο γίνεται διὰ τὸ μηδέπω ἡμᾶς γεγεῦσθαι καὶ
5 ἑωρακέναι ὅτι χρηστὸς ὁ κύριος. Πρῶτον μὲν γάρ, ὡς καὶ ἀνωτέρω ἔφην, κρύπτει τὴν ἑαυτῆς παρουσίαν ἐπὶ τῶν βαπτιζομένων ἡ χάρις, ἐκδεχομένη τὴν τῆς ψυχῆς πρόθεσιν· ἐπειδὰν δὲ ὅλος ἐπιστρέψῃ ὁ ἄνθρωπος πρὸς τὸν κύριον, τότε ἀρρήτῳ τινὶ αἰσθήσει τὴν παρουσίαν αὐτῆς ἐμφαίνει τῇ καρδίᾳ καὶ πάλιν ἐκδέχεται τὴν τῆς ψυχῆς κίνησιν,
10 παραχωροῦσα μέντοι τὰ δαιμονικὰ βέλη ἄχρι τῆς βαθείας αὐτῆς καταφθάνειν αἰσθήσεως, ἵνα θερμοτέρᾳ προθέσει καὶ ταπεινῇ διαθέσει ἐκζητήσῃ τὸν θεόν. Ἐὰν οὖν λοιπὸν ἄρξηται προβαίνειν ὁ ἄνθρωπος τῇ τηρήσει τῶν ἐντολῶν καὶ ἀπαύστως ἐπικαλοῖτο τὸν κύριον, τότε καὶ ἐπὶ τὰ ἐξώτερα αἰσθητήρια τῆς καρδίας τὸ πῦρ τῆς ἁγίας ἐπινέμεται
15 χάριτος τὰ ζιζάνια τῆς ἀνθρωπείας γῆς πληροφορητικῶς καταφλέγουσα· ὅθεν καὶ αἱ δαιμονικαὶ βουλαὶ πόρρω που ἐκείνων τότε καταφθάνουσι τῶν τόπων ἠρέμα λοιπὸν νύττουσαι τὸ ἐμπαθὲς τῆς ψυχῆς. Ὅτε δὴ πάσας τὰς ἀρετὰς ὁ τοῦ ἀγῶνος ἐγκομβώσοιτο ἄνθρωπος καὶ μάλιστα τὴν τελείαν ἀκτημοσύνην, τότε τὴν πᾶσαν αὐτοῦ βαθυτέρᾳ τινὶ αἰσθήσει
20 περιαυγάζει φύσιν εἰς ἀγάπην αὐτὸν λοιπὸν πολλὴν περιθάλπουσα τοῦ θεοῦ. Διόπερ ἐξωτέρω τῆς τοῦ σώματος αἰσθήσεως τότε τὰ δαιμονικὰ ἀποσβέννυται τόξα. Ἡ γὰρ αὔρα τοῦ ἁγίου πνεύματος πρὸς ἀνέμους εἰρήνης κινοῦσα τὴν καρδίαν τὰ τοῦ πυρφόρου δαίμονος εἰς ἀέρα ἔτι φερόμενα κατασβέννυσι βέλη. Πλὴν καὶ τὸν εἰς τοῦτο τὸ μέτρον

---

2 pr. τὸ] τὸ τὰ c || pr. ὁμοῦ om. Nb || alt. ὁμοῦ BNRST: om. AMa || τό τε] τε τὸ BS || 3 ἐν om. Aa || ὑπολαμβάνει A(R)STa: ὑπολαμβάνοι BMN || 4 ὅτι] ὁ τοιοῦτος ὅτι a || μηδέπω] οὕτω a || γεγεῦσθαι] γεύσασθαι R γεύσασθαι ἢ B || 5 χρηστὸς MN: χριστὸς ABRSTa || 6 ἑαυτῆς] ἑαυτοῦ b om. A || 7 ὅλος ABac: ὅλως MN(R)ST || 8 τὸν om. a || 9 τῆς ψυχῆς] αὐτῆς a || 10 τῆς om. a || 11 θερμοτέρᾳ] θερμοτέρα τῇ Sa || καὶ - διαθέσει om. N || 12 ἐκζητήσῃ BNSc: ἐκζητήσει AM(R)Tb ἐκζητῇ a || ἐὰν] ὅταν A || τῇ] ἐν τῇ M ἐν a || 13 ἐπικαλοῖτο] ἐπκαλεῖτο A || κύριον BR: κύριον Ἰησοῦν ceteri || 14 ἐξώτερα αἰσθητήρια] ἔξω τῶν αἰσθητηρίων a || 15 ἀνθρωπείας] ἀνθρωπίνης a || 16 βουλαὶ] ἐπιβουλαὶ a || 17 λοιπὸν om. a || ψυχῆς] ψυχῆς μέρος a || ὅτε] ὅταν a || δὴ N(R): δεῖ b δὲ ABMSTa om. c || 19 τότε] τότε γὰρ c || τὴν om. M || πᾶσαν] ἅπασαν Mc || 21 διόπερ] ὅθεν Aa || 22 ἀποσβέννυται] ἀποσβέννυνται A || 23 εἰρήνης] εἰρηνικοὺς B || 23-24 ἔτι φερόμενα] ἐπιφερόμενα Nb.

85. If anyone assumes that because we consider both good things and foul things at one and the same time, therefore the holy Spirit and the devil dwell together in the intellect, let him understand that this comes about because we have not yet tasted and seen that the Lord is good.[101] For (as I said above) grace first hides its presence in the baptised, awaiting the purpose of the soul; but whenever the whole man returns to the Lord, then grace shows its presence to the heart with an inexpressible sensation and again awaits the movement of the soul–allowing the demonic arrows to fall unawares as far as its most profound Sense, so that the soul might seek God with a more ardent purpose and a humble disposition. So if that man then begins to advance in the keeping of the commandments, and calls upon the Lord unceasingly, the fire of holy grace also encroaches upon the outer sense faculties of the heart, entirely burning down the weeds of human soil; as a result the demonic schemes fall unawares beyond these places, and then prick the impassioned part of the soul slightly. Indeed when the man who contends binds on himself all the virtues (and especially perfect poverty) then grace kindles his whole nature with a more profound sensation, warming him exceedingly into great love of God. And so the demonic bowshots are then extinguished outside the Sense of the body; for the breeze of the holy Spirit, moving the heart into winds of peace, extinguishes the arrows of the fire-bearing demon while still in mid-air. But God sometimes abandons to the wickedness of the demons

---

[101] Psalms 33:9.

ΔΙΑΔΟΧΟΥ

φθάσαντα παραχωρεῖ ποτε τῇ κακίᾳ τῶν δαιμόνων ὁ θεὸς ἀφώτιστον αὐτοῦ τότε τὸν νοῦν καταλιμπάνων, ἵνα τὸ αὐτεξούσιον ἡμῶν εἰς τὸ πᾶν μὴ ᾖ δεδεμένον τῷ δεσμῷ τῆς χάριτος οὐ μόνον διὰ τὸ ἐξ ἀγώνων ἡττηθῆναι τὴν ἁμαρτίαν, ἀλλὰ καὶ διὰ τὸ ὀφείλειν ἔτι προκόπτειν εἰς
5 τὴν πνευματικὴν πεῖραν τὸν ἄνθρωπον. Τὸ γὰρ τοῦ παιδευομένου νομιζόμενον τέλειον ἀτελὲς ἔτι ὡς πρὸς τὸν πλοῦτον τῆς τοῦ παιδεύοντος ἡμᾶς θεοῦ ἐν ἀγάπῃ ὑπάρχει φιλοτιμίας, κἂν ὅλην τὴν τῷ Ἰακὼβ δειχθεῖσαν κλίμακα ἀνελθεῖν τις δυνηθῇ τῇ προκοπῇ τῶν πόνων.

10 πϛ'.
Ὁ κύριος αὐτὸς λέγει τὸν Σατανᾶν ἐκ τῶν οὐρανῶν ὡς ἀστραπὴν πεπτωκέναι, ἵνα μήτε ἀφορᾷ εἰς τὰ τῶν ἁγίων ἀγγέλων ὁ δυσειδὴς ἐνδιαιτήματα. Πῶς οὖν ὁ τῆς τῶν καλῶν δούλων κοινωνίας μὴ καταξιούμενος κοινὸν δύναται ἔχειν μετὰ τοῦ θεοῦ οἰκητήριον τὸν
15 ἀνθρώπινον νοῦν; Ἀλλ' εἰ κατεροῦσιν ὅτι κατὰ παραχώρησιν τοῦτο γίνεται, πλέον οὐδὲν λέξουσιν. Ἡ μὲν γὰρ παιδευτικὴ παραχώρησις οὐδαμῶς τὴν ψυχὴν τοῦ θείου φωτὸς ἀποστερεῖ· κρύπτει δὲ μόνον, ὡς καὶ ἤδη εἶπον, τὰ πολλὰ τὸν νοῦν τὴν ἑαυτῆς παρουσίαν ἡ χάρις, ἵνα προωθοῖτο ὥσπερ τὴν ψυχὴν τῇ πικρίᾳ τῶν δαιμόνων διὰ τὸ μετὰ
20 παντὸς φόβου καὶ πολλῆς ταπεινώσεως ἐκζητεῖν αὐτὴν τὴν ἐκ τοῦ θεοῦ βοήθειαν, τὴν τοῦ ἐχθροῦ αὐτῆς ἐπιγινώσκουσαν κατ' ὀλίγον κακίαν, ὃν τρόπον ἂν μήτηρ ἀτακτοῦν τὸ οἰκεῖον περὶ τοὺς θεσμοὺς τῆς γαλουχίας βρέφος βραχὺ τῶν ἑαυτῆς ἐξωθοίη ἀγκαλῶν, ἵνα καταπληττόμενον ὑπό τινων περιεστώτων αὐτὸ σαπροειδῶν ἀνθρώπων ἢ θηρίων οἰωνδήποτε
25 μετὰ φόβου πολλοῦ καὶ δακρύων εἰς τοὺς μητρῴους ἀνθυποστρέφοι

1 παραχωρεῖ] παρεχώρει A || 2 τότε om. Ra || πᾶν] παντελὲς a || 3 ᾖ] εἴη a || δεδεμένον] δεδομένον Ma || ἀγώνων] ἀγῶνος BR || 4 ἡττηθῆναι] νικηθῆναι Nb || διὰ om. a || προκόπτειν] προσκόπτειν a || 5 τὸ γὰρ τοῦ] τότε γὰρ τοῦ a τότε γὰρ τὸ τοῦ AR || 6 ἔτι] ἐστιν BNb || τῆς τοῦ R: τοῦ ceteri || 7 ἡμᾶς om. MTc || ἀγάπῃ] ἀγάπης a || φιλοτιμίας] φιλοτιμία a φιλοτιμία Nb || 8 δυνηθῇ] δυνηθείη a || προκοπῇ] προσθήκῃ a || 12 μήτε] μὴ ST || 13 ὁ τῆς τῶν καλῶν om. R || τῶν om. a || δούλων om. Nb || 15 εἰ κατεροῦσιν R: ἐροῦσιν ceteri || παραχώρησιν] παραχώρησιν τοῦ θεοῦ M || 19 προωθοῖτο] προωθοῖ R || 20 τὴν ἐκ τοῦ θεοῦ] τὸν θεὸν καὶ τὴν ἐξ αὐτοῦ a || 21 τοῦ ἐχθροῦ] τῶν ἐχθρῶν a || ἐπιγινώσκουσαν] ἐπιγινώσκουσα Aa || κατ' ὀλίγον] κατὰ μικρὸν Aa || 22 ἂν ARSTa: ἐὰν BMN || 23 βραχὺ] βραχύ τι a || 24 περιεστώτων] παρεστώτων T || αὐτὸ MN: αὐτῇ ARSa αὐτῷ B om. T || 25 ἀνθυποστρέφοι AB(R)S: ἀνθυποστρέφῃ Tc ἀνθυποστρέφει MNa.

even someone who is already at this stage, leaving his intellect unilluminated, so that our independence in everything might not be shackled by chains of grace; not only because sin is overcome by contests, but also because man ought to advance further into spiritual testing. For what is thought perfect in one being trained is still imperfect in comparison with the abundance of ambition of the God who trains us in love–even if someone were able, by a progression of labours, to scale the whole ladder which was shown to Jacob.[102]

86. The Lord himself says that Satan fell from the heavens like a flash of lightning,[103] so that he who is malformed might not look straight into the dwelling-places of the holy angels. So how can he who is not deemed worthy of the common life of the good servants have the human intellect as a habitation together with God? But if they counter that this comes about under the terms of being abandoned they will not be making any better sense. In fact the abandonment which pertains to training in no way deprives the soul of the divine light; grace only hides its presence from the intellect in most cases (as I have already said) so that it might as it were urge the soul on in the bitterness of the demons–because it seeks the help which is from God with complete fear and great humility, recognising the evil of its Enemy little by little. In this way a mother might for a short time push away from her arms her own infant who was uncooperative about the proper manner of feeding, so that (terrified by some foul-looking men standing around it, or by any sort of beasts) it might turn round into the

---

[102] Genesis 28:12.
[103] Luke 10:18.

ΔΙΑΔΟΧΟΥ

κόλπους. Ἡ δὲ κατὰ ἀποστροφὴν γινομένη παραχώρησις ὡσανεὶ δέσμιον παραδίδωσι τὴν μὴ θέλουσαν ἔχειν ψυχὴν τὸν θεὸν τοῖς δαίμοσιν. Ἡμεῖς δὲ οὐκ ἐσμὲν ὑποστολῆς τέκνα, μὴ γένοιτο, ἀλλὰ βρέφη γνήσια τῆς τοῦ θεοῦ εἶναι χάριτος πιστεύομεν μικραῖς παραχωρήσεσι καὶ
5 πυκναῖς παρακλήσεσιν παρ' αὐτῆς γαλουχούμενα, ἵνα διὰ τῆς χρηστότητος αὐτῆς φθάσωμεν ἐλθεῖν εἰς ἄνδρα τέλειον εἰς μέτρον ἡλικίας.

πζ'.

10 Ἡ παιδευτικὴ παραχώρησις φέρει μὲν λύπην πολλὴν καὶ ταπείνωσιν καὶ ἀπελπισμὸν δὲ σύμμετρον τῇ ψυχῇ, ἵνα τὸ φιλόδοξον αὐτῆς καὶ εὐπτόητον μέρος πρεπόντως εἰς ταπείνωσιν ἔρχηται· εὐθέως δὲ φόβον θεοῦ καὶ δάκρυον ἐξομολογήσεως ἐπάγει τῇ καρδίᾳ καὶ τῆς καλλίστης σιωπῆς πολλὴν ἐπιθυμίαν. Ἡ δὲ κατὰ ἀποστροφὴν τοῦ θεοῦ γινομένη
15 ἀπελπισμοῦ ὁμοῦ καὶ ἀπιστίας καὶ ὀργῆς καὶ τύφου τὴν ψυχὴν πληρωθῆναι παραχωρεῖ. Δεῖ οὖν ἡμᾶς εἰδότας τὴν πεῖραν τῶν ἀμφοτέρων παραχωρήσεων καὶ κατὰ τὸν ἑκάστης τρόπον προσιέναι τῷ θεῷ. Ἐκεῖ μὲν γὰρ εὐχαριστίαν μετὰ τῆς ἀπολογίας προσάγειν αὐτῷ ὀφείλομεν ὡς τὸ τῆς γνώμης ἡμῶν ἀκόλαστον τῇ σχολῇ τῆς
20 παρακλήσεως κολάζοντι, ἵνα ἀρετῆς ἡμᾶς καὶ κακίας ὡς πατὴρ ἀγαθὸς διδάσκοι τὴν διαφοράν· ἐνταῦθα δὲ ἐξαγόρευσιν τῶν ἁμαρτημάτων ἄπαυστον καὶ δάκρυον ἀνελλιπὲς καὶ ἀναχώρησιν πλείονα, ὅπως κἂν οὕτω δυνηθῶμεν τῇ προσθήκῃ τῶν πόνων δυσωπῆσαί ποτε τὸν θεὸν ἐπιβλέψαι ὡς τὸ πρὶν εἰς τὰς καρδίας ἡμῶν. Πλὴν δεῖ εἰδέναι ὅτι, ὅταν

2 θεὸν] θεὸν ἐν ἑαυτῇ RSa ‖ 5 παρ'] BMNR: ὑπ' ASTa ‖ γαλουχούμενα BMNRT: γαλουχούμενοι ASa ‖ τῆς om. R ‖ 6 αὐτῆς] τῆς αὐτῆς R om. MNbc ‖ ἐλθεῖν om. Aa ‖ εἰς ἄνδρα τέλειον om. a ‖ 7 ἡλικίας] ἡλικίας τοῦ πληρώματος τοῦ χριστοῦ Ta ‖ 10 πολλὴν] τὰ πολλὰ a om. Nb ‖ δὲ om. Nb ‖ 12 ἔρχηται ABRSTc: ἔρχεται MNb ἔρχοιτο a ‖ 13 ἐπάγει τῇ καρδίᾳ om. R ‖ καρδίᾳ] ψυχῇ ASa ‖ 14 τοῦ ABMRTab: om. NS ‖ γινομένη] γινομένη παραχώρησις A ‖ 15 ἀπελπισμοῦ . . . ἀπιστίας . . . ὀργῆς . . . τύφου] ἀφελπισμῷ . . . ἀπιστίᾳ . . . ὀργῇ . . . τύφῳ A ‖ ὁμοῦ om. c ‖ ult. καὶ om. R ‖ 16 πληρωθῆναι] παραδοθῆναι Aa ‖ τὴν πεῖραν om. A ‖ 17 καὶ κατὰ Mc: καὶ R κατὰ ceteri ‖ 18 γὰρ om. N ‖ μετὰ BMNRST: διὰ Aa ‖ ἀπολογίας BMNRST: ἀπολογήσεως A ἐχομολογήσεως a ‖ προσάγειν ABSTa: προσοίσειν MN ‖ 19-20 τῆς παρακλήσεως] τῶν παρακλήσεων a ‖ 20 αρετῆς] τῆς ἀρετῆς AB ‖ ἡμᾶς om. a ‖ 21 διδάσκοι BM: διδάσκει AN(R)ST ἐκδιδάσκῃ a ‖ 22 κἂν R: ἂν ceteri ‖ 23 ποτε] τότε A ‖ 24 ἐπιβλέψαι] ἐπιβλέπειν Aa.

maternal bosom with great fear and tears. But the abandonment which comes about under the terms of dereliction delivers up the soul which decides not to have God, as a captive to the demons. But we are not children of evasion[104]–heaven forbid!–rather we believe we are legitimate infants of the grace of God, fed by it in the midst of minor abandonments and frequent consolations, so that through its excellence we might be quick to come into perfect manhood, into the full measure of age.[105]

87. The abandonment which pertains to training carries much grief, and humility, and moderate despair into the soul, so that its glory-loving and easily excited part might come into humility as is fitting; and it immediately brings fear of God into the heart, and tears of full confession, and great desire for most beautiful silence. But that abandonment which comes about under the terms of dereliction from God allows the soul to be full of hopelessness, together with faithlessness and anger and folly. So knowing the evidence of both abandonments we must also approach God after the manner of each. Thus in the first we ought to bring thanks to him with an apology–since this came about by his disciplining the undisciplined quality of our judgement with an interruption in consolation, so that he might teach us (as a good father) the distinction between virtue and wickedness; while in the second we ought to bring a ceaseless confession of sins, and unfailing tears, and further withdrawal - in such a way that we might thus also be able, with the assistance of labours, eventually to prevail upon God to look on our hearts as before. One must know in addition that whenever the fight comes to be under the terms of an

---

[104] See Hebrews 10:39; (Timothy 1:2, Titus 1:2; Galatians 4:21ff?).
[105] See Ephesians 4:13.

ΔΙΑΔΟΧΟΥ

κατὰ οὐσιώδη συμβολὴν τῇ ψυχῇ καὶ τῷ Σατανᾷ ἡ μάχη γίνηται, ἐπὶ τῆς παιδευτικῆς δὲ λέγω παραχωρήσεως, ὑποστέλλει μέν, ὡς καὶ ἤδη εἶπον, ἡ χάρις ἑαυτήν, ἀγνώστῳ δὲ τῇ ψυχῇ συνεργεῖ βοηθείᾳ, ἵνα τὴν νίκην τῆς ψυχῆς εἶναι μόνον ἐπιδείξῃ τοῖς ἐχθροῖς αὐτῆς.

πη'.

Ὥσπερ ὅταν τις τῇ χειμερινῇ ὥρᾳ ἐν ὑπαιθρίῳ που ἑστηκὼς τόπῳ, ἀφορῶν δὲ πρὸς ἀνατολὰς ὅλος ἐν ἀρχῇ τῆς ἡμέρας, τὰ μὲν ἐμπρόσθια αὐτοῦ μέρη πάντα ὑπὸ τοῦ ἡλίου ὑποθερμαίνοιτο, τὰ δὲ ὀπίσθια αὐτοῦ πάντα ἄμοιρα ᾖ τῆς θέρμης διὰ τὸ μὴ εἶναι κατὰ κεφαλῆς αὐτοῦ τὸν ἥλιον, οὕτω καὶ οἱ εἰς ἀρχὴν ὄντες τῆς πνευματικῆς ἐνεργείας περιθάλπονται μὲν μερικῶς ὑπὸ τῆς ἁγίας χάριτος τὴν καρδίαν. Διόπερ καὶ πνευματικὰ τότε ὁ νοῦς αὐτῶν καρποφορεῖν ἄρχεται φρονήματα, φανερὰ δὲ αὐτῆς μέρη μένουσι κατὰ σάρκα φρονοῦντα διὰ τὸ μηδέπω ἅπαντα τὰ μέλη τῆς καρδίας ἐν βαθείᾳ αἰσθήσει ὑπὸ τοῦ φωτὸς καταυγάζεσθαι τῆς ἁγίας χάριτος. Ὅπερ τινὲς μὴ νοήσαντες δύο ὑποστάσεις ἐνόμισαν ἑαυταῖς ὥσπερ ἀντικαθεστώσας ἐν τῷ νοΐ τῶν ἀγωνιζομένων εἶναι. Οὕτως οὖν ἐν τῇ αὐτῇ ῥοπῇ καὶ καλὰ καὶ οὐ καλὰ συμβαίνει τὴν ψυχὴν ἐννοεῖν, ὃν τρόπον ὁ τοῦ ὑποδείγματος ἄνθρωπος ἐν τῇ αὐτῇ θίξει καὶ ῥιγοῖ καὶ θάλπεται. Ἀφ' οὗ γὰρ ὁ νοῦς ἡμῶν εἰς τὸ διπλοῦν τῆς γνώσεως ἀπωλίσθησεν, ἀνάγκην ἔχει ἔκτοτε, κἂν μὴ θέλῃ, κατὰ τὴν αὐτὴν ῥοπὴν καὶ καλὰ καὶ φαῦλα φέρειν διανοήματα μάλιστα ἐπὶ τῶν εἰς λεπτότητα διακρίσεως ἐρχομένων. Ὡς γὰρ σπεύδει ἀεὶ τὸ καλὸν ἐννοεῖν, εὐθὺς καὶ τοῦ κακοῦ μέμνηται, ἐπειδὴ εἰς διπλῆν τινα ἔννοιαν ἔσχισται ἀπὸ τῆς Ἀδὰμ παρακοῆς ἡ τοῦ ἀνθρώπου μνήμη.

1 ἡ ANSTa: om. BMR || γίνηται Sac: γίνεται BMNRT γένηται A || 2 δὲ] μὲν A om. Ta || καὶ om. RST || ἤδη] δεῖ Nb || 3 ἀγνώστῳ] ἀγνώστως A || βοηθείᾳ] βοηθείαν A || 4 ἐπιδείξῃ Μ: ἐπιδεικνύει ABRST ὑποδεικνύει N ἐπιδεικύοι a || 7 τῇ om. B || που] ποτε Aa || 8 ὅλος] ὅλως M om. A || 9 μέρη - αὐτοῦ om. Nb || μέρη] μέλη Aa || ὑποθερμαίνοιτο] θερμαίνοιτο Mc θερμαίνεται a || 10 πάντα] ἅπαντα B || ἄμοιρα ᾖ] ἀμοιρά ἐστιν R ἀμοιρῇ Mc || αὐτοῦ om. Aa || 11 εἰς ἀρχὴν] εἰς τὴν ἀρχὴν B ἐν ἀρχῇ RS || τῆς om. c || 12 μερικῶς ABMa: μερικῶς ποτε NRST || ἁγίας] θείας a || 13 φρονήματα om. a || 15 μέλη] μέρη AS || 17 ὑποστάσεις] ὑποθέσεις ABa || 18 ἐν om. A || pr. καὶ om. R || 20 ῥιγοῖ] ῥιγᾷ RSac || 21 ἀνάγκην] ἀνάγκη Μa || ἔχει om. Mc || 22 φέρειν] περιφέρειν M || 23 εἰς λεπτότητα διακρίσεως] ἐπὶ λεπτοτάτην διάκρισιν Aa || ὡς] ὃς b || 24 τοῦ om. A || κακοῦ] οὐ καλοῦ Aa || 25 Ἀδὰμ] τοῦ Ἀδὰμ RSa.

essential encounter between the soul and Satan (I speak of training abandonment) grace (as I have already said) contracts itself, and acts with the soul as an unperceived aid, so that it might make it appear to the soul's enemies that the victory is the soul's alone.

88. In the case of anyone standing in an open place in the winter-time looking due east at the beginning of the day, all his front parts are slightly warmed by the sun, but all his back parts are without a share of the warmth because the sun is not over his head. It is the same also for those who are at the beginning of Spiritual activity. The heart is partially warmed by holy grace; and so their intellect then also begins to bear fruit of spiritual resolutions, but the superficial parts of the heart remain thinking according to flesh, because all its parts are not yet shone upon with a profound sensation by the light of holy grace. And so some, not thinking, supposed that there are, as it were, two subjects in the intellect of those who contend, competing with each other. And so it happens that the soul conceives at the same instant both things that are good and things that are not good, in the same way as the man of the example both shivers and is warmed by the same touch. For from the time our intellect slipped into the dichotomy of perception it is forced to bring forth both good and foul thoughts at the same instant, even if it does not intend to; especially in the case of those who come into a refined discernment. For as the intellect is always eager to conceive what is good, it immediately also recollects what is bad, since from the disobedience of Adam the recollection of man has

ΔΙΑΔΟΧΟΥ

Ἐὰν οὖν ἀρξώμεθα θερμῷ ζήλῳ τὰς ἐντολὰς τοῦ θεοῦ διαπράττεσθαι, ἄπαντα ἡμῶν λοιπὸν τὰ αἰσθητήρια ἐν βαθείᾳ τινὶ αἰσθήσει φωτίζουσα ἡ χάρις τὰ μὲν ἡμέτερα ὥσπερ καταφλέγει ἐνθυμήματα, ἡδύνουσα δὲ ἡμῶν τὴν καρδίαν ἐν εἰρήνῃ τινὶ φιλίας ἀνενδότου πνευματικά τινα καὶ
5 οὐκέτι κατὰ σάρκα λογίζεσθαι ἡμᾶς παρασκευάζει. Τοῦτο δὲ τοῖς ἐγγίζουσι τῇ τελειότητι συνεχῶς ἄγαν συμβαίνει, οἵτινες ἄπαυστον ἔχουσιν ἐν τῇ καρδίᾳ τὴν μνήμην τοῦ κυρίου.

πθ'.
10 Δύο ἡμῖν καλὰ ἡ ἁγία χάρις διὰ τοῦ βαπτίσματος περιποιεῖ τῆς ἀναγεννήσεως, ὧντινων τὸ ἓν ἀπείρως τοῦ ἑνὸς ὑπερβάλλει. Ἀλλὰ τὸ μὲν ἓν εὐθέως χαρίζεται· ἀνακαινίζει γὰρ ἡμᾶς ἐν αὐτῷ τῷ ὕδατι καὶ πάσας τὰς γραμμὰς τῆς ψυχῆς, τοῦτ᾽ ἔστιν τὸ κατ᾽ εἰκόνα, λαμπρύνει, πᾶσαν ῥυτίδα τῆς ἁμαρτίας ἡμᾶς ἀπονίπτουσα. Τὸ δὲ ἓν ἐκδέχεται ἵνα
15 σὺν ἡμῖν ἐργάσηται, ὅπερ ἐστὶ τὸ καθ᾽ ὁμοίωσιν. Ὅταν οὖν ἄρξηται ὁ νοῦς ἐν πολλῇ αἰσθήσει γεύεσθαι τῆς χρηστότητος τοῦ ἁγίου πνεύματος, τότε ὀφείλομεν εἰδέναι ὅτι ἄρχεται ἡ χάρις ὥσπερ ἐπιζωγραφεῖν εἰς τὸ κατ᾽ εἰκόνα τὸ καθ᾽ ὁμοίωσιν. Ὃν γὰρ τρόπον οἱ ζωγράφοι πρῶτον μὲν ἑνὶ χρώματι διαγράφουσι τὸ σχῆμα τοῦ ἀνθρώπου,
20 χροιᾷ δὲ τὴν χροιὰν κατ᾽ ὀλίγον ἐπανθίζοντες οὕτως τὸ τοῦ ὁμοιογραφουμένου ἄχρι καὶ τῶν τριχῶν ἀποσῴζουσιν εἶδος· οὕτω καὶ ἡ χάρις τοῦ θεοῦ πρῶτον μὲν διὰ τοῦ βαπτίσματος εἰς τὸ ὅπερ ἦν, ὅτε ἐγένετο ὁ ἄνθρωπος, ῥυθμίζει τὸ κατ᾽ εἰκόνα. Ὅτε δὲ ἡμᾶς ἴδῃ ἐκ πάσης προθέσεως ἐπιθυμοῦντας τοῦ κάλλους τῆς ὁμοιώσεως καὶ ἑστῶτας
25 γυμνούς τε καὶ ἀπτοήτους εἰς τὸ ταύτης ἐργαστήριον, τότε, ἀρετῇ τὴν ἀρετὴν ἐπανθίζουσα καὶ ἀπὸ δόξης εἰς δόξαν τὸ τῆς ψυχῆς εἶδος

---

1 ἀρξώμεθα] ἀρξόμεθα NTb || 3 δὲ] γὰρ a || 5 κατὰ σάρκα] σαρκικὰ Aa || 7 κυρίου RT: θεοῦ Nb κυρίου Ἰησοῦ ceteri || 10 διὰ om. Nb || περιποιεῖ] περιποιεῖται Mac || 11-12 τὸ μὲν ἓν ABSTa: τὸ μὲν MN τὸ ἓν R || 12 γὰρ om. c || 13 τὸ] τοῦ Nb || 14 πᾶσαν MNR: πᾶσαν τὴν ABSTa || ἡμᾶς BNRSa: ἡμῶν MT om. A || ἀπονίπτουσα] ἀπονίπτουσαν Nb ἀπορρύπτουσα T || τὸ δὲ ἓν ABNRSTa: τὸ δὲ M || 15 τὸ om. c || ὅταν ABMRS: ὅτε NTa || 18 ἐπιζωγραφεῖν] ζωγραφεῖν A || pr. τὸ ARSTc: τὸν BMNa || alt. τὸ RSTp.c.: καὶ τὸ B τὸν ANTa.c.ac καὶ τὸν M || 20 κατ᾽ ὀλίγον] κατὰ λόγον A || 21 ὁμοιογραφουμένου BMNR: ὁμοιογραφομένου ASTa || 22 χάρις BMN: ἁγία χάρις ARSTa || 23 τὸ c: τὸν ceteri || 25 τε om. Tc || ταύτης] αὐτῆς Aa || 26 ψυχῆς] γραφῆς Nb.

been divided into a double intellectual conception. Therefore if we ever begin to accomplish the commandments of God with ardent zeal, then grace (illuminating all our sense faculties with a profound sensation) burns down (as it were) our devices, gladdening our heart in a peace of unwavering affection, and prepares us to reckon what is spiritual, and no longer in terms of the flesh. This is what so often happens to those who continually draw near to perfection, who have a ceaseless recollection of the Lord in the heart.

89. Through the baptism of regeneration holy grace procures two good things for us, of which one infinitely surpasses the other. It freely gives the first straight away; for it renews us in water itself, and restores all the outlines of the soul (that is, what is 'in the image') washing us clean from all the smudges of sin.[106] But the other waits so that it might make the 'in the likeness' together with us. So whenever the intellect begins to taste the excellence of the holy Spirit with a great sensation, then we should know that grace begins to portray, as it were, the 'in the likeness' in the 'in the image'. For in the way portraitists first draw the shape of the man in one colour, but then decorate it little by little colour on colour (thus preserving the form of the sitter, even down to the hair), so the grace of God also first composes the 'in the image', through baptism into that which man was when he came into being. But when grace sees us desiring the beauty of the likeness with a complete purpose, and standing naked and undaunted in its studio, then, colouring virtue upon virtue, and restoring the form of the soul from glory unto glory,[107] it preserves the character of the

---

[106] See Ephesians 5:27.
[107] See 2 Corinthians 3:18.

ΔΙΑΔΟΧΟΥ

ἀναφέρουσα, τὸν χαρακτῆρα τῆς ὁμοιώσεως αὐτῇ περιποιεῖ. Ὥστε οὖν ἡ μὲν αἴσθησις δηλοῖ ἡμᾶς μορφοῦσθαι τὸ καθ' ὁμοίωσιν· τὸ δὲ τέλειον τῆς ὁμοιώσεως ἐκ τοῦ φωτισμοῦ γνωσόμεθα. Πάσας μὲν γὰρ τὰς ἀρετὰς διὰ τῆς αἰσθήσεως ὁ νοῦς κατὰ μέτρον τι καὶ ῥυθμὸν ἄρρητον
5 προκόπτων ἀπολαμβάνει· τὴν δὲ πνευματικὴν οὐ δύναταί τις ἀγάπην κτήσασθαι, εἰ μὴ ἐν πάσῃ πληροφορίᾳ φωτισθῇ παρὰ τοῦ ἁγίου πνεύματος. Ἐὰν γὰρ μὴ τελείως τὸ καθ' ὁμοίωσιν διὰ τοῦ θείου φωτὸς ἀπολάβῃ ὁ νοῦς, πάσας μὲν τὰς ἄλλας σχεδὸν ἔχειν ἀρετὰς δύναται, τῆς δὲ τελείας ἀγάπης ἔτι ἄμοιρος μένει. Ὅταν γὰρ ὁμοιωθῇ τῇ τοῦ θεοῦ
10 ἀρετῇ, ὡς χωρεῖ δὲ ἄνθρωπος, λέγω, ὁμοιωθῆναι θεῷ, τότε καὶ τῆς θείας ἀγάπης φέρει τὴν ὁμοίωσιν. Ὡς γὰρ ἐπὶ τῶν ὁμοιογραφουμένων τὸ ἀνθηρὸν ὅλον τῶν χρωμάτων χρῶμα προστεθὲν τῇ εἰκόνι ἄχρι καὶ τοῦ μειδιάσαι ἀποσώζει τὴν τοῦ ὁμοιογραφουμένου ὁμοιότητα, οὕτως καὶ ἐπὶ τῶν εἰς τὴν θείαν ὁμοίωσιν παρὰ τῆς θείας χάριτος ἀναζωγραφουμένων ὁ
15 φωτισμὸς τῆς ἀγάπης προστεθεὶς εἰς τὴν τοῦ καθ' ὁμοίωσιν ὁλοκλήρως εὐπρέπειαν δηλοῖ εἶναι τὸ κατ' εἰκόνα. Οὔτε γὰρ ἀπάθειαν ἄλλη ἀρετὴ δύναται περιποιῆσαι τῇ ψυχῇ, εἰ μὴ ἡ ἀγάπη μόνη. Πλήρωμα γὰρ νόμου ἡ ἀγάπη. Ὥστε οὖν ἀνακαινοῦται μὲν ἡμέρα καὶ ἡμέρα ὁ ἔσω ἡμῶν ἄνθρωπος ἐν τῇ γεύσει τῆς ἀγάπης, πληροῦται δὲ ἐν τῇ ταύτης
20 τελειότητι.

ϟ'.

Γεύει μὲν οὖν τὸ ἅγιον πνεῦμα ἐν ἀρχαῖς τῆς προκοπῆς, εἴπερ θερμῶς ἐρασθῶμεν τῆς ἀρετῆς τοῦ θεοῦ, τὴν ψυχὴν ἐν πάσῃ αἰσθήσει

---

1 αὐτῇ] ἑαυτῇ B ‖ περιποιεῖ] περιποιεῖται M ‖ 2 pr. τὸ BS: τὸν AMNRTa ‖ 3 γὰρ] οὖν N om. Bb ‖ 5 προκόπτων] προκόπτον AT ‖ οὐ] οὐδεὶς A ‖ τις om. A ‖ 6 ἐν πάσῃ] ἐναργεῖ a ‖ παρὰ] ἐκ a ‖ 7 θείου om. a ‖ 8 ἀπολάβῃ B: ἀπολάβοι AN(R)STac ἀπολάβοιεν M ‖ ἔχειν] κτήσασθαι Nb ‖ 9 ὅταν Ba: ὅτε AMNRST ‖ ὁμοιωθῇ] ὁμοιώθη A ‖ 10 δὲ] δὲ ὁ Ba ὁ A ‖ θεῷ] τῷ θεῷ a ‖ 11 ὡς] ὥστε M ‖ ὁμοιογραφουμένων] ὁμοιογραφομένων Nb ‖ 12 ἀνθηρὸν MNRT: ἀνθηρότερον ABSa ‖ ὅλον bc: ὅλων ABMN(R)S ὅλως a om. T ‖ χρῶμα om. A ‖ καὶ om. R ‖ 13 ὁμοιογραφουμένου] ὁμοιογραφομένου ANS ‖ 14 ὁμοίωσιν] ὁμοιότητα Nb ‖ ἀναζωγραφουμένων BMN: διαζωγραφουμένων ARSTa ‖ 15 τοῦ om. R ‖ 16 εἶναι] γενέσθαι Aa ‖ τὸ ANSTa: τὸν BMR ‖ 17 δύναται om. a ‖ τῇ om. R ‖ ἡ NRST: om. ABMa ‖ γὰρ BMNT: γὰρ ἅπαξ ARSa ‖ 18 ἡ om. R ‖ οὖν om. Nb ‖ 19 ταύτης] αὐτῆς AB ‖ 23 οὖν om. AT ‖ ἀρχαῖς] ἀρχῇ T.

likeness. And so the Sense shows that we are being shaped according to the 'in the likeness', but it is from illumination that we will perceive the perfection of the likeness. For the intellect receives all the virtues through the Sense, as it progresses according to a measure and inexpressible rhythm; but one is not able to acquire spiritual love unless one is illuminated with absolute complete assurance by the holy Spirit; since unless the intellect receives the 'in the likeness' perfectly through the divine light, it can have nearly all the other virtues but still remain without a share of perfect love. Because whenever it is made like to the virtue of God (I mean, inasmuch as a man accepts to be made like God) then the intellect also carries the likeness of divine Love. And as in portraits the whole brilliance of colours added to the image preserves the likeness of the sitter even to the point of smiling, so it is also for those who are painted in the divine likeness by divine grace; the illumination of love being added indicates that the 'in the image' is entirely in the comeliness of the 'in the likeness'. For no other virtue can procure dispassion for the soul, only love alone; for 'love is the completion of the law'.[108] So as our inner man is renewed day by day[109] by the taste of love, he is completed in its perfection.

90. So in the beginnings of progress (if indeed we ardently yearn for the virtue of God) the holy Spirit gives the soul a taste of the sweetness of God with a whole Sense and complete assurance, so that the intellect

---

[108] Romans 13:10.
[109] See 2 Corinthians 4:16.

ΔΙΑΔΟΧΟΥ

καὶ πληροφορίᾳ τῆς γλυκύτητος τοῦ θεοῦ, ἵνα ἔχῃ εἰδέναι ὁ νοῦς ἐν ἀκριβεῖ ἐπιγνώσει τὸ τέλειον ἔπαθλον τῶν φιλοθέων πόνων. Κρύπτει δὲ λοιπὸν ἐπὶ πολὺ τὴν τοῦ ζωοποιοῦ τούτου δώρου πολυτέλειαν, ἵνα, κἂν πάσας τὰς ἄλλας ἀρετὰς κατεργαζώμεθα, μηδὲν ὅλως ἑαυτοὺς ὑπονοῶμεν
5 εἶναι διὰ τὸ μηδέπω ὥσπερ εἰς ἕξιν ἔχειν τὴν ἁγίαν ἀγάπην. Οὕτως οὖν τότε πλέον ὁ τοῦ μίσους δαίμων ταῖς τῶν ἀγωνιζομένων διοχλεῖ ψυχαῖς, ὥστε καὶ αὐτοὺς τοὺς ἀγαπῶντας αὐτοὺς πρὸς μῖσος διαβάλλειν, καὶ ἄχρι σχεδὸν τοῦ φιλήματος φέρει τὴν φθοροποιὸν τοῦ μίσους ἐνέργειαν. Ὅθεν πλέον ἀλγύνεται ἡ ψυχὴ φέρουσα μὲν τὴν μνήμην τῆς
10 πνευματικῆς ἀγάπης, μὴ δυναμένη δὲ αὐτὴν ἐν αἰσθήσει κτήσασθαι διὰ τὴν τῶν τελειοτάτων πόνων ὑστέρησιν. Χρεία οὖν ἐκ βίας αὐτὴν τέως κατεργάζεσθαι, ἵνα εἰς τὴν γεῦσιν αὐτῆς ἐν πάσῃ αἰσθήσει καταφθάσωμεν καὶ πληροφορίᾳ. Τὸ γὰρ τέλειον αὐτῆς οὐδεὶς ἐν τῇ σαρκὶ ὢν ταύτῃ δύναται κτήσασθαι, εἰ μὴ μόνον οἱ ἄχρι μαρτυρίου καὶ
15 τελείας ἀνθομολογήσεως ἐλθόντες ἅγιοι. Ἐπειδὴ ὁ τούτου τυχὼν ἀλλάσσεται ὅλος καὶ οὔτε τροφῆς εὐχερῶς ὀρέγεται. Τῷ γὰρ ὑπὸ τῆς θείας ἀγάπης τρεφομένῳ ποία ἔσται ἐπιθυμία τῶν ἐν τῷ κόσμῳ καλῶν; Διὰ τοῦτο ὁ σοφώτατος Παῦλος, τὸ μέγα δοχεῖον τῆς γνώσεως, τὴν μέλλουσαν τρυφὴν τῶν πρώτων δικαίων ἡμᾶς ἐκ τῆς αὐτοῦ πληροφορίας
20 εὐαγγελιζόμενος οὕτως λέγει· Οὐκ ἔστιν ἡ βασιλεία τῶν οὐρανῶν βρῶσις καὶ πόσις, ἀλλὰ δικαιοσύνη καὶ εἰρήνη καὶ χαρὰ ἐν πνεύματι ἁγίῳ, ἅτινά ἐστιν ὁ καρπὸς τῆς τελείας ἀγάπης. Ὥστε οὖν γεύεσθαι μὲν αὐτῆς ἐνταῦθα συνεχῶς οἱ εἰς τελειότητα προκόπτοντες δύνανται, τελείως δὲ αὐτὴν οὐδεὶς δύναται κτήσασθαι, εἰ μὴ ὅταν καταποθῇ
25 τελείως τὸ θνητὸν ὑπὸ τῆς ζωῆς.

1 γλυκύτητος] χάριτος B ‖ ἔχῃ] ἔχει ANb ‖ 2 ἔπαθλον om. A ‖ 3 ἐπὶ πολὺ om. a ‖ 4 κατεργαζώμεθα] κατεργαζόμεθα Nb κατεργασώμεθα A ‖ ὅλως om. a ‖ ὑπονοῶμεν ARSTac: ὑπονοοῦμεν BMN ‖ 8 φέρει MNR: φέρειν ABSTa ‖ 9 πλέον ἀλγύνεται] πλείονα γλυκαίνεται Ha ‖ 11 τῶν τελειοτάτων] τελειοτάτων τῶν RS ‖ πόνων om. Nb ‖ χρεία BMNTa: χρὴ ARS χρεὶ b ‖ τέως om. a ‖ 12 κατεργάζεσθαι] κατεργάσασθαι A ‖ ἵνα] ἵνα καὶ B ‖ εἰς τὴν γεῦσιν] ὃν τὴν πεῦσιν A ‖ αὐτῆς om. Aa ‖ 12-13 αἰσθήσει καταφθάσωμεν καὶ] φθάσωμεν Nb ‖ 14 οἱ om. a ‖ 15 ἀνθομολογήσεως] ὁμολογίας T ‖ 16 ἀλλάσσεται] ἐναλλάσσεται S ‖ ὅλος ABN(R)Sac: ὅλως MT ‖ τῷ] τῶν A ‖ 17 ἀγάπης] ἀγάπης εὐχερῶς B ‖ τρεφομένῳ] τρεφομένων A ‖ 18 σοφώτατος] σοφὸς a ‖ 19 τρυφὴν] τροφὴν BS ‖ αὐτοῦ] ἑαυτοῦ A ‖ 21 καὶ εἰρήνη om. a ‖ 22 γεύεσθαι] γεύσασθαι Nab ‖ 23 αὐτῆς om. N ‖ ἐνταῦθα MNRS: ἐντεῦθεν ABa ‖ δύνανται om. M ‖ 24-25 ὅταν καταποθῇ τελείως R: ἂν ὅταν τελείως καταποθῇ AB ἂν ὅτε τελείως καταποθῇ a ὅταν καταποθῇ MNS ἂν ὅταν καταποθῇ c ‖ ζωῆς] ζωῆς πόθῳ A.

might have knowledge of the final prize of godly labours, with precise recognition. But then it hides the wealth of this life-giving gift for a long time, so that even if we acquire all the other virtues we suppose ourselves to be nothing at all because of not yet having holy love as a habit. As a result the demon of hate then troubles the souls of contenders even more, so as to set them at variance even with those who love them, to the point of hatred; and it even carries the ruinous activity of hatred almost as far as the kiss. And so the soul is further distressed, carrying the recollection of spiritual love, but unable to procure it in the Sense for want of the most perfect labours. So it is necessary to acquire love by force in the meantime, so that we might seize its taste with a whole Sense and complete assurance. For no one can procure the perfection of love while in this flesh, except only those saints who come as far as martyrdom and perfect confession, because whoever attains this is completely transformed and does not reach out recklessly for food–since what sort of desire will there be for the good things which are in the world, to someone who is fed by divine love? This is why the most wise Paul (that great reservoir of perception), proclaiming to us from his complete assurance the coming delight of the first of the just, speaks in this way: 'The kingdom of heaven is not food and drink, but righteousness and peace and joy in the holy Spirit'[110]–which is the fruit of perfect love. And so those who are progressing into perfection are able to taste it here continually, but no one is able to acquire it perfectly until the mortal is perfectly swallowed up by life.[111]

---

[110] Romans 14:17.
[111] 2 Corinthians 5:4.

ΔΙΑΔΟΧΟΥ

ϟα'.

Διηγήσατό μοί τις τῶν ἀπλήστῳ τινὶ γνώμῃ ἀγαπώντων τὸν κύριον ὅτι, ἐπιθυμήσαντί μοι γνωστῶς γνῶναι τὴν ἀγάπην τοῦ θεοῦ, παρέσχε τοῦτο ἐν αἰσθήσει πολλῇ καὶ πληροφορίᾳ ὁ ἀγαθὸς καὶ τοσοῦτον, φησίν,
5 τῆς τοιαύτης ἐνεργείας ᾐσθόμην, ὥστε ἐπείγεσθαι μὲν τότε τὴν ψυχὴν μετὰ ἀνεκλαλήτου τινὸς χαρᾶς καὶ ἀγάπης ἐκβῆναι τοῦ σώματος καὶ ἀπελθεῖν πρὸς τὸν κύριον, ἀγνοεῖν δὲ ὥσπερ τῆς προσκαίρου ταύτης τὸν τρόπον ζωῆς. Ὁ δὲ ταύτης τῆς ἀγάπης ἐν πείρᾳ γενόμενος, κἂν μυρία παρά τινος ὑβρισθῇ ἢ ζημιωθῇ, συμβαίνει γὰρ ἔχειν ἔτι τι τῶν
10 τοιούτων μέλλοντι διαπονεῖσθαι, οὐκ ὀργίζεται κατ' αὐτοῦ, ἀλλὰ μένει ὡσανεὶ κεκολλημένος καὶ τῇ τοῦ ὑβρίσαντος αὐτὸν ἢ καὶ ζημιώσαντος ψυχῇ. Κατ' ἐκείνων δὲ μόνων ἀνάπτεται οἵτινες ἢ κατὰ πενήτων ἔρχονται ἢ κατὰ τοῦ θεοῦ, ὡς λέγει ἡ γραφή, λαλοῦσιν ἀδικίαν ἢ ἄλλως πως βιοῦσι πονηρῶς. Ὁ γὰρ ὑπὲρ ἑαυτὸν λοιπὸν πολὺ φιλῶν τὸν θεόν,
15 μᾶλλον δὲ ὁ μηκέτι ἑαυτὸν φιλῶν ἀλλὰ τὸν θεὸν μόνον οὐκέτι τὴν ἑαυτοῦ τιμὴν ἐκδικεῖ, ἀλλὰ μόνον τὴν τοῦ τιμήσαντος αὐτὸν ἐν τιμῇ αἰωνίῳ θέλει τιμᾶσθαι δικαιοσύνης· τοῦτο δὲ οὐκέτι ὡς ἐκ θελήσεώς τινος ὀλίγης ἔχει, ἀλλ' ὥσπερ λοιπὸν εἰς ἕξιν ἔχει τὴν τοιαύτην διάθεσιν διὰ πολλὴν πεῖραν τῆς τοῦ θεοῦ ἀγάπης. Πρὸς δὲ τούτοις δεῖ
20 εἰδέναι ὅτι ὁ εἰς τοιαύτην ἀγάπην ἐνεργούμενος ὑπὸ τοῦ θεοῦ ἐπάνω καὶ πίστεως γίνεται ἐν τῷ καιρῷ τῆς τοιαύτης ἐνεργείας, ὡς ἐν αἰσθήσει λοιπὸν τῆς καρδίας κρατῶν διὰ τῆς πολλῆς ἀγάπης τὸν πίστει τιμώμενον. Ὅπερ ἡμῖν σαφῶς κατασημαίνει ὁ ἅγιος ἀπόστολος λέγων· Νυνὶ δὲ μένει τὰ τρία ταῦτα, πίστις, ἐλπίς, ἀγάπη· μείζων δὲ τούτων ἡ
25 ἀγάπη. Ὁ γὰρ ἐν πλούτῳ ἀγάπης, ὡς ἔφην, κρατῶν τὸν θεὸν μείζων ἐστὶ πολὺ τότε τῆς ἑαυτοῦ πίστεως ὡς ὅλος ὢν ἐν πόθῳ.

2 τινὶ om. R || ἀγαπώντων] ἀγαπησάντων b || κύριον] θεὸν Β || 5 ᾐσθόμην] ἠσθόμην Αa || 8 ζωῆς] τῆς ζωῆς Μ || 9 συμβαίνει] συμβαίνειν a || τι om. ARSa || 9-10 τῶν τοιούτων BMa: τὸν τοιοῦτον AN(R)Sc || 10 μέλλοντι ABSa: μελλόντων R μέλλον N μέλλων M || διαπονεῖσθαι] διαπολεῖσθαι BR || 11 pr. καὶ MNR: om. ABSa || ἢ om. Aa || 12 ψυχῇ] ψυχὴν A || μόνων] μόνον BM || ἢ om. A || 13 τοῦ om. A || γραφή] ἁγία γραφή R || 14 βιοῦσι] ποιοῦσι a || πονηρῶς] πονηρὰ Αa || ἑαυτὸν] ἑαυτοῦ N || 15 ὁ om. ac || 16 ἐκδικεῖ] ζητεῖ B || τὴν om. M || ἐν om. Mc || 17 αἰωνίῳ BMSb: αἰωνίᾳ ANa || 18 ὀλίγης] ὀλίγως Aa || 20 ὁ om. R || ἀγάπην om. A || 22 αἰσθήσει] αἰσθήσει πολλῇ a || λοιπὸν] λοιπὸν πολλῇ A || τὸν] τῶν A || 23 τιμώμενον] τιμωμένον A || ἀπόστολος] παῦλος A || 24 νυνὶ] νῦν a || μείζων] μείζω Νb || τούτων] πάντων A || 25 ὁ - ἀγάπης om. a || ἔφην] ἔφη ὁ a || 26 τότε om. Aa || ὡς - πόθῳ om. B || ὅλος] ὅλως MNb || πόθῳ] τόπῳ Nb.

91. One of those who love the Lord with an insatiable intent told me: 'Since I desired to perceive the love of God perceptively, he who is good provided this with a whole Sense and complete assurance; and', he said, 'I sensed this activity to such a degree that my soul was then urged on with an unutterable joy and love; it stepped out of the body and went away to the Lord[112] and did not, as it were, perceive the manner of this transient life.' And he who came into evidence of this love is not angry at anyone, even if he is insulted or cheated countless times by him (because it happens that such things still pertain for one who is going to labour); he does not become angry with him, rather he remains clinging (as it were) even to the soul of the one who insulted or cheated him. He flares up only at those who proceed either against the destitute or against God (as Scripture says: 'they speak injustice'[113] or live evilly in other ways). For then, having more affection for God than for himself (or rather no longer having affection for himself but for God alone) he no longer avenges his own honour, but only wants the justice of the one who honoured him to be honoured with eternal honour; and he then no longer holds to this with a weak will, but rather has such a disposition as a habit, because of great evidence of love for God. So in addition to these things one must know that whoever is activated by God into such love comes to be beyond even faith in the time of such activity–as with the Sense of the heart, through great love, he gets hold of him who is honoured in faith. The holy Apostle indicates this to us clearly, saying: 'But now these three things remain, faith, hope, and love; but the greatest of these is love.'[114] For whoever gets hold of God with an abundance of love (as I said) is then much greater than his own faith, being completely in a state of longing.

---

[112] See 2 Corinthians 12:2f.
[113] See Psalms 74:6.
[114] 1 Corinthians 13:13.

ΔΙΑΔΟΧΟΥ

μβ'.

Ἡ μεσότης τῆς ἐνεργείας τῆς ἁγίας γνώσεως οὐ μικρῶς ἡμᾶς λυπεῖσθαι παρασκευάζει, ὅταν ἐκ παροξυσμοῦ τινος ὑβρίσαντές τινα ἐχθρὸν αὐτὸν ἑαυτῶν κατασκευάσωμεν. Διόπερ οὐδεπώποτε ἐνδίδωσι
5 νύττουσα τὴν συνείδησιν ἡμῶν, ἕως ὅτε διὰ πολλῆς ἀπολογίας εἰς τὴν πάλαι ἐπαναγάγωμεν τὸν ὑβρισθέντα διάθεσιν. Ἡ δὲ ἀκροτάτη αὐτῆς κατάνυξις, καὶ ὅταν ἀδίκως τις τῶν τοῦ βίου ἀνθρώπων καθ' ὑμῶν ὀργισθῇ, ἀδολεσχεῖν ἡμᾶς καὶ φροντίζειν ἄγαν ποιεῖ, ἐπειδὴ ὅλως πρόσκομμά τινι τῶν ἐκ τοῦ αἰῶνος τούτου λαλούντων γινόμεθα. Ὅθεν
10 καὶ ἀργὸς τότε ὁ νοῦς περὶ τὴν θεωρίαν γίνεται· ἀγάπης γὰρ ὢν ὅλος ὁ λόγος τῆς γνώσεως οὐ συγχωρεῖ τὴν διάνοιαν πλατυνθῆναι πρὸς σύλληψιν θεωρημάτων θείων, εἰ μὴ πρῶτον ἀπολάβωμεν ἐν τῇ ἀγάπῃ καὶ τὸν εἰκῇ ἡμῖν ὀργιζόμενον. Εἰ δὲ ἐκεῖνος οὐ θέλει τοῦτο γενέσθαι ἢ πάλιν ἀπέστη τῶν ἡμετέρων διατριβῶν, τὸν χαρακτῆρα ἡμᾶς τοῦ
15 προσώπου αὐτοῦ λοιπὸν ἐπείγει τῇ ἑαυτῶν ἐν ἀσυστάλτῳ τινὶ τῷ τῆς ψυχῆς χύματι προστιθέντας διαθέσει οὕτως ἐν τῷ βάθει τῆς καρδίας τῆς ἀγάπης ἀποπληροῦν τὸν νόμον. Δεῖ γάρ, φησίν, καὶ τὰ τῶν χολούντων ἀκαίρως πρόσωπα ἀχόλῳ τῇ ἐννοίᾳ ἐν τῇ ἑαυτῶν ἐνορᾶν διανοίᾳ τοὺς θέλοντας γνῶσιν ἔχειν θεοῦ. Τούτου δὲ γενομένου οὐ μόνον περὶ τὴν
20 θεολογίαν ὁ νοῦς ἡμῶν ἀπταίστως κινηθήσεται, ἀλλὰ καὶ εἰς τὴν ἀγάπην τοῦ θεοῦ μετὰ πολλῆς ἀναβήσεται παρρησίας ὡς ἐκ δευτέρας βαθμίδος εἰς πρώτην ἀνεμποδίστως ἐπειγόμενος.

---

2 ἐνεργείας] ἐργασίας a ‖ 4 αὐτὸν] αὐτῶν A ‖ ἑαυτῶν] ἑαυτὸν Nb ‖ κατασκευάσωμεν BM: κατασκευάσομεν AN παρασκευάσωμεν aR γενέσθαι παρασκευάσωμεν S ‖ οὐδεπώποτε MR: οὐτεπώποτε N οὐδέποτε ASa οὐτέποτε B ‖ 6 ἐπαναγάγωμεν] ἐπαναγάγομεν Nb ‖ ὑβρισθέντα] ὑβρίσαντα A ‖ αὐτῆς] ταύτης a ‖ 7 κατάνυξις] διάνοιξις AS ‖ βίου] κόσμου S ‖ 8 ἄγαν] ἀγαπᾶν A ‖ 9 τινι] τι c ‖ τῶν om. M ‖ ἐκ om. MNb ‖ 10 θεωρίαν] θεολογίαν Nb ‖ 12 ἀπολάβωμεν B(R)Sac: ἀπολάβομεν AMN ‖ 13 ἡμῖν om. N ‖ γενέσθαι] γίνεσθαι Ap.c. ‖ 14 ἀπέστη] ἄπεστιν Nb ἀποστῇ S ‖ 14-15 τοῦ προσώπου] τῷ προσώπῳ A ‖ 15 ἐπείγει AMRa: ἐπείγειν NS ἐπὶ B προσήκει F ‖ ἑαυτῶν] ἑαυτὸν b ‖ ἀσυστάλτῳ RS: ἀσυστάτῳ ABN συστάτῳ Ma ‖ 16 χύματι] σχήματι B ‖ προστιθέντας] προτιθέντας B ‖ 18 ἀχόλῳ] ἀχόλως A ‖ ἐν om. a ‖ ἐνορᾶν] ὁρᾶν b ‖ 19 θεοῦ] τοῦ θεοῦ Aa ‖ γενομένου] γινομένου Nab ‖ 20 νοῦς ἡμῶν ABMRSTa: νοῦς Nc.

92. The mid-point of the activity of holy perception prepares us to grieve not a little, whenever we insult anyone due to his provocation and make him our enemy. It will never stop nudging our conscience, until, through much apologising, we lead the one who was insulted back into his former disposition. But perception's highest compunction is whenever one of the men of this life is unjustly angry at us; it makes us talk about it and dwell on it immoderately, since we are becoming a stumbling-block for those who speak from this world.[115] For this reason the intellect then becomes lazy about contemplation also; for the rationale of perception, being completely of love, does not allow the reason to be broadened so as to receive divine contemplations unless we first receive back in love even him who is angered at us rashly. But if he does not want this to be, or again avoids our company, then perception urges us to add the character of his face to our own disposition, in an uncontainable overflowing of the soul–thus fulfilling the law of love in the depth of the heart. Because those who decide to have perception of God must, it says, observe in their own reasoning, with an unangered intellectual conception, the faces even of those who are unduly angered. When this comes to pass, not only is our intellect moved without stumbling concerning divine converse, but it also ascends to the love of God with great boldness,[116] being urged on unhindered as from a second level onto the first.

---

[115] See Romans 14:13.
[116] See especially Ephesians 3:12 and Hebrews 10:19.

ΔΙΑΔΟΧΟΥ

μγ'.

Ἡ τῆς ἀρετῆς ὁδὸς τοῖς μὲν ἀρχομένοις ἐρᾶν τῆς εὐσεβείας τραχεῖα λίαν καὶ κατάστυγνος φαίνεται οὐ διὰ τὸ ἐκείνηνδε τοιαύτην εἶναι, ἀλλὰ διὰ τὸ τὴν ἀνθρωπείαν φύσιν εὐθὺς ἐκ γαστρὸς τῷ πλάτει
5 συναναστρέφεσθαι τῶν ἡδονῶν· τοῖς δὲ τὸ μέσον αὐτῆς παρελθεῖν δυναμένοις προσηνὴς ὅλη καὶ ἄνετος δείκνυται. Τῷ γὰρ καλῷ ἔθει τὸ φαῦλον ὑποταγὲν διὰ τῆς ἐνεργείας τοῦ ἀγαθοῦ τῇ τῶν ἀλογίστων ἡδονῶν συναπόλλυται μνήμῃ. Ὅθεν λοιπὸν ἡδέως ἡ ψυχὴ τὰς τρίβους ἁπάσας διαπορεύεται τῶν ἀρετῶν. Διὰ τοῦτο ὁ κύριος εἰσάγων μὲν ἡμᾶς
10 εἰς τὴν ὁδὸν τῆς σωτηρίας λέγει· Τί στενὴ καὶ τεθλιμμένη ἡ ὁδὸς ἡ ἀπάγουσα εἰς τὴν βασιλείαν καὶ ὀλίγοι δι' αὐτῆς εἰσπορεύονται. Πρὸς δὲ τοὺς θέλοντας πολλῇ τῇ προθέσει προσιέναι τῇ τῶν ἁγίων αὐτοῦ ἐντολῶν τηρήσει φησίν· Ὁ γὰρ ζυγός μου χρηστὸς καὶ τὸ φορτίον μου ἐλαφρόν ἐστιν. Δεῖ οὖν παρὰ τὴν ἀρχὴν τῆς ἀγωνίας βιαίῳ τινὶ
15 θελήματι τὰς ἁγίας τοῦ θεοῦ κατεργάζεσθαι ἐντολάς, ἵνα θεωρήσας ἡμῶν ὁ ἀγαθὸς κύριος τὸν σκοπὸν καὶ τὸν κόπον ἕτοιμον ἡμῖν καὶ τὸ θέλημα ἡδέως ἄγαν τοῖς αὐτοῦ ὑπηρετοῦν ἐνδόξοις θελήμασι καταπέμψῃ· παρὰ γὰρ κυρίου τότε ἑτοιμάζεται θέλησις· ὥστε ἐν πολλῇ τινι ἡμᾶς χαρᾷ ἐργάζεσθαι ἀπαύστως τὸ ἀγαθόν. Τότε γὰρ ὄντως αἰσθησόμεθα ὅτι θεός
20 ἐστιν ὁ ἐνεργῶν ἐν ἡμῖν καὶ τὸ θέλειν καὶ τὸ ἐνεργεῖν ὑπὲρ τῆς εὐδοκίας.

2 εὐσεβείας] ἀληθείας Mc ‖ 3 λίαν AMRa: ἄγαν BN om. ST ‖ ἐκείνηνδε MNRS: ἐκείνην ABTa ‖ 4 διὰ τὸ] τὸ διὰ GNa.c. τὸ διὰ τὸ Np.c. ‖ εὐθὺς om. A ‖ 6 ἄνετος] ἀνετή A ἄνετη S ‖ 7 ἐνεργείας] συνεργείας BNb ‖ 9 μὲν om. ASc ‖ 12 pr. τῇ om. B ‖ προσιέναι] ἰέναι T ‖ 15 κατεργάζεσθαι] ἐγκατεργάζεσθαι M ‖ ἡμῶν] ἡμᾶς M ‖ 16 καὶ τὸν κόπον om. AM ‖ κόπον RSTac: πόνον BN ‖ ἡμῖν] ἡμῶν T om. AR ‖ καὶ τὸ MRSa: τὸ NT τι B om. A ‖ θέλημα] βούλημα A ‖ 17 ὑπηρετοῦν] ὑπηρετοῦσι T ‖ ἐνδόξοις om. T ‖ καταπέμψῃ] καταπέμψει (R)S καταπέμψῃ τὴν χάριν αὐτοῦ c καταπέμψει τὴν χάριν αὐτοῦ M ‖ 18 τότε om. N ‖ ἐν om. ASb ‖ 19 ἐργάζεσθαι] ἐξεργάζεσθαι Bp.c. ‖ γὰρ om. Mc ‖ αἰσθησόμεθα AB(R)Sac: αἰσθησώμεθα MNT ‖ θεός MNR: ὁ θεός ABSTac ‖ 20 ἐν om. A ‖ τῆς om. R.

138

93.   The path of virtue appears very harsh and gloomy to those who are beginning to yearn for piety; not because it is so, but rather because human nature is brought up amid the expanse of the pleasures straight from the womb. But to those who are able to pass beyond the mid-point of this path, it is shown to be completely smooth and easy, since that which is foul is subordinated by good habit through the activity of the good; it perishes together with the recollection of irrational pleasures, and so the soul then goes gladly along all the paths of the virtues. For this reason the Lord (leading us into the way of salvation) says: 'How narrow and oppressive is the road which leads into the kingdom, and few there are who enter in through it.'[117] But to those who decide, with a great purpose, to arrive at keeping his holy commandments he says: 'For my yoke is easy and my burden is light.'[118] Therefore one must perform the holy commandments of God at the beginning of the contest with a strong will– so that our good Lord, contemplating our watchfulness and labour, might also send us a ready will to serve his glorious wishes very gladly; for then the will shall be prepared by the Lord,[119] so that we do good unceasingly, in great joy. And then we shall truly sense that it is God 'who activates in us both to decide and to act for his approval.'[120]

---

[117] Matthew 7:14.
[118] Matthew 11:30.
[119] Proverbs 8:35.
[120] Philippians 2:13.

ΔΙΑΔΟΧΟΥ

μη'.

Ὃν τρόπον μὴ θερμανθεὶς ἢ μηδὲ μαλαχθεὶς ὁ κηρὸς ἐπὶ πολὺ οὐ δύναται τὴν ἐπιτιθεμένην αὐτῷ σφραγῖδα δέξασθαι, οὕτως οὐδ᾽ ὁ ἄνθρωπος, ἐὰν μὴ διὰ πόνων καὶ ἀσθενειῶν δοκιμασθῇ, οὐ δύναται χωρῆσαι τῆς τοῦ θεοῦ ἀρετῆς τὴν σφραγῖδα. Διὰ τοῦτο ὁ μὲν κύριος λέγει τῷ θεσπεσίῳ Παύλῳ· Ἀρκεῖ σοι ἡ χάρις μου· ἡ γὰρ δύναμίς μου ἐν ἀσθενείᾳ τελειοῦται. Αὐτὸς δὲ ὁ ἀπόστολος καυχᾶται λέγων· Ἥδιστα οὖν μᾶλλον καυχήσομαι ἐν ταῖς ἀνθενείαις μου, ἵνα ἐπισκηνώσῃ ἐπ᾽ ἐμὲ ἡ δύναμις τοῦ Χριστοῦ. Ἀλλὰ καὶ ἐν ταῖς παροιμίαις γέγραπται· Ὃν γὰρ ἀγαπᾷ κύριος, παιδεύει· μαστιγοῖ δὲ πάντα υἱὸν ὃν παραδέχεται. Καὶ ὁ μὲν ἀπόστολος ἀσθενείας λέγει τὰς ἐπαναστάσεις τῶν ἐχθρῶν τοῦ σταυροῦ, αἵτινες συνεχῶς αὐτῷ τε καὶ πᾶσι τοῖς τότε ἁγίοις συνέβαινον, ἵνα μὴ ὑπεραίρωνται, ὡς αὐτὸς λέγει, τῇ ὑπεροχῇ τῶν ἀποκαλύψεων, ἀλλὰ μᾶλλον ἐνέμενον διὰ τῆς ταπεινώσεως ἐν τῷ σχήματι τῆς τελειότητος διὰ τῶν πυκνῶν ἐξουδενώσεων τὸ θεῖον δῶρον ὁσίως φυλάττοντες· ἡμεῖς δὲ νῦν ἀσθενείας τοὺς πονηροὺς λογισμοὺς λέγομεν καὶ τὰς σωματικὰς ἀνωμαλίας. Τότε μὲν γὰρ ἐπειδὴ αἰκίαις θανατηφόροις καὶ διαφόροις ἑτέραις θλίψεσι τὰ σώματα τῶν κατὰ τῆς ἁμαρτίας ἀγωνιζομένων ἁγίων παρεδίδοντο, ἐπάνω ἦσαν πολὺ τῶν τῇ ἀνθρωπίνῃ φύσει ἐκ τῆς ἁμαρτίας ἐπεισελθόντων παθῶν. Νυνὶ δ᾽ ἐπειδὴ εἰρήνη πληθύνεται διὰ τὸν κύριον τῶν ἐκκλησιῶν, διὰ τοῦτο δεῖ συνεχέσι μὲν ἀνωμαλίαις τὸ σῶμα λογισμοῖς δὲ πονηροῖς τὰς ψυχὰς τῶν ἀγωνιστῶν τῆς εὐσεβείας δοκιμάζεσθαι, καὶ μάλιστα παρ᾽ οἷς ἡ γνῶσις ἐν πάσῃ αἰσθήσει καὶ πληροφορίᾳ ἐνεργεῖ, ἵνα καὶ πάσης κενοδοξίας ἢ

2 ἢ μηδὲ R: μηδὲ S ἢ καὶ B ἢ ceteri ‖ 3 ἐπιτιθεμένην] ἐπιτηθημένην A ἐπιτεθημένην S ‖ οὐδ᾽ ὁ MNRST: οὐδ᾽ Bc καὶ ὁ Aa ‖ 4 ἐὰν] εἰ a ‖ πόνων] ἀγώνων a ‖ οὐ om. b ‖ 5 μὲν om. a ‖ 7 ἀσθενείᾳ] ἀσθενείαις Nb ‖ αὐτὸς] οὗτος Sc οὕτως a ‖ ἀπόστολος] παῦλος BNb ‖ 8 μᾶλλον om. A ‖ ἐπισκηνώσῃ BM(R)Sa: ἐπισκηνώσει ANT ‖ 10 γὰρ om. N ‖ 11 μὲν] μὲν οὖν Mc ‖ ἀσθενείας] ἀσθένειαν a ‖ 12 σταυροῦ ANSTa: σταυροῦ τοῦ χριστοῦ B σωτηρίου MRb ‖ 13 ὑπεραίρωνται] ὑπεραίρονται BNb ‖ λέγει] λέγει· ἐδόθη - ὑπεραίρωμαι (2 Cor. 12:7) a ‖ ὑπεροχῇ BMNRS: ὑπερβολῇ ATa ‖ 14 ἐν τῷ AB: τῷ ceteri ‖ 15 τελειότητος ABNT: τελειώσεως MRSa ‖ 18 καὶ om. a ‖ ἑτέραις] ἑτέροις b om. Aa ‖ τῶν] τὰ τῶν c ‖ 19 ἁγίων om. Nb ‖ παρεδίδοντο] παρεδίδοτο B ‖ 20 ἀνθρωπίνῃ BMN: ἀνθρωπίνῳ b ἀνθρωπείᾳ ARSTa ‖ νυνὶ MNRS: νῦν ABTa ‖ 21 διὰ τοῦτο om. Mc ‖ δεῖ om. Nb ‖ 22 σῶμα] σῶμα θλίβεσθαι B ‖ 23 τῆς εὐσεβείας om. Mc ‖ 24 ἢ om. B.

94. In the way beeswax cannot receive the seal placed upon it without being warmed or softened for a long time, neither can man accept the seal of the virtue of God unless he is tested by labours and weaknesses. Because of this the Lord says to the inspired Paul: 'My grace is sufficient for you; for my power is made perfect in weakness.' But the Apostle himself boasted, saying: 'Therefore I will rather boast more gladly in my weaknesses, that the power of Christ might dwell in me.'[121] And again in Proverbs it was written: 'Whom the Lord loves, he corrects; he scourges everyone he accepts as a son.'[122] The Apostle terms 'weaknesses' the rebellions of the enemies of the Cross (which assailed him and all the saints of that time constantly, that they might not be raised up, as he says, to the height of revelations;[123] but through humility they rather remained in the pattern of perfection, preserving the divine gift devoutly through many occasions of being humiliated); but we now speak of evil imaginings and bodily indispositions as weaknesses. For then since the bodies of the saints who contended against sin were handed over to deadly outrages and various other afflictions, they were very much above the passions which entered into human nature from sin. But now, since a peace of the churches flourishes due to the Lord,[124] those who contend for piety must be tested: the body by continual indispositions and souls by evil imaginings–and especially among those whom perception activates with a whole Sense and complete assurance; so that being outside all vainglory

---

[121] 2 Corinthians 12:9.
[122] Proverbs 3:12.
[123] 2 Corinthians 12:7.
[124] See 1 Peter 1:2.

ΔΙΑΔΟΧΟΥ

καὶ μετεωρισμοῦ ἐκτὸς ὑπάρχωσι καὶ χωρῆσαι δυνηθῶσιν, ὡς ἔφην, ἐν ταῖς καρδίαις διὰ τῆς πολλῆς ταπεινώσεως τοῦ κάλλους τοῦ θείου τὴν σφραγῖδα κατὰ τὸν λέγοντα ἅγιον· 'Εσημειώθη ἐφ᾿ ἡμᾶς τὸ φῶς τοῦ προσώπου σου, κύριε. Δεῖ οὖν εὐχαριστοῦντας ὑπομένειν τὴν βουλὴν
5 τοῦ θεοῦ· τότε γὰρ ἡμῖν εἰς λόγον δευτέρου μαρτυρίου τό τε συνεχὲς τῶν νόσων καὶ ἡ πρὸς τοὺς δαιμονιώδεις λογισμοὺς μάχη λογισθήσεται. Ὁ γὰρ τότε λέγων τοῖς ἁγίοις μάρτυσι διὰ τῶν ἀνόμων ἐκείνων ἀρχόντων· Ἀρνήσασθε τὸν Χριστόν, ποθήσατε δὲ τὰς βιωτικὰς δόξας, καὶ νῦν ταῦτα ἐφέστηκε δι᾿ ἑαυτοῦ τοῖς δούλοις τοῦ θεοῦ ἀδιαλείπτως
10 λέγων. Ὁ τότε ἀλγύνων τὰ τῶν δικαίων σώματα καὶ ὑβρίζων ἐσχάτως τοὺς τῆς τιμῆς διδασκάλους διὰ τῶν ὑπηρετούντων τοῖς διαβολικοῖς ἐκείνοις φρονήμασιν αὐτὸς καὶ νῦν τοῖς τῆς εὐσεβείας ὁμολογηταῖς ἐπάγει τὰ διάφορα πάθη μετὰ ὕβρεων πολλῶν καὶ ἐξουδενώσεων, ὅτε μάλιστα πολλῇ δυνάμει τοῖς καταπονουμένοις πένησι διὰ τὴν δόξαν τοῦ
15 κυρίου βοηθοῦσιν. Καὶ διὰ τοῦτο ἐχρῆν μετὰ ἀσφαλείας καὶ ὑπομονῆς τὸ μαρτύριον τῆς συνειδήσεως ἡμῶν κατεργάζεσθαι ἐνώπιον τοῦ θεοῦ· Ὑπομένων γάρ, φησίν, ὑπέμεινα τὸν κύριον καὶ προσέσχε μοι.

ϟε'.

20 Δυσπόριστον μὲν πρᾶγμα ἡ ταπεινοφροσύνη· ὅσῳ γὰρ μέγα ἐστίν, τοσούτῳ μετὰ πολλῶν ἀγώνων κατορθοῦται. Παραγίνεται δὲ τοῖς μετόχοις τῆς ἁγίας γνώσεως κατὰ δύο τρόπους. Ὅτε μὲν γὰρ ἐν μεσότητί ἐστι τῆς πνευματικῆς πείρας ὁ τῆς εὐσεβείας ἀγωνιστής, ἢ δι᾿ ἀσθένειαν σώματος ἢ διὰ τοὺς ἀκαίρως ἐχθραίνοντας τοῖς τοῦ
25 δικαίου φροντίζουσιν ἢ διὰ λογισμοὺς πονηροὺς ταπεινότερόν πως ἔχει τὸ φρόνημα. Ὅτε δὲ ἐν αἰσθήσει πολλῇ καὶ πληροφορίᾳ ὁ νοῦς ὑπὸ τῆς ἁγίας χάριτος καταυγασθῇ, τότε ὥσπερ φυσικὴν ἔχει τὴν ταπεινοφροσύνην ἡ ψυχή. Καταπιαινομένη γὰρ ὑπὸ τῆς θείας χρηστότητος οὐ δύναται οὐκέτι εἰς τὸν ὄγκον τῆς φιλοδοξίας

---

1 pr. καὶ om. ARS || ὑπάρχωσι] ὑπάρχουσι NSb || 2 τῆς om. STa || 4 δεῖ] ἔδει M || 5 θεοῦ ARS: κυρίου ceteri || 8 ἀρνήσασθε BMRST: ἀρνήσασθαι ANa || 9 δι᾽ ἑαυτοῦ om. A || θεοῦ] χριστοῦ N || 10 δικαίων] ἁγίων MS || 11 τῆς τιμῆς MNR: τιμῆς b τιμίους ABSTa || 13 ὕβρεων] τῶν ὕβρεων c || 15 κυρίου] θεοῦ a || 16 κατεργάζεσθαι ABNa: κατεργάζεσθαι ἡμᾶς MRSTb || 20 μὲν] μέντι B om. FT || ὅσῳ ABRSTab: ὡς MN || 21 τοσούτῳ ABM(R)a: τοσοῦτο N τοσοῦτον ST || 28 καταπιαινομένη] καταπονουμένη M || 29 χρηστότητος] χάριτος B || οὐ δύναται om. A.

142

and even elation, they might be able (as I said) to receive in their hearts the seal of divine beauty through great humility, according to the holy one who says: 'The Light of your countenance, O Lord, was printed on us.'[125] And so rejoicing we must be steadfast in the intention of God, since the continuation of diseases and the fight against demonic imaginings will then be reckoned to us on the principle of a second martyrdom. For he who said to the martyrs through those lawless rulers: 'Deny Christ, long for the glory of this life,' he it is who even now causes these things through ceaselessly speaking, himself, to the servants of God. He who then afflicted the bodies of the just, and insulted the teachers of honour exceedingly through those who served those diabolical purposes, he himself now also induces various passions in those who confess piety, with many insults and humiliations–especially when with great power they help those subjected to penury, for the sake of the glory of the Lord. And for this reason it is necessary that the witness of our conscience be performed before God with assurance and steadfastness. For 'being steadfast,' it says, 'I was steadfast in the Lord, and he upheld me.'[126]

95. Humble-mindedness is a thing which is hard to acquire–for it is just as great as the extent to which it is accomplished with many contests; but it supports those who participate in holy perception, in two ways. For when he who contends for piety is in the midst of spiritual trial (either because of a weakness of the body, or because of people who are unduly hostile to those who take thought of what is just, or because of evil imaginings), this is how he holds to a humbler mentality. But when the intellect is shone upon by holy grace with a whole Sense and complete assurance, then the soul has humble-mindedness just as if it were natural. For being greatly swollen by divine excellence it is no longer able to be

---

[125] Psalms 4:7.
[126] Psalms 39:2.

ΔΙΑΔΟΧΟΥ

ἐπαίρεσθαι, κἂν ἀπαύστως τὰς ἐντολὰς κατεργάζοιτο τοῦ θεοῦ, ταπεινοτέραν δὲ μᾶλλον ἑαυτὴν πάντων διὰ τὴν τῆς θείας ἐπιεικείας κοινωνίαν ἡγεῖται. Ἔχει δὲ ἐκείνη μὲν ἡ ταπεινοφροσύνη λύπην τὰ πολλὰ καὶ ἀθυμίαν, αὕτη δὲ χαρὰν μετ' αἰδοῦς πανσόφου. Διόπερ ἡ μὲν τοῖς ἐν μέσῳ, ὡς ἔφην, τῶν ἀγώνων οὖσι παραγίνεται, ἡ δὲ τοῖς ἐγγίζουσι τῇ τελειότητι καταπέμπεται. Διὰ τοῦτο ἐκείνη μὲν ὑπὸ τῶν βιωτικῶν πολλάκις εὐπραγιῶν ὀνειδίζεται, αὕτη δέ, κἂν ὅλας τὰς βασιλείας τοῦ κόσμου τις αὐτῇ προσαγάγῃ, οὔτε πτοεῖται οὔτε ὅλως τῶν δεινῶν βελῶν τῆς ἁμαρτίας αἰσθάνεται· πνευματικὴ γὰρ ὅλη ὑπάρχουσα ἀγνοεῖ πάντως τὰς σωματικὰς δόξας. Ἐχρῆν δὲ δι' ἐκείνης παντὶ τρόπῳ παρελθόντα τὸν ἀγωνιστὴν ἐπὶ ταύτην ἐλθεῖν· εἰ μὴ γὰρ δι' ἐκείνης τῇ ἐπιφορᾷ τῶν παιδευτικῶν παθῶν δοκιμαστικῶς, οὐ γὰρ ἀναγκαστικῶς, τὸ αὐτεξούσιον ἡμῶν προμαλάξοι ἡ χάρις, οὐκ ἂν τὴν ταύτης ἡμῖν δωρήσηται πολυτέλειαν.

ϟϛ'.

Οἱ τῶν τοῦ παρόντος βίου ἡδονῶν ὄντες φίλοι ἐκ τῶν λογισμῶν ἐπὶ τὰ πταίσματα ἔρχονται· ἀδιακρίτῳ γὰρ γνώμῃ φερόμενοι πάσας αὐτῶν σχεδὸν τὰς ἐμπαθεῖς ἐννοίας εἴς τε λόγους ἀνόμους καὶ ἔργα ἀνόσια ἐπιθυμοῦσι φέρειν. Οἱ δὲ τὸν ἀσκητικὸν ἐπιχειροῦντες κατορθοῦν βίον ἐκ τῶν πταισμάτων εἰς τοὺς πονηροὺς λογισμοὺς ἢ εἰς πονηρά τινα καὶ ἐπιβλαβῆ ἔρχονται ῥήματα. Ἐὰν γὰρ οἱ δαίμονες τοὺς τοιούτους ἢ λοιδορίας ἀνεχομένους ἡδέως ἢ ἀργά τινα καὶ ἄκαιρα ὁμιλοῦντας ἢ γελῶντας ὡς οὐ δεῖ ἢ θυμουμένους ἀμέτρως ἢ τῆς κενῆς καὶ ματαίας ἐπιθυμοῦντας ἴδωσιν δόξης, τότε ὁμοθυμαδὸν κατ' αὐτῶν ἐξοπλίζονται· τὴν γὰρ φιλοδοξίαν μάλιστα εἰς πρόφασιν τῆς ἑαυτῶν κακίας λαμβάνοντες δι' ἐκείνης ὥσπερ διὰ θυρίδος τινὸς σκοτεινῆς εἰσπηδῶντες τὰς ψυχὰς διαρπάζουσιν. Ἐχρῆν οὖν τοὺς θέλοντας συνδιαιτᾶσθαι τῷ

---

2 πάντων ANa: τῶν πάντων MRT πάντων ἀνθρώπων S om. B ‖ διὰ om. B τὴν om. AB ‖ 3 κοινωνίαν] καὶ κοινωνίας A ‖ 4 αὕτη] αὐτὴ b ‖ 7 αὕτη] αὐτὴ A ‖ 8 αὐτῇ] αὐτὴν R ‖ προσαγάγῃ FT: προσάγοι NRc προσαγάγοι ABMSa ‖ 9 δεινῶν βελῶν B: δεινῶν MN βελῶν ARSTa ‖ αἰσθάνεται] αἰσθάνεσθαι A ‖ 10 δι' ἐκείνης] ἐκείνην R ‖ 12 παθῶν] πόνων R ‖ 14 ταύτης AB: αὐτῆς MNRST ‖ 18 πάσας] πάσα A ‖ αὐτῶν om. Aa ‖ 19 τε om. Aa ‖ καὶ] καὶ εἰς B ‖ 24 ὡς om. c ‖ κενῆς BRSTbc: καινῆς AMNa ‖ 25 ἐπιθυμοῦντας] ὀρεγομένους Nb ‖ 26 φιλοδοξίαν] κενοδοξίαν Ba ‖ ἑαυτῶν] αὐτῶν R ‖ 28 τὰς ψυχὰς om. A ‖ διαρπάζουσιν] ἁρπάζουσιν b.

raised into the pretension of liking glory; even if it performs the commandments of God ceaselessly, it holds itself rather to be most lowly of all, due to participating in divine reasonableness. The former humble-mindedness has grief and dispiritedness for the most part, while the latter has joy, with a completely wise modesty. And so the first (as I said) supports those who are in the midst of contests, but the second is sent down to those who are drawing near to perfection. For this reason the former is often mocked by the prosperity of this life, while the latter is neither excited nor does it sense the fearful arrows of sin at all, even if someone offers it all the kingdoms of the world;[127] for being completely spiritual, it is altogether without perception of bodily glories. Yet it is in every way necessary for the contender to come to the latter by passing through the former; for unless grace pre-softens our independence through the first by an impetus of educative passions (by testing, not by compulsion) it would not give us the abundance of the second.

96. Those who are friends of the pleasures of this present life come into lapses from imaginings; for borne by an undiscriminating inquisitiveness, they long to carry almost all their impassioned intellectual conceptions into lawless words and profane works. But those who undertake to succeed in the ascetic life come into evil imaginings or into evil and harmful statements *through* lapses. Because whenever the demons see such men either gladly tolerating raillery, or conversing in idle and undue terms, or joking in a way one ought not, or being in an immoderate temper, or desiring vain and empty glory, then they stand in armed array with one accord against them. Taking up affection for glory in particular as an opportunity for their own evil, they leap through it just as through a shadowy window, and snatch souls. And so those who intend to dwell

---

[127] See Matthew 4:8.

ΔΙΑΔΟΧΟΥ

πλήθει τῶν ἀρετῶν μήτε δόξης ἐφίεσθαι μήτε πολλοῖς συντυγχάνειν μήτε προόδοις συνεχέσι κεχρῆσθαι ἢ λοιδορεῖν τινας, κἂν οἱ λοιδορούμενοι τῆς λοιδορίας ὑπάρχωσιν ἄξιοι, μήτε πολλὰ ὁμιλεῖν, κἂν πάντα καλὰ λέγειν δύναιντο. Ἡ γὰρ πολυλογία ἀμέτρως διαφοροῦσα
5 τὸν νοῦν οὐ μόνον περὶ τὴν πνευματικὴν αὐτὸν ἐργασίαν ἀργὸν ἀπεργάζεται, ἀλλὰ καὶ τῷ τῆς ἀκηδίας αὐτὸν παραδίδωσι δαίμονι, ὅστις αὐτὸν ὑπεκλύων ἀμέτρως τοῖς τῆς λύπης λοιπὸν δὲ καὶ τοῖς τῆς ὀργῆς παραδίδωσι δαίμοσιν. Δεῖ οὖν ἀεὶ εἰς τὴν τῶν ἁγίων ἐντολῶν τήρησιν ἀπασχολεῖσθαι τὸν νοῦν καὶ εἰς βαθεῖαν μνήμην τοῦ κυρίου τῆς δόξης.
10 Ὁ γὰρ φυλάσσων, φησίν, ἐντολὴν οὐ γνώσεται ῥῆμα πονηρόν, τοῦτ' ἔστιν, εἰς φαύλους λογισμοὺς ἢ λόγους οὐκ ἐκτραπήσεται.

ϟζ'.

Ὅτε μετὰ ζεστῆς τινος ἀλγηδόνος ἡ καρδία εἰσδέχεται τὰ τόξα τῶν
15 δαιμόνων ὡς αὐτὰ οἴεσθαι φέρειν τὰ βέλη τὸν πολεμούμενον, μισεῖ μετὰ πόνου ἡ ψυχὴ τὰ πάθη ὡς ἐν ἀρχῇ οὖσα τοῦ καθαίρεσθαι· ἐὰν γὰρ μὴ ἀλγήσῃ μεγάλως ἐπὶ τῇ ἀναιδείᾳ τῆς ἁμαρτίας, οὐκ ἂν δυνηθείη πλουσίως χαρῆναι ἐπὶ τῇ τῆς δικαιοσύνης χρηστότητι. Ὁ τοίνυν θέλων τὴν ἑαυτοῦ καθαρίσαι καρδίαν τῇ μνήμῃ τοῦ κυρίου διὰ παντὸς
20 διαπυρούτω αὐτήν, τοῦτο μόνον μελέτην καὶ ἔργον ἄπαυστον ἔχων. Οὐ γὰρ ποτὲ μὲν εὔχεσθαι δεῖ ποτὲ δὲ μὴ τοὺς τὴν ἑαυτῶν σαπρίαν ἀποβαλεῖν ἐθέλοντας, ἀλλὰ ἀεὶ τῇ προσευχῇ σχολάζειν ἐν τῇ τηρήσει τοῦ νοῦ, κἂν ἔξω που αὐλίζοιτο τῶν εὐκτηρίων δόμων. Ὃν γὰρ τρόπον ὁ θέλων καθαρίσαι χρυσίον, ἐὰν κἂν πρὸς βραχὺ τὸ πῦρ ἐάσῃ σχολάσαι

---

2 προόδοις] προσόδοις B ‖ 3 ὑπάρχωσιν MRa: ὑπάρχουσιν ABNS εἰσιν T ‖ μήτε Bac: μήτε δὲ MNRST μηδὲ A ‖ 4 δύναιντο ABMRSp.c.Ta: δύνοιτο N δύνανται Sa.c. ‖ ἀμέτρως] ἡ ἄμετρος A ‖ 4 διαφοροῦσα - 7 ἀμέτρως om. Aa ‖ 5 περὶ om. M ‖ 7 pr. τοῖς] τῷ B ‖ δὲ om. Aa ‖ alt. τοῖς MNRST: τῷ B om. Aac ‖ 8 δαίμοσιν] δαίμονι B ‖ ἀεὶ om. Aa ‖ 9 κυρίου] κυρίου Ἰησοῦ ATa ‖ 10 ῥῆμα om. c ‖ 11 ἢ λόγους BMRST: om. ANa ‖ 14 ὅτε ARSTa: ὅταν MN ‖ 17 ἀλγήσῃ] ἀλγήσει Tb ‖ δυνηθείη] δυνηθῇ ARS ‖ 19 καθαρίσαι] ἐκκαθάραι T ‖ μνήμῃ] μνήμη τῇ B ‖ κυρίου RST: κυρίου Ἰησοῦ ceteri ‖ 20 διαπυρούτω] πυρούτω NTb ‖ ἄπαυστον] ἀδιάλειπτον Aa ‖ 21 ποτὲ δὲ μὴ om. AMa ‖ 22 ἀποβαλεῖν MNRSTa: ἀποβάλλειν Bc ἀποβαλλεῖν A ἀποβεῖν T ‖ ἐθέλοντας MNRST: θέλοντας Bc θέλοντας ποτὲ δὲ οὐ δεῖ Aa ‖ ἀεὶ] δεῖ ASa ‖ σχολάζειν] σπουδάζειν Nb ‖ 23 κἂν - δόμων om. MRSc ‖ 24 ἐὰν κἂν MNRS: ἐὰν ABa κἂν T ‖ τὸ πῦρ om. Nb ‖ ἐάσῃ] ἐάσει (R)S.

with the fullness of the virtues must neither aim at glory nor fall in with the many, nor indulge in constant excursions, nor revile anyone (even if those who are reviled are worthy of reviling), nor converse a lot (even if they are able to say all things well). For speaking a lot disperses the intellect immeasurably, not only making it idle concerning spiritual work, but also delivering it up to the demon of restlessness, which (breaking it down immeasurably by degrees) then delivers it up to the demons of grief and of anger. So the intellect must always be kept employed in keeping the holy commandments and in profound recollection of the Lord of glory; for 'he who keeps the commandment,' it says, 'will not perceive evil speech;'[128] that is, he will not turn aside into foul imaginings or words.

97. When the heart receives the bowshots of the demons with a burning pain (in such a way that he who is warred against supposes he sustains real arrows) it is with difficulty that the soul hates the passions, since it is at the beginning of being cleansed; for if it were not severely distressed by the impudence of sin, it could not rejoice abundantly in the excellence of righteousness. So whoever intends his heart to be cleansed, let him set it on fire by the recollection of the Lord at all times, having this alone as his concern and unceasing work. For those who decide to cast off their own rottenness must not sometimes pray and sometimes not; rather one must always devote oneself to prayer in guarding the intellect, even if one dwells outside the houses of prayer. Because in the way one who intends to purify gold, if he permits the fire of the smelting furnace to ease off even for a short period, he makes the matter being purified hard again; so also

---

[128] Ecclesiastes 8:5.

ΔΙΑΔΟΧΟΥ

τοῦ χωνευτηρίου, σκληρίαν πάλιν τῇ καθαιρομένῃ ὕλῃ ἐμποιεῖ, οὕτως καὶ ὁ ποτὲ μὲν μεμνημένος τοῦ θεοῦ ποτὲ δὲ μή, ὅπερ δοκεῖ κτᾶσθαι διὰ τῆς εὐχῆς, τοῦτο ἀπόλλυσι διὰ τῆς σχολῆς. Ἀνδρὸς δέ ἐστι φιλαρέτου ἴδιον τὸ ἀεὶ τῇ μνήμῃ τοῦ θεοῦ τὸ τῆς καρδίας
5 καταναλίσκειν γεῶδες, ἵν' οὕτω κατ' ὀλίγον τοῦ κακοῦ ὑπὸ τοῦ πυρὸς τῆς τοῦ ἀγαθοῦ μνήμης δαπανωμένου τελείως 'εἰς τὴν φυσικὴν αὐτῆς ἡ ψυχὴ μετὰ πλείονος δόξης ἐπανέλθοι λαμπρότητα.

ϟη'.
10 Ἀπάθειά ἐστιν οὐ τὸ μὴ πολεμεῖσθαι ὑπὸ τῶν δαιμόνων, ἐπεὶ ἄρα ὀφείλομεν ἐξεληλυθέναι κατὰ τὸν ἀπόστολον ἐκ τοῦ κόσμου, ἀλλὰ τὸ πολεμουμένους ὑπ' αὐτῶν ἀπολεμήτους μένειν. Καὶ γὰρ οἱ σιδηροφόροι πολεμισταὶ τοξεύονται μὲν ὑπὸ τῶν ἀντιπάλων καὶ τοῦ ἤχου τῆς τοξείας ἀκούουσιν, ἀλλὰ καὶ αὐτὰ βλέπουσι τὰ πεμπόμενα κατ' αὐτῶν
15 σχεδὸν ἅπαντα βέλη, οὐ πλήττονται δὲ διὰ τὴν τῶν πολεμικῶν ἐνδυμάτων στερρότητα. Ἀλλ' ἐκεῖνοι μὲν σιδήρῳ φραττόμενοι ἐν τῷ πολεμεῖσθαι τὸ ἀπολέμητον ἔχουσιν· ἡμεῖς δὲ τῇ τοῦ φωτὸς τοῦ ἁγίου πανοπλίᾳ καὶ τῇ τοῦ σωτηρίου περικεφαλαίᾳ διὰ πάντων τῶν καλῶν ἔργων καθωπλισμένοι τὰς σκοτεινὰς τῶν δαιμόνων διακόψωμεν φάλαγγας.
20 Οὐ γὰρ τὸ μηκέτι πρᾶξαι τὰ κακὰ μόνον καθαρότητα φέρει, ἀλλὰ τὸ ἐπιμελείᾳ τῶν καλῶν κατὰ κράτος ἀθετῆσαι τὰ κακά.

---

1 τοῦ] ἐκ τοῦ ABa ǁ 3 εὐχῆς] προσευχῆς S ǁ 5 καταναλίσκειν] ἀναλίσκειν RS καταλίσκειν A ǁ κατ' ὀλίγον] κατολίγων A λίγοντος T ǁ 5 τοῦ κακοῦ - 6 τῆς om. A ǁ 7 ἐπανέλθοι] ἐπανέλθῃ T ǁ 11 ὀφείλομεν] ὀφείλαμεν B ὠφείλαμεν a ǁ ἐκ om. R ǁ 12 ἀπολεμήτους] ἀτρώτους S ǁ 13 ὑπὸ] παρὰ B ἐκ a ǁ τοῦ ἤχου] τοῦ ἤχους MR τοὺς ἤχους A τὸν ἤχον a ǁ 14 ἀλλὰ - βλέπουσι om. Nb ǁ πεμπόμενα] πετόμενα R βαλλόμενα B ǁ 17 ἁγίου] ἁγίου πνεύματος a ǁ 19 καθωπλισμένοι MNRa: καθοπλισάμενοι AST καθοπλιζόμενοι B ǁ διακόψωμεν] διακόψομεν N ǁ 20 κακὰ] καλὰ B ǁ alt. τὸ] τῷ N τὸ τῇ S.

for someone who recollects God sometimes but sometimes not; that which he seems to gain through prayer, he loses through taking time off. It is characteristic of a man who loves virtue always to consume the earthiness of the heart in the recollection of God, so that as the bad is consumed little by little by the fire of the recollection of the good, the soul might return to its natural brightness perfectly, with additional glory.

98. Dispassion does not consist in not being attacked by the demons, since for that we would have to 'go out of the world,' according to the Apostle;[129] rather it is to remain unattacked when attacked by them. For those warriors who wear armour are shot by their antagonists and hear the report of the bows firing, and they see almost all the arrows sent against them; but because of the hardness of the clothing of war they are not wounded. But they sustain 'being unattacked while being attacked,' through being shielded by iron; but let us, being armed with the full armour of the holy light and the helmet of salvation[130] through all good works, cut through the shadowy phalanxes of the demons; for it is not only no longer doing evil deeds which brings purity, but rejecting evil things with all one's might, by attention to those which are good.

---

[129] 1 Corinthians 5:10.
[130] Ephesians 6:11ff.

ΔΙΑΔΟΧΟΥ

μθ'.

Ὅταν σχεδὸν ἅπαντα τὰ πάθη νικήσῃ ὁ τοῦ θεοῦ ἄνθρωπος, δύο δαίμονες αὐτῷ ἀπομένουσι προσπαλαίοντες, ὧν ὁ μὲν τῇ ψυχῇ παρενοχλεῖ ἀπὸ πολλῆς θεοφιλίας εἰς ζῆλον αὐτὴν ἄκαιρον φέρων, ὥστε μὴ θέλειν ἄλλον τινὰ κατ' αὐτὴν ἀρέσαι τῷ θεῷ· ὁ δὲ τῷ σώματι εἰς ἐπιθυμίαν συνουσίας αὐτὸ ἐμπύρῳ τινὶ κινῶν ἐνεργείᾳ. Τοῦτο δὲ συμβαίνει τῷ σώματι πρῶτον μὲν διὰ τὸ τῆς φύσεως εἶναι ταύτην τὴν ἡδονὴν ἰδίαν ὡς διὰ τὴν παιδογονίαν καὶ διὰ τοῦτο εὐχερῶς ἡττωμένην· λοιπὸν δὲ καὶ διὰ παραχώρησιν τοῦ θεοῦ. Ὅταν γὰρ ἴδῃ τινὰ τῶν ἀγωνιστῶν μεγάλως ἀκμάζοντα τῷ πλήθει τῶν ἀρετῶν ὁ κύριος, παραχωρεῖ αὐτόν ποτε ὑπὸ τοῦ τοιούτου καταρρυποῦσθαι δαίμονος, ἵνα πάντων τῶν τοῦ βίου ἀνθρώπων εὐτελέστερον ἑαυτὸν ὑπολαμβάνῃ. Ἀμέλει ἢ ἕπεται ἡ ὄχλησις τοῦ πάθους τοῖς κατορθώμασιν ἢ καὶ προλαμβάνει ταῦτά ποτε, ἵνα τῇ προλήψει ἢ τῇ ἐπιφορᾷ τοῦ πάθους ἀχρεία πως ἡ ψυχὴ φαίνηται, κἂν ὁποῖα ἢ μεγάλα αὐτῆς τὰ κατορθώματα. Ἀλλὰ τῷ μὲν ἐν ταπεινοφροσύνῃ πολλῇ καὶ ἀγάπῃ μαχησώμεθα, τῷ δὲ ἐν ἐγκρατείᾳ καὶ ἀοργησίᾳ καὶ ἐννοίᾳ βαθείᾳ τοῦ θανάτου, ἵνα ἀπαύστως ἐντεῦθεν τῆς ἐνεργείας αἰσθόμενοι τοῦ ἁγίου πνεύματος ἐπάνω καὶ τούτων γενώμεθα ἐν κυρίῳ τῶν παθῶν.

2 ἅπαντα] πάντα MR || νικήσῃ BMN(R)S: νικήσει ATab || 3 τῇ ψυχῇ] τὴν ψυχὴν c || 4 θεοφιλίας] θεοσεβείας ABa || αὐτὴν om. T || 5 θέλειν] θέλειν αὐτὴν NTb || εἰς] τὴν Mc || 6 αὐτὸ BN: αὐτῷ Ap.c.MT αὐτῶν Aa.c. αὐτὸν Sa αὐτῆς R || 8 τοῦτο] τοῦτο δὲ BR || ἡττωμένην] ἡττωμένης T || 9 τοῦ om. Aa || γὰρ om. Aa || 10 ὁ κύριος om. Aa || 11 τοῦ BNRST: om. AMa || 12 ὑπολαμβάνῃ a: ὑπολαμβάνει N(R)ST ὑπολαμβάνοι ABM || 13 κατορθώμασιν MNRST: κατορθουμένοις ABa || 14 ἵνα MNRSa: ἵνα ἢ ABT || τῇ προλήψει om. a || ἢ] καὶ R || 15 ἀχρεία] ἀχρείαν T || πως AMRSa: ποιεῖ BN ποιῇ T || ἡ ψυχὴ AMRSa: τὴν ψυχὴν T τῇ ψυχῇ BN || φαίνηται MRS: φαίνεσθαι NT γίνηται A γένηται a γίνεσθαι B || ἢ om. R || αὐτῆς] αὐτὴν R || 16 ἀλλὰ - 17 μαχησώμεθα om. T || 16 τῷ] τὸ AM || ἐν om. ASa || 17 μαχησώμεθα BMN: μαχησόμεθα A(R)Sa || ἐν MN: om. ABRSa || καὶ ἀοργησίᾳ] καὶ ἐν ἀοργησίᾳ Mbc || ἐννοίᾳ ANRST: ἐν ἐννοίᾳ BM συννοίᾳ a || βαθείᾳ om. Aa || 18 ἐντεῦθεν] ἔνθεν Aa || αἰσθόμενοι] αἰθανόμενοι MTc || 19 γενώμεθα] γενόμεθα AN γινόμεθα b || ἐν κυρίῳ om. R.

99. Whenever the man of God is victorious over almost all the passions, two demons remain fighting with him: the first of them makes trouble in the soul, bearing it from great love of God into undue zeal, so that it does not want another to please God as much as it does; but the other makes trouble in the body, moving it into desire for intercourse, by an inflamed activity. But this takes place in the body first because this pleasure is inherent in its nature (presumably due to reproduction and because nature is therefore easily prevailed upon), and then also by the permission of God. For whenever the Lord sees one of those who contend greatly flourishing in the fullness of the virtues, he permits him sometimes to be soiled by such a demon, so that the contender might apprehend himself as being more worthless than all the men of this life. Of course the disturbance of passion either follows successes or indeed at times precedes them, so that the soul might appear useless[131] in the anticipation or conclusion of the passion, however great its successes might be. But let us fight the first by great humble-mindedness and love, and the second by self-control and freedom from anger, and a profound intellectual conception of death; so that as a result, sensing the activity of the holy Spirit ceaselessly, we might come, in the Lord, to be above these passions also.

---

[131] See Luke 17:10.

ΔΙΑΔΟΧΟΥ

ρ'.

Ὅσοι τῆς ἁγίας γνώσεως γινόμεθα μέτοχοι, καὶ τῶν ἀκουσίων μετεωρισμῶν ἁπάντων λόγον ὑφέξομεν. Ἐπεσημήνω γάρ, φησὶν ὁ Ἰώβ, καὶ εἴ τι ἄκων παρέβην, καὶ δικαίως. Ἐὰν γὰρ μὴ σχολάσῃ τις τοῦ μεμνῆσθαι τοῦ θεοῦ καὶ τῶν ἁγίων αὐτοῦ μὴ παραμελήσῃ ἐντολῶν, οὐκ ἂν ἢ ἀκουσίῳ ἢ ἑκουσίῳ ὑποπέσοι πταίσματι. Δεῖ οὖν εὐθέως καὶ περὶ τῶν ἀκουσίων πταισμάτων ἐξομολόγησιν σύντονον προσφέρειν τῷ δεσπότῃ, τοῦτ' ἔστι περὶ τὴν ἐργασίαν τοῦ συνήθους κανόνος (οὐ γὰρ ἔστιν ἄνθρωπον ὄντα μὴ πταίειν ἀνθρώπινα), ἄχρις οὗ πληροφορηθῇ ἡ συνείδησις ἡμῶν ἐν δακρύῳ ἀγάπης περὶ τῆς τούτων ἀφέσεως. Ἐὰν γάρ, φησίν, ὁμολογῶμεν τὰς ἁμαρτίας ἡμῶν, πιστός ἐστι καὶ δίκαιος, ἵνα ἀφῇ ἡμῖν τὰς ἁμαρτίας καὶ καθαρίσῃ ἡμᾶς ἀπὸ πάσης ἀδικίας. Προσέχειν δὲ δεῖ ἀδιαλείπτως τῇ αἰσθήσει τῆς ἐξομολογήσεως, μή που ἄρα ἡ συνείδησις ἡμῶν ψεύσηται ἑαυτὴν ὑπονοήσασα ἀρκούντως ἐξομολογήσασθαι τῷ θεῷ, ὅτι πολὺ κρείττων ἐστὶν ἡ τοῦ θεοῦ κρίσις τῆς ἡμετέρας συνειδήσεως, κἂν μηδὲν ἑαυτῷ τις ἐν πάσῃ σύνοιδεν πληροφορίᾳ, καθὼς ὁ σοφώτατος ἡμᾶς Παῦλος διδάσκει λέγων· Ἀλλ' οὐδὲ ἐμαυτὸν ἀνακρίνω· οὐδὲν γὰρ ἐμαυτῷ σύνοιδα, ἀλλ' οὐκ ἐν τούτῳ δεδικαίωμαι, ὁ δὲ ἀνακρίνων με κύριός ἐστιν. Ἐὰν γὰρ μὴ πρεπόντως καὶ περὶ αὐτῶν ἐξομολογησώμεθα, δειλίαν τινὰ ἄδηλον ἐν τῷ καιρῷ τῆς ἐξόδου ἡμῶν εὑρήσομεν ἐν ἑαυτοῖς. Ἐχρῆν δὲ ἡμᾶς εὔχεσθαι τοὺς ἀγαπῶντας τὸν κύριον ἐκτὸς παντὸς φόβου τότε εὑρίσκεσθαι· ὁ μὲν γὰρ ἐν φόβῳ εὑρισκόμενος τότε ἐλευθερίῳ τρόπῳ τοὺς ταρταρίους οὐ παρελεύσεται ἄρχοντας· συνήγορον γὰρ ἔχουσιν ὥσπερ ἐκεῖνοι τὴν τῆς ψυχῆς δειλίαν τῆς ἑαυτῶν κακίας. Ἡ δὲ ἐν τῇ ἀγάπῃ ἀγαλλιωμένη

3 ἁπάντων MN: πάντως ABRSTa || ὑφέξομεν M(R)STa: ὑφέξωμεν AB ὑφαίξωμεν N || γάρ, φησὶν ὁ ἰώβ, καὶ om. B || ὁ om. Nb || 4 μὴ om. BNb || σχολάσῃ] σχολάσει Nb σχολάσοι Mc || τοῦ] τὸ N τοῦ ἀεὶ T || 5 παραμελήσῃ MN(R)S: παραμελήσει Tb παραμελοίη Aa || 6 pr. ἢ MN: om. ABRSTa || ἀκουσίῳ ἢ ἑκουσίῳ NRSc: ἀκουσίως ἢ ἑκουσίως M ἑκουσίῳ ἢ ἀκουσίῳ ATa ἀκουσίῳ B || πταίσματι] πτώματι Nb || 9 ἀνθρώπινα om. Aa || 11 ὁμολογῶμεν] ὁμολογοῦμεν A || 12 ἡμῖν] ἡμῶν Nb || ἁμαρτίας] ἁμαρτίας ἡμῶν B || 13 ἀδιαλείπτως] λείπτως Nb || που BNR: πῶς MST τι Aa || 14 ἑαυτὴν] ἑαυτῇ Sc om. B || 15 ἐξομολογήσασθαι BMRT: ἐξομολογεῖσθαι ANSa || κρείττων ab: κρεῖττον ABMN(R)ST || 17 σοφώτατος] σοφὸς Aa || 18 ἀνακρίνω] ἀνακρινῶ A || 20 καὶ περὶ αὐτῶν om. Aa || ἐξομολογησώμεθα] ἐξομολογησόμεθα A || 21 εὑρήσομεν AN(R)Sac: εὑρήσωμεν BMT || ἐν om. a || ἑαυτοῖς] ἑαυτῷ R || δὲ] οὖν b || 25 ἐν om. a.

100. As many of us as participate in holy perception will be held accountable for all the elations, even involuntary ones. For Job says, 'I am marked even if I transgress involuntarily,'[132] and justly so. For if one does not leave off from the recollection of God and does not disregard his holy commandments, he will not fall by either an involuntary or a voluntary lapse. Therefore one must immediately offer to the Master earnest full confession about involuntary lapses–that is in terms of the execution of one's usual rule (for it is not possible for someone who is human not to lapse in a human way)–until our conscience is completely assured about their forgiveness, with tears of love. For it says, 'if ever we confess our sins, he is faithful and just, so that he would forgive us our sins and cleanse us from all unrighteousness.'[133] But we must give heed incessantly to the sensation of full confession; lest our conscience be deceived, supposing itself to have confessed fully to God abundantly; for the judgement of God is much better than our conscience, even if, with complete assurance, one has no consciousness of it; just as the most wise Paul teaches us saying: 'Yet I do not judge myself; for I am conscious of nothing, but I am not justified in this, rather it is the Lord who judges me.'[134] For if we do not make full confession as is fitting of these lapses also, we will find in ourselves an unnoticed cowardice at the time of our departing. We who love the Lord must rather pray to be found outside all fear then, since he who is found in fear at that time will not go past the rulers of Tartaros in a free manner, because they have the cowardice of the soul as an ally of their own wickedness. But the soul which rejoices in

---

[132] Job 14:17.
[133] 1 John 1:9.
[134] 1 Corinthians 4:3f.

ΔΙΑΔΟΧΟΥ

ψυχὴ τοῦ θεοῦ ἐν τῇ ὥρᾳ τῆς ἀναλύσεως ἐπάνω πασῶν τῶν σκοτεινῶν παρατάξεων σὺν τοῖς ἀγγέλοις τῆς εἰρήνης φέρεται. Ἐπτέρωται γὰρ ὥσπερ τῇ πνευματικῇ ἀγάπῃ ὡς τὸ πλήρωμα ἀνελλιπῶς φέρουσα τοῦ νόμου τὴν ἀγάπην. Διόπερ καὶ ἐν τῇ παρουσίᾳ τοῦ κυρίου μετὰ πάντων
5 τῶν ἁγίων οἱ μετὰ τοιαύτης παρρησίας ἐξιόντες τοῦ βίου ἁρπαγήσονται. Οἱ δὲ κἂν ἐν βραχεῖ δειλιῶντες ἐν τῷ καιρῷ τοῦ θανάτου ἐν τῇ πάντων τῶν ἄλλων ἀνθρώπων καταλειφθήσονται πληθύι ὡς ὑπὸ κρίσιν ὄντες, ἵνα διὰ τοῦ πυρὸς δοκιμασθέντες τῆς κρίσεως τοὺς κεχρεωστημένους αὐτοῖς κατὰ τὰς αὐτῶν πράξεις ἀπολάβωσι κλήρους παρὰ τοῦ ἀγαθοῦ ἡμῶν θεοῦ
10 καὶ βασιλέως Ἰησοῦ Χριστοῦ· ὅτι αὐτός ἐστιν θεὸς τῆς δικαιοσύνης καὶ αὐτοῦ ἐστιν ἐφ᾽ ἡμᾶς τοὺς ἀγαπῶντας αὐτὸν ὁ πλοῦτος τῆς χρηστότητος τῆς βασιλείας αὐτοῦ εἰς τὸν αἰῶνα τοῦ αἰῶνος. Ἀμήν.

1 ψυχὴ om. R ‖ ἐν om. a ‖ ἀναλύσεως] ἀναπαύσεως RS ‖ 2 γὰρ om. B ‖ 6 κἂν] καὶ a ‖ 7 ἄλλων om. A ‖ 8 δοκιμασθέντες AMRST: καθαρισθέντες BNa ‖ αὐτοῖς] ἑαυτοῖς A αὐτοὺς M ‖ 9 ἀπολάβωσι] ἀπολάβουσιν A ‖ 9-10 θεοῦ καὶ βασιλέως om. A ‖ 10 θεὸς BMNRS: ὁ θεὸς ATa ‖ 11 αὐτοῦ] αὐτὸς ABR ‖ τοὺς] τοῦ R ‖ 12 αὐτοῦ] αὐτοῦ καὶ αὐτῷ πρεπει τιμὴ καὶ δόξα Aa ‖ εἰς B: καὶ εἰς AMNRSTa ‖ τὸν αἰῶνα τοῦ αἰῶνος NRST: τοῦ αἰῶνος B τοὺς σύμπαντας αἰῶνας τῶν αἰώνων AMa ‖ post ἀμήν colophon τοῦ ἁγίου διαδόχου ἐπισκόπου πόλεως φωτικῆς τῆς ἠπείρου τοῦ ἰλλυρικοῦ λόγοι ἀσκητικοί κεφάλαια ρ΄ στίχοι Βτ΄ Β τέλος τῶν ρ΄ κεφαλαίων τοῦ ἁγίου διαδόχου ἐπισκόπου φωτικῆς τῆς ἠπείρου τοῦ ἰλλυρικοῦ τοῦ μακαρίου καὶ θεοφιλοῦς τῷ ὄντι S τέλος τῶν ἑκατὸν κεφαλαίων διαδόχου φωτικῆς T.

love for God at the hour of release is borne up with the angels of peace over all the shadowy battle ranks, since it takes flight in spiritual love, bearing unfailingly the love which is the fulfilment of the law.[135] And so at the coming of the Lord, those who depart this life with this sort of boldness[136] will be snatched up with all the saints.[137] But if they are even briefly cowardly at the time of death they will be left behind in the crowd of all other men, as being under judgement–so that through being tested by the fire of judgement[138] they might receive the portions due to them according to their deeds, from our good God and King, Jesus Christ; for he is a God of justice, and the wealth of the excellence[139] of his kingdom is for us who love him, unto the age of the age, Amen.

---

[135] See Romans 13:10.
[136] See 1 John 4:17.
[137] See 1 Thessalonians 4:17.
[138] 1 Peter 1:7.
[139] See Ephesians 2:7.

Commentary

Commentary

Title and introduction
The title here follows manuscript R, which is the only one to retain the 'Old' of 'Old Epiros'. 'Practical' refers to the practice of ascesis, particularly in the Evagrian tradition. Evagrios's λόγος πρακτικός, or *practical account* of the ascetic life distinguishes three elements of ascetic prayer:[1] the day to day practice of asceticism (πρακτική), discernment of the nature of things (φυσική), and contemplation of God (θεολογική). The ascetic way of life is intended to lead to an ability to perceive the divine principles (λόγοι) inherent in the created world, and this in turn is meant to lead to a relationship with the Logos of God, from whom these principles derive. As explained in the Introduction to this volume, Diadochos's concern is with an accurate understanding of Scripture and spiritual experience, and it is these which he explores for evidence of the nature of eternal reality, rather than the natural world. It is quite likely that Diadochos himself called his composition *practical texts*; it consists of 100 passages or 'texts', after the Evagrian model[2]. At first these texts are short and pithy, like those of Evagrios. But soon the theological complexity of his purpose leads him to write longer and longer passages, which themselves often merge into one another. The inter-relatedness of his themes means that although his composition is 'practical', ultimately he must deal with all three aspects of ascetic life—practice, valid discrimination of divine and demonic nature, and ultimate union with God. It is important to note that γνῶσις has been translated throughout as 'perception.' It will be necessary in reading Diadochos to realise that he relates *gnosis* specifically to the intellect's Sense;[3] it does not relate to rational knowledge, but to direct experience of the presence of grace in the soul, which the intellect's Sense must accurately discern, and Reason accurately understand. This use of γνῶσις is fully consistent with that of Evagrios.[4]

The ten definitions and introductory words which follow were most likely composed by someone other than Diadochos. They exhibit a

---

[1] λόγος πρακτικός, ed. A. and C. Guillaumont, *Évagre le pontique, Traité pratique ou Le moine* (Paris, 1971), 498.
[2] See λόγος πρακτικός (above), κεφάλαια γνωστικά, ed. A. Guillaumont, *PO*, 28.i, περὶ προσευχῆς, ed. J. Migne, *PG*, 79, 1165-1200. These works will be referred to henceforth as *Praktikos*, *Gnostic chapters*, and *On prayer*.
[3] See Introduction, 5.
[4] See in particular *Praktikos* 2, 3, (498-500), and *Gnostic chapters* generally.

COMMENTARY

general understanding of Diadochos's use of terminology, but are vague and often tautologous. These definitions are however familiar to many who have read Diadochos in other editions, so they are included here in italics rather than being omitted altogether.

Text 1

As has been explained in the Introduction, Diadochos founds all his arguments on Scripture, whether explicitly stated or implicitly assumed to be understood by the reader. The most authoritative scriptural statements are those from the Gospels. We will see that Diadochos emphasises the importance of regarding Christ's earthly life as a pattern for our own, and his Incarnation as the foundation for the activity of grace in the human soul. Diadochos's major hermeneutical battle with Messalianism will concern the interpretation of the Johannine prologue. On the vexed question of how to interpret the gospels, Diadochos's short fragment from a sermon on the Ascension provides a valuable clue, which is borne out by his hermeneutical method in dealing with the Gospel passages in the *100 practical texts*. In the sermon on the Ascension, Diadochos explicitly states that the psalms contain insights into the Incarnation revealed by God in advance, while the epistles provide inspired explanations of the truth of the gospels.[5] We will see that Diadochos consistently turns to the epistles to explain a point. In doing so his understanding of Scripture is quite literal; unlike the elaborate typology we find in the Makarian *Homilies*,[6] Diadochos assumes that the instruction of the epistles, like the example of Christ in the gospels, is to be taken at face value. Faith, hope, and love therefore are assumed by Diadochos to have a precise meaning, and to be distinguishable features of spiritual experience; they are much more than the general attributes of a devout life. We will see that he regards faith as the discernible influence of grace on the Reason, as hope is for the Sense. Love has a very multi-faceted and complex significance for Diadochos, which only unfolds in the course of reading the entire composition. It is the product of the total human integration for which we strive–[7] the restoration of proper relationship with both God and neighbour. Love will thus be used of love between individuals, and also of our integrated impetus towards God in prayer. But most importantly love is the image and likeness of God, in which the soul was made and into which it must be restored–Love is ultimately the essence of God (as 1 John 3 explicitly states–and this is a passage to which we will return).

---

[5] *Sermon on the Ascension*, 1, 2 ,3 ,5.
[6] See *Homilies*, 47, and throughout; compare Evagrios, *Praktikos*, 38.
[7] See Introduction, 5.

COMMENTARY

Thus God's Son and Logos is Love manifest in creation, and present in the illumined intellect. As we read Diadochos all these aspects of love unfold; but they are also all present implicitly whenever Diadochos speaks of love. Maximos Confessor's understanding of union with God through love is highly influenced by Diadochos. In the present passage we see how necessary it will be for the intellect's Sense[8] to discriminate love unerringly, in order, as it were, to 'lock on' to God.

Text 2

The formation of healthy, integrative habits is extremely important to Diadochos, since the fragmented human Sense and Reason can only be held in a steady disposition towards God by efforts of a damaged human Will. All references to 'willing' therefore have an extremely important significance for Diadochos. The Greek word for willing which corresponds to Diadochos's word for the human Will is translated throughout as 'decide' or 'intend', since these words give an accurate idea of what Diadochos is trying to say, as well as being more natural English. The damaged human Will is still able to decide to turn towards God, and in some measure to hold the intellect together by force through prayer; acquiring a habit of prayerful disposition towards God lightens the burden of perpetual, conscious acts of will. Diadochos's understanding of the Will influenced Maximos Confessor in his distinction between the original pre-fallen human will, which Christ shared with us, and the damaged *gnomic* will which human nature had as a result of original sin, and which therefore did not afflict Christ.[9]

Text 3

For Diadochos our creation in the 'image and likeness' of God (which he will elaborate later) entails very powerful creative ability, which is dangerous when misused through flawed acts of will. We shall see how he develops his understanding of 'imaginings', fantasies and daydreams which we can willingly acquiesce in, or not. As part of the formation of the habit of Godward disposition it is necessary to eradicate habits of imagining earthly pleasures. Implicit here is the gospel passage Diadochos will quote later (Matthew 5:27-28), in which imagining adultery is regarded as equivalent to its performance.

---

[8] Evagrios also speaks of an intellectual Sense in both the *Praktikos* and the *Gnostic chapters*, though for him it is not so highly developed as a technical term as it is for Diadochos.

[9] See A. Louth, *Maximus Confessor* (London, 1996), Introduction.

COMMENTARY

Text 4

Here also Diadochos touches on themes which will only receive elaboration later. This short and seemingly simple paragraph is actually a condensed summary of the heart of Diadochos's understanding of the human predicament and our hope of salvation. It is only much later in the text that Diadochos will explain his belief that the original 'image' of God, in which we were created, is restored in baptism. This will lie at the heart of his argument against Messalianism about the efficacy of baptism for casting sin out of the soul. But Diadochos will distinguish between the 'image' of God and the 'likeness' of God. We are only transformed into the likeness of God when the human Will holds the intellect together in love towards God long enough for grace to heal and re-pattern the soul in the form of divine Love, the illumination of Christ's risen presence in the intellect.

Text 5

The Greek word which appears throughout as 'intellectual conception' is translated in this rather ponderous way because it has a precise technical significance which is not adequately expressed by 'thought' (since the imaginings of the demons are also, generally speaking, thoughts). Intellectual conceptions are the product of Will acting on Reason. They are the 'reasonings', so to speak, which Reason uses to assess the evidence provided by Scripture and Sense. Here Diadochos again emphasises the importance of accurately assessing what is diving so that habits of erroneous thinking of all kinds can be eradicated.

Text 6

Light for Diadochos is always the light of the Johannine prologue–the presence of Christ the Logos in creation, and of the risen Christ illumining the intellect. To have 'true perception' is only possible when the human Will enables grace to illumine the intellect, thus safeguarding our valid assessment of things. This text throws down the gauntlet to Messalianism, and states Diadochos's intention of refuting their errors. He is very conscious of the importance Evagrios gives to remaining free from anger, since anger is one of the passions which fragment the intellect and make accurate judgement impossible. He retains Evagrios's distinction between anger and dispassionate temper, by which we calmly reject things. But whereas Evagrios reserves the use of temper for repulsing demonically inspired imaginings, Diadochos believes that temper can legitimately be used against people who are in error.[10] In

---

[10] Compare *Praktikos*, 11, 20, 21, 24.

COMMENTARY

Diadochos the difference between anger and temper appears to be one of degree–temper is a calm force for repelling things, but when it becomes too heated it is referred to as anger, which disrupts intellectual integration.

Texts 7-8

Words which are genuinely inspired by the holy Spirit will be experienced in a way which carries complete conviction to the intellect in which grace is operative. We shall see later that Diadochos regards this conviction as precise evidence that the light of illumination is effective in a perfectly integrated human being. *Logos* has been translated here as 'expression' to remind us that it is not mere words that are meant when Diadochos uses this word. Whenever Diadochos writes of spiritual speech he is assuming the presence of the illumining Word of God in the intellect. The *Logos* is for Diadochos the Principle, or Rationale, of God manifest in creation, the expression of his nature Incarnate as man but also as divinely inspired words. Thus *theologia* will be translated as 'divine expression' or 'divine converse', since it involves much more than we are used to including under the heading of 'theology'.*Theologia* is the communication of the *Logos* to the intellect via the Spirit, conveying truths which the individual then puts into words for the edification of others. Since speech is a product of Reason, it is faith which is mentioned here with particular reference to it. Love, as has been explained above, is the presence of grace in the intellect perfecting the imperfectly Godward disposition of the soul. The soul is 'unaccused', in that it is completely convinced of the presence of grace and therefore not subject to doubts about its own imperfections, and thus drawn to self-examination, which would be evidence that the soul is deficient in illumination. The Diadochan vocabulary explained thus far should enable a clear appreciation of text 8.

Text 9

Perception, as has been explained, is the capacity of the Sense to have evidence of the presence of grace. Wisdom on the other hand is the product of grace on the Reason and is manifested in words.

COMMENTARY

Text 10
Diadochos accepts the tripartite division of the soul into intellect, entempered part, and impassioned part; but he does not deal with the latter two in any detail.[11]

Text 14
The reference to sensing from 'one's bones' is extremely important. Diadochos does not believe at all that our ultimate goal is to be freed from our bodies. Discussion of human nature in his *Vision* confirms the evidence in this work that for Diadochos to be human is to have a body, and to be saved is to be saved body and soul. He will later speak of the necessity to effectively de-materialise the body. The body must also be part of human reintegration and reorientation, and consequently evidence of the presence of grace in the soul will include the body. Everything the body does must be in keeping with the soul's longing for God, and for this reason Diadochos will pay attention to all aspects of physical asceticism, and particularly to our treatment of other people. This understanding of human integration is also important to bear in mind with regard to the emphasis Diadochos gives to physically praying, both psalms, and the prayer 'Lord Jesus'. The integration of body and soul is one example of the usefulness Diadochos found in Makarian ascetic culture. 'Heart' for him is not a poetical equivalent for 'intellect'; rather the heart is the interface of soul and body, pertaining to both of them and experiencing through both of them. This will be developed later when Diadochos talks about evidence of demonic assaults, in refuting Messalian interpretation of spiritual evidence.

Text 17
Fear is the first form of 'evidence' which Diadochos discusses. When Sense and Reason are functioning properly, Sense receives an experience which it recognises accurately, and which Reason can use to assess the soul's state in relation to God. By a process of self-examination the Reason can determine what the experience Sense has received means about the degree to which grace is present in the soul, and the extent to which our own efforts are succeeding. This will enable the Will to make valid decisions about what action needs to be taken. Again, these are themes which will be explained more fully later when Diadochos deals with penitence and full confession.

---

[11] See *Praktikos*, 89.

COMMENTARY

Text 18
The withdrawal referred to here is the physical retreat of ascetics from the world, including the society of other people–traditionally this was into the desert (and later, in Russia particularly, into the deep forest), but ultimately to any place where there are no distractions from recollection of God.

Texts 31-33
When Diadochos discusses discerning whether dreams are of divine or demonic origin, he is not digressing from his purpose in refuting Messalianism–he is deliberately leading up to it; because the source of error is the same. The evidence dreams provide during sleep constitutes spiritual experience in the same way as do feelings of fear, faith, longing and love, etc. during prayer. At the end of text 33 Diadochos makes the link between Messalian error and demonic deception explicit. As a result of baptism, as he will explain later, grace inhabits the intellect and Satan can only influence it from the body. Messalians, as explained in the Introduction, believed that even the presence of the holy Spirit in the soul did not expel Satan from it.[12] Here Diadochos warns that it is necessary to know exactly what is happening within our intellects in order to be able to interpret the things we see and feel in dreams. In these texts Diadochos again touches on a theme which he will develop extensively later–the practice of using the Jesus prayer to hold the intellect steady in integrated recollection of God.

Text 34
When Diadochos speaks of what is 'natural' to humanity, he is almost always referring to what the human condition is now as a result of the fall of Adam and Eve. But it is also useful to remember that Diadochos is going to elaborate a theory of divine illumination in which the end result of the activity of grace is to elevate the recipient to a state which is superior even to the original nature of humanity before the fall.

Text 36
The claim to see visible light or fire as a divine manifestation was a prevalent feature of Messalian ascetic culture from the fourth century onwards. The tension between Evagrios's and Diadochos's understanding of the 'light of the intellect' as an immaterial, spiritual experience of divine illumination, and the Messalian conviction that the operation of grace could be seen visibly as light or fire, remained throughout the

---
[12] See Introduction, 3-4.

history of Byzantine asceticism. This tension was ultimately resolved by a synthesis achieved by the hesychasts of Mt Athos in the fourteenth century, whereby the eyes of the enlightened can perceive the uncreated light which was seen by the disciples during Christ's transfiguration on Mt Tabor.[13] This light is obviously not to be confused with the visions of figures of light and fire which Diadochos criticises here. One suspects that the solid grounding of the hesychastic experience in the example of the gospels would have satisfied Diadochos as to the legitimacy of the experience. The hesychasts were, and Athonite monasticism still is, much influenced by the synthesis between Evagrian and Makarian asceticism which Diadochos achieved, particularly in the use of the Jesus prayer to acquire the recollection which is necessary for contemplative prayer, and in the harmonisation between prayer of the intellect, and prayer of the heart–which for hesychasts, as for Diadochos, necessarily involves the body. In Athonite terms this is expressed as putting 'the mind in the heart'. The influence of Diadochos can also be seen in the hesychastic understanding that the divine light can only be seen visibly by those who have first refined, or 'thinned down', as this translation puts it, their bodies to a more spiritual state through prayer.

Text 37

The status of grief and tears as evidence of the activity of grace is another feature of Makarian asceticism which Diadochos is determined to preserve for orthodoxy. He will go on to take great pains to distinguish between sadness which is spiritually healthy, and sadness which is a danger signal that we are in great spiritual error. Assessing the true significance of emotional responses to prayer is of course at the heart of his argument against Messalianism; and he is determined to preserve emotion as a legitimate, and indeed necessary, source of spiritual evidence.

Text 40

See the note on text 36. The phrase 'with a whole Sense and complete assurance' is a very characteristic Makarian phrase. Diadochos makes it the centre-piece of his teaching on the necessity of fully integrating the whole human being in order to allow grace unhindered activity in the intellect, allowing accurate assessment of things. Characteristically he consolidated this significance with reference to the gospels. This is a very good example of Diadochos's use of Messalian terminology against Messalians, since ultimately he will accuse them of having fallen into

---

[13] See Matthew 17:1-8; Mark 9:2-8.

error through not having the spiritual integration necessary to interpret evidence accurately.

Text 41

References to obedience in ascetic literature usually pertain to the relationship between a monk and his spiritual father. But in the context in which Diadochos is writing (particularly to a dispersed audience, some of whom will be hermits), he is concentrating on how to sustain an integrated disposition towards God–and as he points out repeatedly, this is through prayer and the reading of Scripture. So obedience here is really referring to obedience to God, particularly by following Christ's example of prayerful obedience to the Father's decision that he must suffer and die. Christ is always the focus of prayer for Diadochos–in imitation of his gospel example, by participation in the sacraments his Incarnation have made possible, through prayerful use of his prophetic voice in the Psalms, and by illumination with his risen presence while praying 'Lord Jesus'. Diadochos has a very profound sense of the central place the Incarnation holds in the status of everything vis-à-vis God; this is not at first evident to Western readers, since we are accustomed to incarnational theology centring on the crucifixion. But although Diadochos's purpose in this work does not lead him into a discussion of the passion or the sacrament of communion, the Incarnation is implicit in everything he posits, deriving from his central argument about baptism. Christ–as Son and Logos in creation, as visible example in the gospels, as interface of divine and human nature in his Incarnation, and as risen presence in prayer–is at all times for Diadochos God manifest in creation. Diadochos's understanding of the distinct roles played by each of the persons of the Trinity will be elaborated further later.

Text 42

For the phrase 'committing adultery with the demon of disobedience' see Makarios, *Homilies*, 26.

Texts 45-53

Diadochos's emphasis on moderation in the physical aspects of ascetic practice is part of his wider emphasis on moderation.[14] With regard to spiritual experience, it is reasonableness, gentleness, and calmness which characterise the activity of grace. Extremes of all kinds, whether physical or emotional, destroy the fragile reintegration of intellect, soul, and body in a Godward disposition. This is why Diadochos puts such strong

---

[14] Compare *Praktikos*, 17, which advocates going for long periods without water.

emphasis on humility. Presumption and vainglory are particularly dangerous vices since they obliterate one's ability to assess spiritual evidence of grace and sin, inflating the intellect into a completely wrong assessment of itself.

Texts 54-57

Apatheia is used by Diadochos with its Evagrian sense. It is translated literally as 'dispassion', since that is what both Evagrios and Diadochos mean–freedom from being influenced by the passions, either those which destroy our integration spiritually, like anger, or those which destroy it through matter, like gluttony. Whatever its source, passion fragments our intellect's recollection and pulls it in other directions than God. So dispassion is complete freedom to see clearly and to make valid decisions; it is neither apathetic nor unfeeling. We have seen how important feelings are for Diadochos; they are after all part of the whole human being which must return to God as a unity.

Text 58

Akedia is another Evagrian term which Diadochos uses in its original sense. It has sometimes been translated as 'sloth', since it prevents a monk or hermit from getting on with ascetic practice and prayer. But it has been translated here as 'restlessness', since for both Evagrios and Diadochos it operates by preventing one from settling down to a task or indeed a place–and so Diadochos sees it as *causing* sloth. For Evagrios, in *Praktikos*, 12, *akedia* makes a monk keep looking out of his window, going out of his cell, and seeking other monks to talk to; it can even make a monk think of moving to another place, and prevents him settling to his manual work. The end result is a cooling of love towards his brother monks. Diadochos would see all of this as symptomatic of severe fragmentation and disorientation. Although not always given this name in early ascetic literature, the phenomenon was well known. The traditional advice to someone exhibiting this sort of behaviour was to 'go, sit in your cell and be still'.

Text 59

See the note on text 36.

Text 60

In order to appreciate the importance of joy for Diadochos and its significance as spiritual evidence, it is necessary to realise that implicit in all his teaching on this experience is the Pauline statement in Galatians

COMMENTARY

5:22 that 'the fruit of the Spirit is love, joy, peace, patience, kindness, goodness, faithfulness, gentleness, self-control'. There are many similar references to joy in the Pauline epistles, and Diadochos regards them all as literal instruction that all the things mentioned are actual evidence of grace. Here Diadochos begins to elaborate how to assess feelings of joy– which, we must remember, is calm and balanced and not a delirious happiness.

Text 61

See the note on texts 54-57. In this text Diadochos gives a very beautiful account of the necessary synergy between the human will and grace. He also articulates the distinct roles of the three Persons of the Trinity in prayer, while managing to convey their essential Unity. The assistance of the holy Spirit enables us to pray 'Lord Jesus' validly, which in turn enables the illumination of Christ to direct us unerringly towards the Father. This short statement of the harmonious activity of the Persons of the Trinity comes close to conveying in words the poised balance and dynamic unity which Rublev achieved in his famous icon of the Trinity. Diadochos's high awareness of the distinct roles of the Persons of the Trinity is one of the chief ways in which he differs from Evagrios. Evagrios states in *Praktikos*, 3, that 'the kingdom of God is perception of the holy Trinity, coextensive with the composition of the intellect and surpassing its incorruptibility', which Diadochos would certainly agree with. But neither in the *Praktikos* nor in the *Gnostic chapters* does Evagrios elaborate what he means by perception of the Trinity. The *Gnostic chapters* contain several references to both 'perception of the holy Trinity' and 'perception of the holy Unity', but do not give any account of the difference between them.

Text 62

Diadochos does not explicitly state what the four virtues are. He founds his thinking on faith, hope and love (see the note on text 1), and regards self-control as the foundation of all the virtues (see text 42), so these may be what he is referring to. On the other hand he may be speaking of the four Platonic and Aristotelian virtues of temperance, justice, courage, and practical wisdom.

COMMENTARY

Text 66

We have already seen the importance Diadochos attaches to our treatment of others.[15] In text 43 Diadochos praises the degree of abstinence which leaves enough food for an ascetic to share with beggars. So this text is not advocating an abdication of our responsibility to care for other people. In the context of the preceding texts, Diadochos is rather trying to point out, in the strongest possible terms, that private property must inevitably be a source of distraction for an ascetic. He is warning of the many excuses one can find to avoid the necessity of being literally impoverished. There is probably also a Scriptural passage implicit in his thinking: 'Children, how hard it is to enter the kingdom of God! It is easier for a camel to go through the eye of a needle than for a rich man to enter the kingdom of God.' (Mark 10:24f; see also Matthew 19:23f).

Texts 70-74

For a discussion of divine converse and perception, see the notes on the title and introduction, and on texts 7 and 9. The 'activity' referred to in text 72 is the activity of grace in the intellect. Likewise the 'deficiency' referred to in text 74 is deficiency of the activity of grace in the intellect. For a discussion of the heart see the note on text 14.

Text 76

Here Diadochos introduces the main themes he will use in countering the Messalian belief that sin and grace co-exist in the intellect after baptism. He makes his criteria for judgement clear: Scripture, and a properly functioning intellectual Sense. As we shall see, the main battleground will be about interpreting the significance of the fact that after baptism the intellect still spontaneously imagines wicked things. Messalians believed that this was evidence of the continuing presence of the Devil in the soul, despite the sacramental gift of grace–the presence of the holy Spirit in the soul. It is for this reason that they believed that only continuous, demonstrative prayer and penitence could drive Satan to the extremities of the soul and prevent him from tormenting the soul with wicked thoughts. Diadochos's argument against this will be built on using the Messalian emphasis on the 'heart' against them. As the material interface and unifying focus of soul and body, the heart for Diadochos is vulnerable to allowing demonic influence to insinuate itself into the soul through the body–which is the only place Satan can dwell after baptism. This is why he introduces in this text the notion of the 'malleability' of the body. Of all the component parts of the human being which Will is

---

[15] See text 15.

COMMENTARY

trying to get hold of in an integrated disposition towards God, the body is necessarily the most liable to being imposed on by Satan. The five bodily senses are, after all, the result of the fragmentation of the original unitive Sense. Diadochos states that as a result of original sin the body became mortal.[16] He correspondingly believed that to be in perfect communion with the holy Spirit the body must be 'thinned down'![17] It is thus possible, but by no means certain, that he believed that the body became material as a result of the fall of Adam and Eve. Thus there would be a permanent flaw in the body in this life, which renders it particularly susceptible to demonic influence. Also introduced in this text is Diadochos's argument that the activity of demonic delusion is not the result of our remaining in a state of sin after baptism, but of God's beneficent instruction spurring the Will to further efforts of integration. The argument that evil imaginings are evidence of Satan's continuing presence in the soul can be found in the Makarian *Homilies*, 17:4ff and 26:15.

Text 77
Diadochos continues the themes of text 76 here, but also clarifies the significance of his previous comments on owning property: material possessions pertain to the material body in a particularly dangerous way. Whereas Diadochos will argue that thoughts of material pleasures, like eating, sexual gratification, and property ownership, are instigated by Satan, actual physical ownership of things is an act of Will. If the Will cannot renounce them, it is concrete evidence that the intellect is not completely focused on God. We have already seen in text 3 that to accept demonic imaginings in some way gives them substance, and that the physical performance of such things gives them concrete reality.

Text 78
Here Diadochos begins to explain his distinction between humanity being in the image, and in the likeness, of God; this is an important element of the baptismal theology he develops to counter Messalianism. In Genesis 1:26 God states his intention to make humanity in his image and likeness. We have seen that as a result of the sin of Adam and Eve, Diadochos believed that the intellect is permanently fragmented. Here he refers to this as an obscuring of the clear outline of the image of God within us. The body has fallen into mortality, inevitably vulnerable to physical passions, and, through the heart, to the infiltration of demonic influences which entice both soul and body away from integrated concentration on

---

[16] See text 78.
[17] See text 24.

COMMENTARY

God. Diadochos now develops his theory of the efficacy of baptism for healing the damage done by original sin. He has already stated that before baptism this damage results in the ability of Satan to reside in the intellect, whereas after baptism Satan is cast out and the holy Spirit resides in the intellect. He sees this as the restoration of the image of God in the intellect, which (as he will later explain) returns the soul to its pre-fallen state. Of course, not all the damage done by original sin is eradicated. The body remains mortal, and thus continually pulls the intellect out of integrated disposition towards God. It is important to note the incarnational basis of Diadochos's understanding of the efficacy of baptism. Various theories have been posited by theologians as to why Jesus, being sinless, presented himself for John's baptism of repentance. For Diadochos Christ's participation in the act of baptism is what makes it sacramentally valid for us, imbuing a physical act with divine presence. Again the synergy between Son and Spirit in the activity of grace is made clear, and we shall see that this is a theme he will return to. The Spirit conveys grace into the human intellect, but the content of grace is the illumination which is the Logos; and this can only reside in humanity because of the intersection of the divine and the human which came about in the Incarnation. Diadochos also reminds us here of the necessary synergy between grace and the damaged Will. The holy Spirit may be in the intellects of the baptised, but they must approach God in an integrated disposition in order for grace to be effective. The quotation from 2 Corinthians introduces the theme of the Johannine prologue, which Diadochos will examine in detail to demonstrate the error of Messalian exegesis.

Text 80

Diadochos bases his refutation of the Messalian interpretation of the Johannine prologue on establishing the precise meaning ofκαταλαμβάνω, here translated as 'apprehend'. His point is that the Messalian argument, that both grace and sin can be in the soul at the same time (see *Homilies*, 16, 26, 47), misinterprets 'did not apprehend', taking the 'darkness' to refer to Satan. With reference to the epistles to clarify the point, he uses Philippians 3:12 to identify 'apprehending' with the intellect's capacity to have γνῶσις, perception, of God. He argues that Satan couldn't be the 'darkness' referred to here as not apprehending God, since Satan is in every respect alien to, and out of relationship with God, whereas perception involves the most profoundly intimate relationship with God. Rather the 'darkness' referred to is simply literal absence of light–the

COMMENTARY

unilluminated, unperceiving human intellect. Diadochos will return to the epistles in text 82 to back up his argument further.

Text 81
Diadochos now elaborates his understanding of the heart as the interface of soul and body. 'The parts of the heart' reflects the Messalian term 'the limbs of the heart'. The heart was considered by Messalians to be like a tree, with many limbs and branches; and this is why they could argue that the devil, not being cast out of the soul completely, had to be chased to the extremities of the heart by ceaseless prayer and penitence. By distinguishing between the soul and the heart, Diadochos can accept the presence of sin in the heart, and the corresponding emphasis on ceaseless prayer and tears–giving them all non-Messalian meanings. We will see later the difference between Messalian and Diadochan penitence. Here Diadochos explains his theory with reference to examples of the experiences we have of the activity of sin within us, so we can know how to react to it. Diadochos does not retain Evagrios's clear-cut distinctions between the various imaginings and their respective demons. Presumption is the equivalent of vainglory. As we have seen, this is the worst affliction of the intellect since it causes a completely erroneous assessment of one's status vis-à-vis both God and neighbour, and thus renders every aspect of spiritual judgement impossible.

Texts 83-85
For the argument Diadochos is refuting, see especially the Makarian *Homilies*, 15:13ff. At the end of this text Diadochos refers to the sin of accepting demonic imaginings. Because of his thesis that inherited sin is cast out of the soul at baptism, he will later explain that in terms of guilt and debt vis-à-vis God, baptism wipes the slate clean. For this reason the distinction between corporate, inherited sin and individually acquired sin is very important. The damaged Will has the power to say 'no' to demonic imaginings. To have bad thoughts is not evidence of a sinful soul, only of demonic activity insinuating things into the soul through the flesh of the heart. But if the intellect entertains such thoughts, even for a moment, the individual has sinned; and it is these failings which the Reason's 'tribunal' must assess and repent of. Confession for Diadochos is thus always to do with one's own deliberate errors, since the gift of baptism has wiped the slate clean of original sin. This text therefore claims that Messalian error has arisen from misinterpretation of the evidence of demonic imaginings. Because they have misinterpreted Scripture, they misinterpret spiritual evidence: they do not understand

COMMENTARY

what is happening in the soul, and attribute bad thoughts to the continuing bondage of the baptised to inherited sin. In text 85 Diadochos suggests that these errors arise from a failure to maintain the necessary integration for correct orientation to God. The reference to a humble disposition is significant. We have seen how Diadochos warns against volatile emotions, since they disrupt integrated recollection of God. Diadochos does not refer explicitly to the more flamboyant and demonstrative features of Messalian ascetic culture, but the emphasis on peace and gentleness which he derives from the epistles, together with Pauline references to the 'whole man' are part of his overall emphasis on moderation, as we have seen. Since the body is meant to be in the process of 'thinning down' so that the soul comes to perceive demonic assaults less and less (and Diadochos again mentions the importance of poverty in achieving this), it is perhaps not reading too much into his argument to suppose that he saw the origins of Messalian error in their overly flamboyant, histrionic demonstrations of penitence, which militated against total human integration and thus proper recollection of the Lord. On the other hand, Diadochos may not have encountered Messalianism except through its literature, and may therefore never have tried to account for this. Whichever is the case, for Diadochos divinely inspired feelings and intuitions are to be recognised precisely on the grounds of their being peaceful, gentle, and in this Pauline sense, joyful and tearful. At the end of text 85 Diadochos reiterates his previous point about the significance of not feeling the activity of the holy Spirit. Once we examine ourselves and are assured that we are behaving as we should, we must be assured that grace is still present within us, but hiding in order to spur the Will to further efforts of loving God.

Texts 86-88

Continuing this theme, Diadochos states that the erroneous, Messalian interpretation extends to just this experience–because of their emphasis on the inherited guilt of original sin, they believe that when we do not feel the activity of the Spirit, it means that the presence of sin has caused grace to leave the soul. Spiritual dereliction on the other hand can be recognised by a complete inability to recollect God. Text 87 gives more details of the difference between evidence of 'training abandonment' and of dereliction, and text 88 deals with the ambiguous experiences of beginners.

COMMENTARY

Text 89

Having dealt with the most important manifestations of spiritual experience, and explained how it is to be assessed accurately, outside Messalian error, Diadochos can at last deal more fully with the main point: what the synergy of grace and free will is actually capable of achieving. Now that restoration into the original 'image of God' has been explained as the achievement of baptismal grace, and post-baptismal experience of sin described, Diadochos can move on to discuss the illumination made possible by willed integration, as the whole person reaches out to God through recollection in the prayer 'Lord Jesus'. When Diadochos discussed the Johannine prologue, he identified the Light of the Logos during creation with the Light of the risen Christ as illumination in the perceptive intellect. Here, to be perfectly God-like, as we were created to be, is to be re-patterned on the original image and likeness of the Father–the Son. The Son is, of course, the Father's essence incarnate–the 'virtue' of God, which is Love itself; thus we are only fully in the image and likeness of God when we love perfectly. Implicit in this text is 1 John 4:7-21, which is worth quoting in full:

> Beloved, let us love one another, since love is of God, and everyone who loves has been born of God and knows (γινώσκει) God. He who does not love does not know God, *since God is Love*. The love of God was made evident among us in this: that God sent his only-begotten Son into the world so that we might live through him. Love is in this: not that we have loved God, but that he loved us and sent his Son to be an atonement for our sins. Beloved, if God loved us like this we also should love each other. No one has ever beheld God; if we love each other, God remains among us and his love is perfected in us. We know that we remain in him and he in us by this: that he has given of his Spirit to us. And we have beheld and testify that the Father has sent the Son to be saviour of the world. If anyone agrees that Jesus is the Son of God, God remains in him, and he in God. And we have known and have believed the love God has for us. God is love, and he who remains in love remains in God, and God remains in him. Love has been perfected among us in this, so that we might have confidence at the day of judgement, that we in this world are also as he is. There isn't fear in love; rather, perfect love casts out fear, since fear has chastisement, and he who fears has not been perfected in love. We love because he first loved us. If anyone were to say 'I love God' and he hated his brother, he is a liar. For he who doesn't love his brother whom he has seen can't love God whom he hasn't seen. And we have this commandment from him, that he who loves God also love his brother.

COMMENTARY

Texts 91-92

The quotation above from 1 John should explain the relationship these texts assume to exist between illuminating Love and love of neighbour. God is love, and it is only through the perfect integration of ourselves into love–body and soul loving God and neighbour–that one is perfected into the image and likeness of divine Love and 'gets hold of' God. This perfect integration into communion with the Trinity gives complete assurance, which is evidence of the validity of the experience.

Texts 93-99

The preceding pages have dealt with all the main aspects of Diadochos's thinking. It should now be possible to see the technical significance of these texts, in which he draws together and summarises many of the themes he has already discussed.

Text 100

Finally, Diadochos concludes with an account of the end of the struggle to recollect God perfectly and continually in this life. As has been remarked, in terms of divine judgement, the inherent debt of original sin has been expunged by baptism. The sins for which one will be called to account are those committed by us after baptism. They are 'deliberate', in that they involve the collusion of the Will; but we will not be aware of all of them. On the other hand, Diadochos is not advocating an excessively scrupulous examination of every movement of our intellects; it is lapses in the rules by which his readers observe the ascetic life to which he refers. Full assurance, as we have seen, is evidence that if all the other things we experience accord with the evidence of Scripture, we have given total assent to grace, in our whole being. But the pliancy of the mortal body gives us a permanent tendency to lapse, so that constant self-examination is necessary, lest the demons insinuate some error into the soul through the heart. Fear, as we have also seen, is evidence that love is not perfected in us; if this is the state of the soul on death, the fearful individual will have to reach God's presence through the process of judgement–purifying fire perfecting that which is still imperfect. Quotations from this text in the middle ages were often accompanied by a gloss by Maximos Confessor to the effect that Diadochos did not believe in apokatastasis, or universal salvation. It should be evident that Diadochos could never have accepted the restoration of Satan, who is the antithesis of grace. In terms of the salvation of humanity, his words do not at all suggest that all will be saved. He is very clear about the power of the human Will to deny grace; where we wilfully remain in sin, our

COMMENTARY

culpability is absolute, as his remarks on spiritual dereliction indicate. Likewise he speaks of impious men, presumably baptised but uninterested in God; he gives no indication that he expects them to be saved. But with regard to those who concern him, who are trying to find God, it is not clear what he anticipates. After all, the divine fire which purifies cannot be unrelated to the divine light which transforms; so if there is anything at all of the image and likeness of God in an individual, Diadochos may have believed that restoration would ultimately be possible through judgement. Would he have held out this hope for Messalians themselves? It is worth remembering how well acquainted Diadochos was with the epistles. He will have been conscious of Paul's comments about the grave responsibility of those who undertake to teach Christianity. So perhaps he would have seen the ultimate fate of Messalians in terms of 1 Corinthians 3:10-15:

> According to the grace of God which has been given to me, I have established a foundation like a wise architect, but another builds upon it. Let each watch out how he builds; for no one can establish another foundation than that which has been laid, which is Jesus Christ. But if someone builds upon the foundation with gold, silver, precious stones, wood, hay, straw–the work of each will become evident; for the day will make it plain. Because it is revealed in fire, and the fire will prove whatever the work of each is. If someone's work which he has built remains, he will receive a reward; if someone's work is burnt down, he will be punished–he himself will be saved, but only as through fire.

Select bibliography

Select bibliography

Primary sources

Diadochos of Photike
κεφάλαια γνωστικὰ ρ', ὅρασις,
λόγος εἰς τὴν ἀνάληψιν,
ed. E. des Places, *Diadoque de Photicé, Œuvres spirituelles* (Paris, 1966)

Evagrios Monachos
λόγος πρακτικός,
ed. A. and C. Guillaumont,
Évagre le Pontique, Traité pratique ou Le moine (Paris, 1971)

κεφάλαια γνωστικά,
ed. A. Guillaumont, *Patrologia Orientalis*, 28.i

περὶ προσευχῆς,
PG, 79, 1165-1200

pseudo-Makarios
εὐχαί,
ed. H. Dörries, E. Klostermann, and M. Kroeger, *Die 50 geistlichen Homilien des Makarios* (Berlin, 1964)

Timothy of Constantinople
περὶ διαφορᾶς τῶν προσερχομένων τῇ εὐαγεστάτῃ ἡμῶν πίστει,
PG, 86.i, 45C-52C

Victor Vitensis
Historia persecutionis Africanae provinciae, ed. E. Schwartz, *Corpus scriptorum ecclesiasticorum Latinorum*, 7 (Vienna, 1866)

BIBLIOGRAPHY

Secondary sources

Christou, P. Διάδοχος ὁ Φοτικῆς, (Thessalonike, 1952)

Dörr, F. *Diadochos von Photike und die Messalianer: Ein Kampf zwischen wahrer und falscher Mystik in fünften Jahrhundert* (Freiburg, 1937)

Dörries, H. 'Diadochos und Symeon: Das Verhältnis der κεφάλαια γνωστικὰ ρ´ zum Messalianismus', *Wort und Stunde*, I (Göttingen, 1966), 352-422

Hausherr, I. *Noms du Christ et voies d'oraison* (Rome, 1960)

Hester, D. 'Diadochos of Photiki: The memory and its purification', *Studia Patristica*, 23 (1989), 49-52

Hick, J. 'Theology and verification', *The philosophy of religion*, ed. B. Mitchell (London, 1971), 53-71

Horn, G. 'Sens de l'esprit d'apres Diadoque de Photicé', *Revue d'Ascetique et de Mystique*, 8 (1927), 402-419

Louth, A. *Maximus the Confessor* (London, 1996)

Louth, A. *The origins of the Christian mystical tradition* (Oxford, 1981)

Madden, N. 'Aisthesis noera (Diadochus-Maximus)', *Studia Patristica*, 23 (1989), 53-60

BIBLIOGRAPHY

Maloney, G.	*pseudo-Makarius: the fifty spiritual homilies and the great letter* (Oxford, 1981)
Marrou, H.-J.	'Diadoque de Photiké et Victor de Vita', *Revue des Études anciennes*, 45 (1943), 225-232
Messana, V.	'San Diadoco de Fotica', *Introduzione ai padri della chiesa. Secoli IV e V*, ed. G. Bosio, E. dal Covolo, and M. Maritano (Turin, 1995)
des Places, E.	'Diadoque de Photicé', *Dictionnaire de spiritualité*, 3 (1955), 817-834
des Places, E.	*Diadoque de Photicé, Œuvres spirituelles* (Paris, 1966)
des Places, E.	'Diadoque de Photicé et le Messalianisme', *Kyriakon*, ed. P. Granfield and A. Jungman (Münster, 1970), 591-595
des Places, E.	'Maxime le Confesseur et Diadoque de Photicé', *Maximus Confessor*, ed. F. Heinzer and C. Schönborn, (Freiburg, 1982)
Rothenhäusler, M.	'Zur asketischen Lehrschrift des Diadochus von Photike', *Die heilige Überlieferung* (Münster, 1938), 86-95
Rutherford, J.	'Byzantine asceticism: a stranger to the church?', *Strangers to themselves: the Byzantine outsider*, ed. D. Smythe (*SPBS*, 8, Aldershot, 1999), 39-45

BIBLIOGRAPHY

Rutherford, J. — 'Sealed with the likeness of God: Logos theology in Diadochos of Photike', *Studies in patristic Christology* (Dublin, 1998), 67-83

Stiernon, D. — 'Diadoque de Photicé', *Dictionnaire d'histoire et de géographie ecclésiastiques*, 14 (1960), 374-378

Spidlik, T. — *La spiritualité de l'Orient chrétien: Manuel systématique* (Rome, 1978)

Ware, K. — 'The Jesus Prayer in St Diadochos of Photice', *Aksum-Thyateira* (Athens, 1985), 557-568

Ware, K. — 'Diadochus von Photice', *Theologische Realenzyclopaedie*, 8, 610-620